Sunlight illuminates a wall of Buddhist statuary at Dunhuang, Gansu Province

Copyright © 2004, 2002 Airphoto International Ltd.
Maps Copyright © 2004, 2002 Airphoto International Ltd.

Airphoto International Ltd., 903 Seaview Commercial Building,
21–24 Connaught Road West, Sheung Wan, Hong Kong
Tel: (852) 2856-3896; Fax: (852) 2565-8004; E-mail: sales@odysseypublications.com

Copyright © 1999, 1998, 1993, 1992, 1990, 1988 Odyssey Publications Ltd.
Maps Copyright © 1999, 1998, 1993, 1992, 1990, 1988 Odyssey Publications Ltd.

Distribution in the United States of America by
W.W. Norton & Company, Inc., 500 Fifth Avenue, New York, NY 10110, USA
Tel: 800-233-4830; Fax: 800-458-6515; World Wide Web: www.wwnorton.com

Distribution in the United Kingdom and Europe by
Cordee Books and Maps, 3a De Montfort Street, Leicester, LE1 7HD, UK
Tel: 0116-254-3579; Fax. 0116-247-1176; www.cordee.co.uk

Library of Congress Catalog Card Number has been requested.

ISBN: 962-217-741-7

Grateful acknowledgment is made to the following authors and publishers:

Routledge for Travels in Tartary, Thibet and China 1844–1846 by Evariste-Régis Huc and Joseph Gabet, translated by William Hazlitt; Random Century Group for An Adventure on the Old Silk Road © 1989 by John Pilkington; Methuen and Co Ltd for Chinese Central Asia by C P Skrine © 1926; Random Century for From Heaven Lake by Vikram Seth © 1983 by Vikram Seth; Unwin Hyman, of Harper Collins Publishers (London) for Monkey by Wu Ch'en En, translated by Arthur Waley © 1942, 1979 by George Allen and Unwin; Harper Collins Publishers for In Xanadu by William Dalrymple © 1989 by William Dalrymple; The Massachusetts Institute of Technology for Spring Silkworms by Mao Tun, taken from Straw Sandals; Chinese short stories 1918–1933, translated by Harold Isaacs © 1974 by the Massachusetts Institute of Technology; Hodder & Stoughton Publishers for The Gobi Desert by Mildred Cable © Hodder & Stoughton Publishers; Macmillan and Co. for Ruins of Desert Cathay by Sir Mark Aurel Stein © 1912; Barry Holstun Lopez for Desert Notes © 1976.

Editor: Jeremy Tredinnick
Series Co-ordinator: Helen Northey
Design: Alex Ng Kin Man
Cover Design: Au Yeung Chui Kwai
Maps: Tom Le Bas, Au Yeung Chui Kwai

Front cover photography: Amar Grover
Back cover photography: How Man Wong
Photography/illustrations courtesy of Museum für Indische Kunst Berlin 23, 96, 111, 226; Xia Ju-xian 64–65, 69; Qiu Ziyu © National Museum of Shaanxi History 1, 8–9, 19, 30, 49, 52, 53, 72, 73, 76, 77, 160, 161, 205, 310, 311; Christoph Baumer 60, 315, 319, 321, 324–325, 329; Kevin Bishop 230–231, 264, 278, 290, 291; William Bleisch 332, 333; Peter Fredenburg 164, 193, 336; How Man Wong 4–5, 12–13, 26, 197, 222–223, 234–235, 260–261, 294–295, 299; William Lindesay 1, 27, 29, 31, 101, 103, 104, 107, 148, 152–153, 156, 169, 172, 173, 298; © National Museum, New Delhi 328; Kazuyoshi Nomachi 149; Julia Wilkinson 283; © Xinjiang Regional Museum 318; Jacky Yip, China Photo Library 81, 88–89, 93, 115, 118–119, 123, 127, 145, 189, 200–201, 208, 214–215, 219, 238–239, 257, 269, 272, 286, 303, 307; Zhong Ling 168

Production by Twin Age Ltd, Hong Kong
Manufactured in Hong Kong

THE SILK ROAD
FROM XI'AN TO KASHGAR

Judy Bonavia

Revised by
Christoph Baumer

Contents

(preceding pages) A golden eagle perches on the arm of a Kirghiz horseman. Each autumn in western Xinjiang, groups of Kirghiz men like this set out in hunting parties. Their eagles and falcons are trained to hunt for animals like gazelles, foxes and rabbits

THE SOUTHERN SILK ROAD ... 293

(preceding pages) Pottery camel with rider from the Tang dynasty (618–907). One of many fine examples of pottery figurines from this period on display in the National Museum of Shaanxi History, Xi'an. Commerce on the Silk Road reached its height during the Tang dynasty, when camel caravans trekked through Western China and Central Asia

(following pages) The Mingsha sand dunes, five kilometres south of Dunhuang. China is fighting a constant battle against the encroachment of the desert on to fertile farmland in its northwest region, where the continual movement of sand has swallowed ancient cities, such as Loulan and Niya, which once thrived on the Silk Road

INTRODUCTION

Nowadays silk is found in all the world's markets. It travels easily and cheaply by sea and air freight. This was not always so.

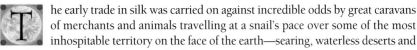

he early trade in silk was carried on against incredible odds by great caravans of merchants and animals travelling at a snail's pace over some of the most inhospitable territory on the face of the earth—searing, waterless deserts and snowbound mountain passes. In high summer, the caravans travelled at night, less afraid of legendary desert demons than of the palpable, scorching heat. Blinding sandstorms forced both merchants and animals to the ground for days on end—their eyes, ears and mouths stifled—before the fury abated. Altitude sickness and snow-blindness affected both man and beast along cliff-hanging and boulder-strewn tracks. Death followed on the heels of every caravan.

For protection against gangs of marauders, who were much tempted by the precious cargoes of silk, gemstones, spices and incense, merchants set aside their competitiveness and joined forces to form large caravans of as many as 1,000 camels under the protection of armed escorts. The two-humped Bactrian camel could carry 350 to 400 pounds of merchandise and was favoured over the single-humped species, which, although capable of the same load, could not keep up the pace.

The journeys of China's emissary, Zhang Qian, in the second century BC brought the Han dynasty (206 BC–AD 220) into political contact with the many kingdoms of Central Asia and opened up the great East–West trade route. But it was only in the 1870s that the German geographer, Ferdinand von Richthofen, gave it the name by which we now know it—the Silk Road.

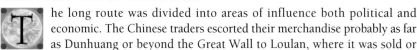

he long route was divided into areas of influence both political and economic. The Chinese traders escorted their merchandise probably as far as Dunhuang or beyond the Great Wall to Loulan, where it was sold or bartered to Central Asian middlemen—Parthians, Sogdians, Indians and Kushans—who carried the trade on to the cities of the Persian, Syrian and Greek merchants. Each transaction increased the cost of the end product, which reached the Roman empire in the hands of Greek and Jewish entrepreneurs.

The Han-dynasty Silk Road began at the magnificent capital city of Chang'an (Xi'an)—Sera Metropolis. The route took traders westwards into Gansu Province and along the Hexi Corridor to the giant barrier of the Great Wall. From here, many caravans favoured the northern route through the Jade Gate Pass (Yumenguan) northwest of Dunhuang, along the southern foothills of the Heavenly Mountains (Tian Shan) and, skirting the northern rim of the Taklamakan Desert, past the rich oasis towns of Hami, Turpan, Yanqi, Korla, Kucha and Kashgar. Others chose the more arduous but direct route through Yangguan Pass southwest of Dunhuang, and along the northern foothills of the Kunlun Mountains—and the southern edge of the Taklamakan—to Loulan, Khotan, Yarkand and Kashgar.

At Kashgar, there were more choices. Some went westwards over the Terek Pass in the Heavenly Mountains into the kingdoms of Ferghana and Sogdiana (in the vicinity of Tashkent and Samarkand) and across the Oxus River to Merv (present-day Mary in Turkmenistan). Others crossed the high Pamirs to the south near Tashkurgan and went along the Wakhan Corridor of Afghanistan to Balkh, in the ancient Graeco-Iranian kingdom of Bactria, to meet up with the northern route in Merv. Still another route from Kashgar passed Tashkurgan and went over the Karakoram Pass and down into India.

From Merv the Silk Road continued west on an easier path to the old capital of Parthia, Hecatompylos (near present-day Damghan), continuing south of the Caspian Sea to Hamadan, southwest of Teheran, then on to the ancient twin cities of Seleuceia and Ctesiphon, near Baghdad on the Tigris River. From here various routes led through Syria to Antioch, Palmyra and the eastern shores of the Mediterranean Sea and the Roman Empire.

lexander the Great's expansion into Central Asia over 2,300 years ago stopped far short of Chinese Turkestan, and he appears to have gained little knowledge of the lands beyond. So the empires of Rome and China, developing almost simultaneously in the second century BC, had only the vaguest consciousness of each other. The Chinese knew of a country called Ta Ts'in or Li Kun, which historians believe was Rome, while the Romans knew of Seres, the Kingdom of Silk. But with the thrust of the Han dynasty into Central Asia, commerce developed between the two distant powers.

The Silk Road flourished until the weakened Han dynasty lost control over the Tarim Basin kingdoms in the third century and political instability hampered trade. In Asia Minor, Parthian power gave way to the Sassanid rulers in Persia, disrupting the traditional overland routes and causing the Mediterranean traders to make greater use of the already long-established sea routes to India. By the sixth century, the southern Silk Road, from Dunhuang via Khotan to Kashgar, was shunned in favour of the new northern Silk Road, which took a course through Hami, over the Heavenly Mountains and along their northern slopes, through the towns of Barkol and Jimusaer, westwards to Yining and beyond to Samarkand and Merv.

The Indo-European Sogdians proved themselves consummate Silk Road traders during the fifth and sixth centuries, selling glass, horses and perfumes to the Chinese, and buying raw silk. Sogdian documents and paintings have surfaced at Dunhuang and Sogdian inscriptions are carved into the stones and rocks strewn along the Indus River Valley, beside the Karakoram Highway in Pakistan.

By the Tang dynasty (618–907), the art of sericulture had been mastered by the Persians and Byzantium, and though silk was not produced in Europe until the 12th century, the heyday of the route was over. However, silk continued to play a most important role as a tributary gift and in local trade with the 'Western barbarians', who were radically to change Chinese culture by introducing new arts, skills and ideas.

CHRONOLOGY OF PERIODS IN CHINESE HISTORY	
NEOLITHIC	7000–2100 BC
HA	2100–1600 BC
SHANG	1600–1027 BC
WESTERN ZHOU	1027–771 BC
EASTERN ZHOU	771–256 BC
SPRING AND AUTUMN ANNALS	770–481 BC
WARRING STATES	480–221 BC
QIN	221–206 BC
WESTERN (FORMER) HAN	206 BC–AD 8
XIN	9–24
EASTERN (LATER) HAN	25–220
THREE KINGDOMS	220–265
WESTERN JIN	265–317
EASTERN JIN	317–420
NORTHERN AND SOUTHERN DYNASTIES	386–589
SIXTEEN KINGDOMS	317–439
FORMER ZHAO	304–329
FORMER QIN	351–383
LATER QIN	384–417
NORTHERN WEI	386–534
WESTERN WEI	535–556
NORTHERN ZHOU	557–581
SUI	581–618
TANG	618–907
FIVE DYNASTIES	907–960
LIAO	916–1125
NORTHERN SONG	960–1127
SOUTHERN SONG	1127–1279
JIN (JURCHEN)	1115–1234
YUAN (MONGOL)	1279–1368
MING	1368–1644
QING (MANCHU)	1644–1911
REPUBLIC OF CHINA	1911–1949
PEOPLE'S REPUBLIC OF CHINA	1949–

A Short History of the Silk Road

amed in the 1870s by the German scholar, Baron Ferdinand von Richthofen, the Silk Road—perhaps the greatest East–West trade route and vehicle for cross-cultural exchange—was first travelled by ambassador Zhang Qian in the second century BC while on a mission from Emperor Wudi (ruled 141–87 BC) of the Han dynasty (206 BC–AD 220). Zhang was sent to recruit the Yuezhi people, who had recently been defeated by the Xiongnu (Huns of Turkish descent) and driven to the western fringes of the Taklamakan Desert. Since the Warring States period (475–221 BC), the Huns had been launching aggressive raids into Chinese territory, which prompted Emperor Qin Shihuangdi of the Qin dynasty (221–207 BC) to build the Great Wall. Eager to defeat these powerful marauders, Wudi heard that the Yuezhi were seeking revenge on the Xiongnu and would welcome help with retaliation from any ally.

Zhang with a caravan of 100 men set out in 138 BC from the Chinese capital of Chang'an (present-day Xi'an) only to be soon captured by the Huns as they passed through the Hexi Corridor in northwest Gansu. The surviving members of the caravan were treated well; Zhang married and had a son. After ten years, he and the remainder of the party managed to escape and continue their journey west along the northern Silk Road to Kashgar and Ferghana. Upon reaching the Yuezhi, Zhang found them to have settled prosperously in the various oases of Central Asia and to be no longer interested in avenging themselves of the Huns. Zhang stayed one year gathering valuable military, economic, political and geographical information and returned via the southern Silk Road, only to be captured again, this time by Tibetan tribes allied with the Xiongnu; once again he escaped. In 125 BC, 13 years later, he returned to Chang'an. Of the original party only he and one other completed the trailblazing journey—the first land route between East and West and one that would eventually link Imperial China with Imperial Rome.

Zhang reported on some 36 kingdoms in the Western Regions, delighting Emperor Han Wudi with detailed accounts of the previously unknown kingdoms of Ferghana, Samarkand, Bokhara and others in what are now the CIS, Pakistan and Persia (Iran) as well as the city of Li Kun, which was almost certainly Rome. Zhang recounted stories he had heard of the famous Ferghana horse, rumoured to be of 'heavenly' stock. Tempted by this fast and powerful warhorse, seemingly far superior to the average steed and having the potential to defeat the marauding Huns, Han Wudi dispatched successive missions to develop political contacts—the first of which Zhang led in 119 BC—and return with foreign envoys, and of course horses, from the courts of Ferghana, Sogdiana, Bactria, Parthia and northern India. Now extinct, these horses were immortalized by artists of both the

Han (206 BC–AD 220) and the Tang dynasties (AD 618–907). The most famous work is the Flying Horse of Gansu, a small bronze sculpture cast by an unknown artist over 2,000 years ago and excavated in 1969 by Chinese archeologists in Wuwei County. Zhang continued seeking allies against the Xiongnu, travelling in 115 BC to the territory of the Wusun, a nomadic tribespeople who lived on the western frontier of the Huns, but again Zhang was unable to enlist support. Upon his return, Zhang died in 113 BC, bearing the Imperial Title of 'Great Traveller'.

lexander the Great's expansion into Central Asia stopped far short of Chinese Turkestan, and he appears to have gained little knowledge of the lands beyond. The Romans, with only a slightly better understanding, were convinced that the Seres (the Silk People, or the Chinese) harvested silk from trees, the 'wool of the forests' according to Pliny. In 53 BC, the seven legions of Marcus Licinius Crassus were the first Romans to see silk in battle whilst pursuing the Parthians, a rough warlike tribe, across the Euphrates. They became the victims of the first 'Parthian shot', which broke the Romans' front line formation and was quickly followed by a tactic that both terrorized and amazed the Romans: the Parthians waved banners of a strange, shimmering material that towered above the defeated soldiers, blinding them in the brilliant heat of the desert. The Romans managed to obtain samples of this marvellous silk from the victorious Parthians, who had traded it for an ostrich egg and some conjurers with a member of Emperor Han Wudi's early trade missions.

The Parthians along with the Sogdians, Indians and Kushans soon became prominent middlemen in the trade of silk, reaping tremendous profits, bartering with Chinese traders who escorted their merchandise to Dunhuang and as far as Loulan, in the heart of the Lop Nor Desert beyond the Great Wall, and carrying the trade on to Persian, Syrian and Greek merchants. Each transaction increased the cost of the end product, which reached the Roman Empire in the hands of Greek and Jewish entrepreneurs. Silk garments became all the rage in Roman society, so much so that in AD 14 men were no longer permitted to wear them, as they were perceived to contribute to an already decadent society. Despite the disapproval of the Empire's moral superiors and its high cost, silk was widely worn amongst even the lowest socio-economic classes. The silk trade flourished up until the second century AD, when it began to arrive in Rome via the sea trade routes.

CARAVANS AND TRADE ROUTES

Silk actually composed a relatively small portion of the trade along the Silk Road: eastbound caravans brought gold, precious metals and stones, textiles, ivory and coral, while westbound caravans transported furs, ceramics, cinnamon bark and

(right) The eastern terminus of the Silk Road, Chang'an (present-day Xi'an) played host to thousands of foreign travellers. Foreign influence can be seen in the dress of this pottery figurine wearing an open fronted robe over trousers

rhubarb as well as bronze weapons. Very few caravans, including the people, animals and goods they transported, would complete the entire route that connected the capitals of these two great empires. The oasis towns that made the overland journey possible became important trading posts, commercial centres where caravans would take on fresh merchants, animals and goods. The oasis towns prospered considerably, extracting large profits on the goods they bought and sold.

uring the Han dynasty, the Chinese referred to the **Taklamakan Desert** as Liu sha, or 'moving sands', since the dunes are constantly moving, blown about by fierce winds. Geographers call it the **Tarim Basin**, after the glacier-fed **Tarim River** that flows east across the Taklamakan Desert to the Lop Nor Lake. The Taklamakan is bordered on three sides by some of the highest mountain ranges in the world: to the north, by the Heavenly Mountains (Tian Shan); to the west, by the Pamirs (Roof of the World); and to the south, by the Karakoram and Kunlun Mountains. To the east lie the Lop Nor and Gobi Deserts. The infamous Taklamakan—which in Turki means 'go in and you will not come out'—has been feared and cursed by travellers for more than 2,000 years. Sir Clarmont Skrine, British consul-general at Kashgar in the 1920s, described it in his book *Chinese Central Asia*:

> To the north in the clear dawn the view is inexpressively awe-inspiring and sinister. The yellow dunes of the Taklamakan, like the giant waves of a petrified ocean, extend in countless myriads to a far horizon with, here and there, an extra large sand-hill, a king dune as it were, towering above his fellows. They seem to clamour silently, those dunes, for travellers to engulf, for whole caravans to swallow up as they have swallowed up so many in the past.

RELIGION AND ART

The most significant innovations carried along the Silk Road to China were the belief systems and religious arts of India, Central Asia and the Middle East. Buddhism began its evolution as a religious doctrine in the sixth century BC, and was adopted as India's official religion in the third century BC. When Buddhism, and to a lesser extent Manicheanism and Nestorianism arrived in China, their art and creed revolutionized Chinese culture. Many of the structures housing ancient religious manuscripts, beautiful frescoes and statuary—built from the first century BC to the end of the Tang dynasty—lay hidden under centuries of sand until their rediscovery at the turn of this century.

According to legend, the Han Emperor Mingdi, who had already heard of Buddhism, dreamt of a golden figure floating in a halo of light—perhaps a flying apsara (Buddhist angel)—that was interpreted by the Emperor's wise men to be the

Buddha himself. Consequently, an envoy was sent to India to learn about the new religion, returning with sacred Buddhist texts and paintings as well as Indian priests to explain the teachings of the Buddha to the Emperor. Monks, missionaries and pilgrims began travelling from India to Central Asia and then on to China, bringing Buddhist writings and paintings, while converts followed the Silk Road west. The new Buddhist art that emerged from Chinese Turkestan, now known as Serindian, absorbed different styles and forms along the way, including those popular in the Kingdom of Gandhara (in what is now the Peshawar valley of northwest Pakistan), where indigenous Indian art forms had already been mixed with those of the Greeks and Persians in the early sixth century BC.

his Graeco-Indian, or Gandharan art was considered revolutionary for its depiction of the Buddha in human form, the temporal earthbound personality of Sakyamuni. Since Sakyamuni had achieved nirvana, escaping the cycles of birth and rebirth, he had essentially ceased to exist. He had previously been symbolized by a footprint, a wheel, a tree, a stupa or Sanskrit characters. The Greek (Hellenistic) influence on traditional Buddhist painting was obvious: instead of a loincloth the Buddha wore flowing robes, had a straight chiselled nose and brow, full lips and wavy hair. Some of the Indian influences that remained were the heavy eyelids and elongated ear lobes, stretched long because of Sakyamuni's former life as a heavily jewelled and worldly prince, a symbol of the life he renounced for the ascetic spiritual life. As a result of rushed and highly unprofessional excavations in the cities and temples of Gandhara (which were already in extremely poor condition), most of the wall paintings and frescoes were destroyed and sculptures are all that remain of this exquisite art form. Nonetheless, it was this art form that travelled across the Pamirs, establishing itself in the oasis towns of the Taklamakan and beyond, where it was again to absorb new influences. Concurrently with the school of Gandhara, the school of Mathura also began to show the Buddha in human form, and its influence is noticeable in figures found in Rawak on the Southern Silk Road.

With the rapid spread of Buddhism along the Silk Road, elaborate cave complexes and monasteries were built in and around the oasis towns, generously supported by powerful local families and merchants to ensure the safe passage of their caravans. Many of the cave frescoes portray these benefactors in pious positions, sometimes by name, since these gifts were believed to help them in their quest for nirvana. Pilgrims from China continued to travel west searching for original manuscripts and holy sites, over the Karakoram range to Gandhara and India.

The first Chinese pilgrim to actually reach India and return with a knowledge of Buddhism was Fa Xian (337–422), a monk who travelled the southern route in 399, through Dunhuang and Khotan and over the Himalayas to India. He studied Buddhism under various Indian masters in Benares, Gandhara and Ceylon (Sri

continued on page 26

THE IMAGE OF THE BUDDHA

ncient Gandhara, comprising modern northwest Pakistan and eastern Afghanistan, was the centre of the great Kusana empire, of which Mathura and the upper Ganges–Jumna Valley represented the outlying areas. While local Indian cultural influences were predominant in those eastern areas, Gandhara had already been open for several centuries to Persian and Greek influences as well as to barbarian influxes from the north. One must not imagine the existence of any well-defined cultural barrier between the Ganges–Jumna Valley and the more central parts of the Kusana empire, for it is certain that Persian and Greek influences had already penetrated, at least to some extent, into the very heartland of India. But whereas such influences are slight and so less clearly definable in India, they were predominant in Gandhara. However, here again one must note that Gandhara was as much open to influence from the Indian side as from the Persian and Greek side. The whole Buddhist religion, the cult of the stupa and its carved decorations, the aniconic symbols of the Buddha and even probably the very idea of creating an anthropomorphic image of the Buddha, not to mention the vast literature on which the whole religion was based, all this was of Indian provenance.

The production of the first anthropomorphic images of the Buddha seemed to coincide with the first attempts at a quasi-historical account of Sakyamuni's life on earth. The earlier Indian art was concerned with a mythical conception of Buddhahood, as represented by symbols and by scenes referring to previous lives of the Bodhisattva (*jatakas*). One may note the stark realism of the scene of the Bodhisattva abandoning his sleeping wife on earth or the scene of his quelling a dangerous snake. It is likely that Gandhara led the way in introducing such realism into Buddhist art, while Hellenistic influences were the motivating force.

Seated or standing, the Buddha is conceived as a short, rather stocky figure, and the position of the body is invariably frontal wherever he appears independently. His hair is arranged in waves gathered together at the top of his head. The eyes are open and there is a little circle (the *urna*, or beauty-spot) between the brows. He often wears a moustache, and it has been suggested that even in cases where the sculpturing does not suggest the presence of one

Seated wooden Buddha, Tumshuk, fifth century AD

nowadays, one may have been painted on. The ear-lobes are distended. The body is covered in a heavy monastic cloak that hangs in deep folds and covers the standing figure to just above the feet, while the seated cross-legged figure may be covered completely. The hands may be held in the gesture of blessing (*abhaya*), or together on the lap in the gesture of repose and meditation (*dhyana*), or together in front of the body in the gesture of teaching (*dharmakra-pravartana*), or touching the earth with the right hand to call the earth-goddess to witness (*bhumisparsa*).

All of these gestures clearly belong to early Indian Buddhist tradition and, except possibly the gesture of blessing, have no association with Western ideas. The mound of hair on the head, corresponding to the *usnisa* (turban or headdress) as well as the circle between the brows and the extended ear-lobes, all relate to Indian tradition. Of these the mound of hair requires special consideration, for it may plausibly be compared with the hair-style of the Greek divinities, and the adoption of this style by the first sculptors of Buddha images in Gandhara has been one of the main arguments in support of the Greek origin of the Buddha image. It is argued that the sculptors preferred to follow a Greek tradition of a divine image with a comely hair-style rather than produce a bald-headed monk as would have been in keeping with the scriptural accounts. This argument may be accepted, especially when one regards the full and radiant face with its sharply chiselled nose and refined proportions.

The Image of the Buddha, edited by David Snellgrove

MAHAYANA AND HINAYANA BUDDHISM

The two most important rival schools of Buddhism, which began in India, were carried to and developed in different parts of Asia. Mahayana and Hinayana Buddhism are both based on the essential teachings of the historical Buddha Sakyamuni but stress different aspects of his teaching. Mahayana Buddhism is also called the 'Greater Vehicle', as opposed to Hinayana, the 'Lesser Vehicle', because it opens the way to salvation for many people; a Mahayana follower seeks to attain enlightenment for the sake of the welfare of all beings. This approach is embodied in the bodhisattvas, 'enlightenment beings' who renounce complete entry into nirvana until all beings are saved; they are guided by compassion and wisdom. The Mahayana places less emphasis on monastic life, holding that all beings can achieve nirvana with the help of the Buddhas and bodhisattvas. Nirvana in this school of thought is not only liberation from the cycles of rebirth, but also the realization that by one's nature one is liberated. Mahayana Buddhism developed during the first century AD; its schools divided and spread to Tibet, China, Korea and Japan.

Hinayana Buddhism is also called Southern Buddhism because of its popularity in Southeast Asia: Sri Lanka, Thailand, Burma, Cambodia and Laos. Hinayana Buddhism evolved after the death of Sakyamuni until the first century BC and represents the original, pure teaching of the Buddha, based on sutras spoken by the Buddha himself. Hinayana followers refer to their teaching as the Theravada, the 'Teaching of the Elders'. Unlike the Mahayana, the Hinayana teachings consider philosophical speculation a hindrance to the attainment of nirvana, yet provide their own analysis of human existence and the structure of individuality. Suffering is seen as real, not just as a state of mind. The supreme goal is liberation from rebirth and attainment of nirvana, which comes through one's own efforts, renouncing the world and overcoming it. A heavy emphasis is therefore placed on a homeless, monastic life, thus excluding laymen from achieving nirvana. The Hinayana equivalent to the bodhisattva is the arhat, a being who has extinguished all desires and defilements, and freed his mind through perfect understanding. Upon his death he will be released from the cycles of existence and not return in another incarnation. The arhat, the ideal of early Buddhism, is unlike a bodhisattva in that the arhat strives to gain only his own salvation.

Lanka), and went as far as Sumatra and Java in Indonesia; altogether he visited over 30 countries, returning to China in 414 via the sea route. The Buddhist monk, Xuan Zang (600–664), is perhaps the most well known of all Chinese travellers on the Silk Road, and one of the four great translators of Buddhist texts. His lasting fame is primarily due to the humorous 16th century novel, *Journey to the West* (also known as *Monkey*), a fictional account of his pilgrimage that includes the various escapades of an odd assortment of characters who accompany the monk on his journey.

Xuan Zang left Chang'an in 629 and travelled along the northern Silk Road to Turpan, Kucha, then onto Tashkent, Samarkand and Bactria, over the Hindu Kush to Gandhara and eventually further south to Sri Lanka. He studied Mahayana Buddhism, particularly the Yogachara school, at various monasteries for 14 years and became a renowned scholar, winning many debates against Hinayana Buddhist scholars. He returned to China in 645 via the southern Silk Road and wrote *Records of the Western Regions*, an excellent account of his travels and the state of Buddhism in the seventh century. With a disciple he co-founded the Fa Xiang school, the Chinese form of Yogachara, which was popular during the Tang dynasty. The central tenet in this belief is that the external world is a product of our consciousness, things exist only as far as they exist in our minds, and nirvana

Uygur man with camel cart and mules braves the harsh conditions of the Southern Silk Road near Hetian

(Buddhahood) is achieved after working through several complex levels of spiritual development and detachment. The Fa Xiang school denies that Buddhahood is possible for everyone, in direct opposition to other Mahayana schools, and it actually contributed to the latter's decline after the Tang dynasty. Xuan Zang translated over 75 Sanskrit works into Chinese, and translated the teachings of the Taoist philosopher, Laozi, into Sanskrit as well. His translations were known for their high literary content and he was instrumental in creating an extensive Buddhist vocabulary in Chinese. The Big Goose Pagoda in Xi'an was built to house the 520 Mahayana and Hinayana texts and various relics that he brought back, and this was where he worked for the remainder of his life, translating sutras.

The religions of Manicheanism and Nestorian Christianity were also introduced, accepted and assimilated along the Silk Road, although neither reached the popularity enjoyed by Buddhism. Manicheanism was started by Manes of Persia in the third century BC and is a religion based on the opposing principles of light and dark (spirit and flesh). Followers of Manicheanism, persecuted by the Sassanian kings in the third to sixth centuries AD, began arriving in Central Asia and flourished during the Sui (581–618) and Tang dynasties. Until the recent discovery of Manichean libraries and wall paintings at Kharakhoja (near Turpan), little was known of this religious

Traders and travellers heading west from Chang'an shadowed the Great Wall for the first leg of their challenging journey. Although left to ruin for centuries, some stretches of this once mighty rammed-earth construction still remain intact

sect, believed by most scholars to have no literature or art. It sustained a substantial following into the tenth century, but then quickly disappeared with the advent of Islam in the West and Buddhism in the East. However, Manicheanism survived in southeastern China until the 17th century.

 ne of the essential beliefs of Nestorian Christianity is that Christ is fully human as well as fully divine, both natures being complete side by side. This belief was condemned in 431 by the Council of Ephesus and hence forbidden in the Roman Empire. The Independent Church of the East, based in Seleucia-Ctesiphon near today's Baghdad, retained this belief. Unable to expand westwards, the Persian Church sent its missionaries east towards China in the seventh century. Nestorian manuscripts were discovered in the Turpan and Khotan regions and Marco Polo found thriving Nestorian communities in cities along the Silk Road as late as the 13th century, even though all foreign religions had been heavily persecuted in 843–845. Eventually, under pressure from Islam these religions disappeared from northwestern China.

THE FALL OF THE SILK ROAD

Not coincidentally, the Silk Road flourished during the highly artistic and prosperous Tang dynasty. Chang'an, the capital, a large cosmopolitan centre, was the departure point and final destination for travellers on the Silk Road. The city in 742 was five by six miles in area and had a population of nearly two million, including over 5,000 foreigners. Numerous religions were represented and the city contained the temples, churches and synagogues of Nestorian Christians, Manicheans, Zoroastrians, Hindus, Buddhists and Jews, to name but a few. Foreigners from Byzantium, Iran, Arabia, Sogdia, Mongolia, Armenia, India, Korea, Malaya and Japan lived in Chang'an. Some Tang tomb murals depict foreigners in the imperial court.

 n addition to Western goods, religious thought and art, Chang'an received caravans from distant lands loaded with exotic treasures such as cosmetics, rare plants including saffron, medicines, perfumes, wines, spices, fragrant woods, books and woven rugs. Strange and unknown animals also arrived: peacocks, parrots, falcons, hunting dogs, lions, and a rare prize, the ostrich or 'camel bird'.

By the end of the eighth century, the sea routes from the southern coastal city of Canton (Guangzhou) to the Middle East were well developed, while the Tibetan occupation of the Tarim Basin from 790 until around 850 AD often disrupted the overland trade routes. The art of sericulture had been mastered by the Persians and Byzantines, and the heyday of the Silk Road was over. The Tang dynasty's downfall led to political chaos and an unstable economy less able to support extravagant foreign imports. At the same time, entire communities, active oasis towns, thriving monasteries and grottoes along the Silk Road were disappearing in the space of weeks, as the glacier-fed streams ran dry or changed course. Since the end of the Ice Age, shrinking glaciers have been consistently reducing the amount of water in the Tarim Basin. Only the most fertile and well-irrigated oasis towns have survived.

The fanatical spread of Islam from the Middle East was one of the most critical factors in the disappearance of the Buddhist civilizations along the Silk Road, and perhaps the most destructive element in the loss of Serindian art. Only those caves and monasteries that had been swallowed by the sands centuries before were able to survive unmutilated by the followers of Allah. Many of the Buddhist cave frescoes, silk paintings and statues had adopted the Gandharan figurative style, portraying 'the almighty' in human form, of which the Muslims were intolerant and even fearful. By the late 15th century, the entire Taklamakan region was thoroughly entrenched in Islam; Buddhist stupas and temples were either destroyed or left to crumble. At this time, the Ming dynasty (1368–1644) virtually shut China off from the outside world, effectively ending the centuries-old influx of foreign ideas and culture. Islam brought a whole new mix of religion, art and architecture that today is the root of Uygur culture in Xinjiang. The surviving remnants of an intensely artistic Buddhist civilization were to remain interned until the late 19th century, when a new generation of 'foreign devils' undertook archaeological excavations in the Tarim Basin.

159. ROWS OF CAVE-TEMPLES, SHOWING DECAYED PORCHES, NEAR MIDDLE OF SOUTHERN GROUP, 'THOUSAND BUDDHAS' SITE.

An exterior view of the Mogao Caves near Dunhuang, taken by Aurel Stein in 1907

FACTS FOR THE TRAVELLER

GETTING THERE

xperiencing the sights and sounds of the Silk Road is for most Westerners the fulfilment of their own Marco Polo adventure fantasy, and the opening of the China–Pakistan border at the Khunjerab Pass in 1986 made that dream an exciting reality. A public bus runs from at least May to October, depending on the weather, and vehicles of various sizes can be chartered for the remainder of the year. Since 1992 there have been flights from Almaty to Urumqi and this is the normal way to cross from China to Central Asia. It is also possible to enter China by rail from Almaty in Kazakhstan, and by road from Bishkek in Kyrgyzstan.

VISAS AND CUSTOMS

All visitors entering China must have a valid passport and visa, but this is usually a straightforward process. Tourists travelling in a group are listed on a single group visa issued in advance to tour organizers. Tourist visas for individual travellers can be obtained directly through Chinese embassies and consulates around the world. Certain travel agents and tour operators can arrange individual visas for their clients. Visa fees and their duration vary considerably, depending on the source of the visa and the time taken to issue it. In Hong Kong, for instance, travel agents can arrange a three-month tourist visa in two to three days for around HK$400, while the same visa obtained from **China Travel Service (HK) Ltd** (4/F CTS House, 78–83 Connaught Road, Central, tel 2853-3533) will cost HK$210. All that is needed is a completed application form and one passport photograph. Six-month multiple-entry business visas are also available and cost HK$850 for most nationalities. Visas can also be obtained directly from the **Visa Office of the Foreign Ministry of the PRC** (7th Floor, 26 Harbour Road, Wanchai, Hong Kong, tel 3413-2424).

ost nationalities require a visa to cross the Khunjerab Pass into Pakistan, regulations change and it is advisable to get one either before leaving home or at the **Embassy of the Islamic Republic of Pakistan** at 1 Dongzhimenwai Dajie, Sanlitun, Beijing, tel (010) 6532-6660. During the tourist season the border is open daily. Travellers can have their Chinese visas extended for 30 days up to three times at Public Security Bureaux in most open towns and cities, although the third extension can be difficult. The service is only granted up to four days before an existing visa or extension expires. At some offices extension charges vary according to nationality, at others there's a flat fee. Beware PSBs which suggest you use an agent to make your application for you (such as Beijing), as overcharging will be the result.

A staple of the Uygur diet is delicious nan bread, made in hot clay ovens in time-honoured tradition

Modern-day travel between northern Xinjiang and the ancient trading city of Kashgar makes it difficult to imagine the horrific hardships suffered by travellers of old

A visa permits visits to all places on a 'list' of open cities, towns and counties. However, an up-to-date full listing is almost impossible to acquire, even from Chinese embassies abroad. In theory, places not on the open list, called closed places, can only be visited if the visitor procures an Alien's Travel Permit, normally in the provincial capital. Alien's Travel Permits are not granted for a third category of places deemed 'forbidden'. Unless otherwise mentioned, all cities and sites described in this book are open to foreign tourists, while the territory in between them may be closed. One might be able to travel through but not stay overnight in such areas. (At present, all major archaeological sites along the Southern Silk Road—including Dandan Oilik, Karadong, Niya, Endere and Loulan—are off-limits. To visit these sites a special permit is required, issued by the Cultural Relics Bureau in Urumqi. These are seldom granted and may carry a fee of several hundreds or even thousands of US dollars.)

If you have purchased antiques in China you may be required to show the official receipts to customs officials. Two litres of alcohol, one pint of perfume, three cartons of cigarettes, 72 rolls of still film and 3,000 feet of movie film, and medicine for personal use may be taken in. Firearms and illicit drugs are strictly forbidden. There is no limit to the amount of foreign currency you can bring into China.

ITINERARIES: ORGANIZED TOURS AND INDEPENDENT TRAVEL

he journey along China's Silk Road can combine air, rail and road travel, requiring careful planning to achieve as much as possible in the time available, given the enormous distances involved, the condition of the roads, the slowness of the trains, and the infrequency of some internal flights. Many tours offered by foreign travel agents begin in Xi'an, with flights to Lanzhou and Dunhuang. The overnight journey by train from Dunhuang to Turpan is followed by a stretch by road to Urumqi, the capital of Xinjiang. You can also fly from Dunhuang to Urumqi, and from Urumqi there are daily flights to Kashgar.

Independent travellers with more time and energy may prefer to take the train from Xi'an to Lanzhou and up the Hexi Corridor, stopping at Jiayuguan, the westernmost section of the Great Wall. From here there is a bus to Dunhuang and then a bus or a train to Turpan or Urumqi. Travel between these latter twin destinations is best accomplished by road. Buses from either Urumqi or Turpan make the run southwest to Kashgar. Fitted with berths rather than seats, they drive non-stop through the night and take about 40 hours.

Although this book follows the Silk Road from east to west, Xi'an to Kashgar, it is equally useful if you are travelling eastwards and arrive from Pakistan, Tibet or the CIS. The summer is peak season, with many travellers going east and west, as well as north to the CIS and south to Qinghai and Tibet. A leisurely tour of the Silk Road could take up to three months, with two of those in Xinjiang, particularly if you begin and end in Xi'an. The amount of time you spend on the Silk Road depends largely on the form of transportation you use, which in turn depends on your budget.

 here are now a wide variety of packages available. **Listed in alphabetic order below are just a sampling of some of those companies.** Tour highlights might include a unique melon and fruit tour, ice climbing on the Qiyi Glacier, gliding across the Gobi Desert, or hunting wild antelope in the grasslands of Gansu. Some tour groups have even undertaken a 70-day desert trek along the Southern Silk Road by camel.

Abercrombie & Kent International, 1520 Kensington Road, Oak Brook, Chicago, Il 60521, USA, tel: 1 630 954 2944, fax: 1 630 954 3324, website: www.abercrombiekent.com

Asia Transpacific Journeys, 2995 Center Green Court, Boulder, Colorado 80301, USA, tel: (1) 303 443 6789 (toll free: 1-800-642-2742), fax: (1) 303 443 7078, email: travel@asiatranspacific.com, website: www.asiatranspacific.com

Beijing Longmen Travel Service, No. A9 Daqudeng Lane, Meishuguan Houjie East District, Beijing, China, tel: 86 10 4012179, 86 10 4074616, fax: 86 10 4012180, email: blts@public.bta.net.cn, website: www.bta.net.cn

Caravan Café, 120 Seman Road, Kashgar, Xinjiang 844000, China, tel: 86 298 2196, 86 298 1864, email: info1@caravancafe.com, website: www.caravancafe.com

Exodus, 9 Weir Rd, London SW12 0LT, UK, tel: (020) 8675 5550, email: info@exodus.co.uk, website: www.exodus.co.uk

Explore, 1 Frederick St, Aldershot, Hants GU11 1LQ, UK, tel: (01252) 319448, email: info@explore.co.uk, website: www.explore.co.uk

Geographic Expeditions, 2627 Lombard Street, San Francisco, CA 94123, USA, tel: 1 800 777 8183, fax: 1 415 346 5535, Email: info@geoex.com, website: www. geoex.com

Golden Bridge International, 6/F, Tak Woo House, 17-19 D'Aguilar St. Central, Hong Kong, China, tel: 852 2801 5591, fax: 852 2523 7293, email: agentdesk@goldenbridge.net, website: www.goldenbridge.net

Helen Wong's Tours, Level 18, 456 Kent Street, Sydney, Australia, tel: 61 2 9267 7833, fax: 61 2 9267 7717, email: info@helenwongstours.com, website: www.helenwongstours.com

MIR Corporation, Suite 210, 85 S. Washington Street, Seattle WA 98104, USA, tel: 1 206 624 7289 and 1 800 424 7289, fax: 1 206 624 7360, email: info@mircorp.com, website: www.mircorp.com

Peregrine Adventures, 258 Lonsdale Street, Melbourne VIC 3000, tel: (03) 9663 8611, fax: (03) 9663 8618, email: websales@peregrine.net.au, website: www.peregrine.net.au

Regent Holidays,15 John Street, Bristol, BS1 2 HR, England, tel: 44 117 921 1711, fax: 44 117 925 4866, email: regent@regent-holidays.co.uk, website: www.regent-holidays.co.uk

Silk Road Travellers Club, St Mary's Court, Henley-on-Thames, Oxfordshire, RG9 2AA, UK, tel: 44 1491 410 510, fax: 44 1491 637 617, email: info@silkraodtravel.co.uk, website: www.silkroadtravel.co.uk

Steppes East, 51 Castle St, Cirencester, Gloucestershire GL7 1QD, UK, tel: (01285) 651010, fax: (01285) 885888, email: sales@steppeseast.co.uk, website: www.steppeseast.co.uk

Sundowners, First Floor, 14 Barley Mow Passage, Chiswick, London W4, 4PH, UK, tel: 44 20 8742 8612, fax: 44 20 8742 3045

Suite 15, 600 Lonsdale Street
Melbourne, Australia, tel: 61 3 9600 1934, fax: 61 3 9642 5838, email: mail@sundowners-travel.com, website: www.sundowners-travel.com

TCS Expeditions, Suite 450, 2025 First Avenue, Seattle WA 98121, USA, tel: 1 800 727 7300 and 727 7477, fax: 1 206 727 7309, email: travel@tcs-expeditions.com, website: www.tcs-expeditions.com

Travel China Guide, Suite 5-B, Kang De Mansion, 447 Chang An Nan Lu, Xi'an 710061, China, tel: 86 29 8523 6688, fax: 86 29 8525 8897, 8526 5801, website: www.travelchinaguide.com

Travelsphere Ltd, Compass House, Rockingham Road, Market Harborough, Leics LE16 7QD, UK, tel: (01858) 410 818, website: www.travelsphere.co.uk

Voyages Jules Verne, Travel Promotions Ltd, 21 Dorset Square, London NW1 6QG, tel: 44 207 616 1000, fax: 44 207 723 8629, website: www.vjv.co.uk

Wild China, No. 70 Dongsi Qitiao, Dongcheng District, Beijing, 100007, China, tel: (86-10) 6403-9737/9724/9726, fax: (86-10) 6403-9703, email: customerservices@wildchina.com, website: www.wildchina.com

Wild Frontiers Adventure Travel, 40A Peterborough Rd, London SW6 3BN, UK, tel: (020) 7736 3968, fax: (020) 7751 0710, email: office@wildfrontiers.co.uk, website: www.wildfrontiers.co.uk

World Expeditions, 580 Market Street, Suite #525, San Francisco, CA, 94104, tel: 1 415 989 2212, fax: 1 415 989 2112, Toll free: 1 888 464 TREK, email: contactus@worldexpeditions.net, website: www.worldexpeditions.net

3 Northfields Prospect, Putney Bridge Road, London SW18 1PE, UK, tel: 020 8870 2600, fax: 020 8870 2615, email: enquiries@worldexpeditions.co.uk, website: www.worldexpeditions.co.uk

Xinjiang Tianshan Tianchi International Travel Service, Huadian Building No.5 Jiankang Road, 83002 Urumqi, Xinjiang, China, tel: 86 991 28 43 832, fax:86 991 28 46 273, email: nature@mail.xj.cninfo.net

USEFUL WEBSITES

The Silk Road Project, an organization founded by classical cellist Yo-Yo Ma, aims to 'illuminate the Silk Road's historical contribution to the diffusion of art and culture'. Its website contains much useful information on the region:

www.silkroadproject.org

Caravan Café, a foreign-owned establishment in Kashgar, has a website containing basic information on the western Xinjiang region and its sights:

www.caravancafe.com

The British Library's International Dunhuang Project has a huge amount of information about the caves of the Dunhuang region, and contains excellent links to other aspects of Silk Road history:

http://idp.bl.uk/

The Silk Road Foundation, Saratoga, California has a vast amount of useful information:

www.silk-road.com

Turfan Research, Berlin-Brandenburgische Akademie der Wissenschaften, Berlin contains all the ancient manuscripts found in Turpan (the text is also in English):

www.bbaw.de/vh/turfan/

www.chinapage.com/silkroad contains information on Silk Road art and culture in both Chinese and English.

www.chinaplanner.com/silkroad also contains comprehensive information on the region.

GETTING AROUND

TRANSPORTATION

 etails of routes, connections, timetables and booking offices are contained in the Practical Information section for each city. China is experiencing a burgeoning demand from domestic travellers, so availability of seats has been affected and where possible booking well ahead is advised.

BY AIR

Airplanes link most of the cities along the Silk Road; frequency of flights can vary from several times each day to once a week. Airplanes are the most efficient, comfortable and expensive way of getting around, costing as much as ten times the price of a bus ticket. The **Civil Aviation Administration of China (CAAC)** is efficient in making reservations; however, tickets are in short supply, so book as far ahead as possible. CITS and some of the larger hotels can also make reservations. You can book air tickets from any reputable travel agency, for example those attached to hotels. Tickets for a variety of Chinese airlines serving Urumqi can be bought at Beijing's Aviation Building in Fuxingmennei Dajie (metro Xidan). From Hong Kong **Dragonair** (4609 Cosco Tower, 183 Queen's Road Central) offers a round-trip service to Xi'an, on Mondays, Wednesdays and Fridays (reservations tel 3193-3888). In Xi'an, bookings can be made at the Dragonair desk in the lobby of the Sheraton Xi'an Hotel (tel 426-2988). China Northwest Airlines offers a similar service every Tuesday, Wednesday, Thursday, Saturday and Sunday.

BY RAIL

The Lanzhou-Urumqi railway line, the iron silk road, was completed in 1963. A spur, from Turpan to Korla, came into use in 1984, and the westward extension of this, a further 975 kilometres as far as Kashgar, is now complete. For those with time to travel in short stages, the railway along most of the Silk Road serves as the backbone for their transport plans. Hardseat tickets can be bought easily, and suffered for the daylight hours. However, travellers taking longer, overnight journeys face difficulties in booking sleepers, unless they are boarding at termini stations or major intermediate ones where travel agents may be able to procure tickets. Regarding accommodation, hardseat carriages are usually dreary, dirty and overcrowded, nevertheless recommended to the curious. Overnight journeys are extremely trying and dampen the spirits of all but the hardiest travellers. Conversation and kindness of the locals can have an anaesthetic effect. Sleeper carriage berths, both hard and soft, are perfectly comfortable, but may sometimes need to be booked months in advance. Travellers making long journeys should prepare ample provisions, even drinks, as boilers often run dry from Gansu westwards. All ticket prices are now standardized, which means foreigners and Chinese pay the same fare.

By Road

There are now express buses along the highway between Turpan and Urumqi; they take about three hours. Public buses are the most inexpensive method and slow-moving one, especially in Xinjiang where they regularly depart one or two hours behind schedule. It should be noted, however, that although schedules are in Beijing time, Xinjiang is in a different time zone by local decree and therefore this two-hour time difference affects bus departure times. The 40-hour bus ride from Urumqi to Kashgar is highly recommended for hardy travellers, offering spectacular views of the Heavenly Mountains and glimpses of the oasis towns along the northern rim of the Taklamakan Desert. Note that in Gansu, foreigners are required to purchase an insurance policy in order to ride inter-city buses and to produce the receipt when buying subsequent tickets. Bus-company employees are fairly rigid about this rule, or may demand a substantial bribe to ignore it.

Another option is to hire a land cruiser or mini-van, enabling you to visit sites far from cities or towns that would otherwise be inaccessible. Costs can be minimized if you are in a group, and bargain the price down to a reasonable level. Travel agencies and many hotels have cars or mini-vans for hire. Prices should be based on the number of days hired and kilometres travelled, an average of US$30 to US$50 per day.

Health and Altitude

here are no mandatory vaccination requirements, but make sure your basic immunizations are up to date: polio, diphtheria and tetanus. Vaccinations against the following are recommended, although need may vary according to time of year and part of China to be visited: meningococcal meningitis, cholera, hepatitis A and B, and Japanese B encephalitis. There are two different prophylactic regimens against malaria depending on the part of China to be visited. Contact your nearest specialist travel clinic or tropical medicine hospital, and plan well ahead.

Travellers crossing the Khunjerab Pass and overnighting at Tashkurgan, where the altitude is over 3,300 metres (10,800 feet), may suffer altitude sickness. This is caused by an insufficient flow of oxygen to the brain and other vital organs. It can affect anybody at above 3,000 metres (10,000 feet).

The symptoms of altitude sickness include headache, nausea and shortness of breath. In 99 per cent of these cases, rest and two aspirins relieve the discomfort. However, the serious, sometimes fatal, conditions of pulmonary and cerebral oedema also begin with these same symptoms. Overexertion and dehydration contribute to mountain sickness. Drink plenty of fluids, do not smoke, and avoid sleeping pills or tranquillisers, which tend to depress respiration and limit oxygen intake. Diamox (acetozolamide), a mild prescription diuretic that stimulates oxygen intake, is used by doctors of the Himalayan Rescue Association in Kathmandu for climbers making sudden ascents.

CLIMATE AND CLOTHING

Conditions along the Silk Road vary from a typical inland China climate around Xi'an (similar to that of Eastern Europe) to a severe desert climate for most of its westward extension. The latter entails an extremely hot and arid summer, a short, barely noticeable autumn and spring, and a relatively cold winter, with snow on high ground. The oases have micro-climates similar to conditions in the hot Mediterranean areas, with moisture provided from underground channels and wells.

lthough the hottest, the summer months are the most rewarding time to travel—the oasis towns are full of life, flowers are in bloom, fruit is in season, and the smell of sweet melons and resinating hemp fills the air. In Xinjiang June is already hot, with summer temperatures averaging 30°C (86°F) in Urumqi and rising to the mid-40°sC (110°F) in the Turpan area. Precipitation is minimal and the air is very dry. Throughout July, August and September, the temperatures in Xi'an reach an average high of 38°C (100°F) and can be extremely humid. Visitors in the summer should wear light cotton garments and a hat to guard against sunburn. In deference to Muslim sensibilities, long pants or skirts should be worn by both sexes whenever possible. Visitors would do well to imitate the locals by staying in the shade around midday. Shoes should be solid and comfortable; even in the summer it is advisable to have thick-soled shoes, for the ground temperature can get extremely hot, especially at sites in the desert.

Winters are raw and severe. During December and January, Xi'an averages around –4° or –5°C (25° or 23°F). The average temperature in Urumqi is –10°C (14°F) and is considerably lower in the mountains and northern Junggar Basin. Wool and fleece layers, topped with a coat or jacket of down or *thinsulate* with a wind-breaking shell, should constitute the main defence against the cold. Pay attention also to extremities: hats, scarves, gloves and good socks in thick-soled boots are essential. Even in spring and autumn, the most comfortable seasons for travel, one's feet can freeze to numbness while sitting motionless on a long distance bus. Two thin pairs of all-wool socks are better than a thick pair of acrylic ones.

Travellers should also be prepared for dust storms, especially in Turpan, which often begin in the early afternoon and last for several hours: abrasive, blasting sands whipped up by strong winds, bringing all activity to a halt. The dust is particularly bad news for your camera. (Fuji, Kodak and Konica colour film is widely available, but, with the exception of Xi'an, neither slide nor black-and-white film can be found.) It is important to carry a good torch, especially when visiting unlit Buddhist caves. A sturdy pair of sunglasses and water bottle are also highly recommended. (The ideal time for visiting the Southern Silk Road is autumn—in spring there is often fog and powerful sandstorms, and temperatures in summer and winter are too extreme.)

MONEY AND COSTS

CHINESE CURRENCY

The Chinese currency is called Renminbi (meaning people's currency) and this is abbreviated to Rmb. It is denominated in yuan, referred to as *kuai* in everyday speech. The *yuan* is divided into ten *jiao* (colloquially called *mao*). Each *jiao* is divided into 10 *fen*. There are large notes for 100, 50, 10, 5 and 1 *yuan*, small notes for 5, 2 and 1 *jiao*, and coins for 1 *yuan*, 5 and 1 *jiao*, and 5, 2 and 1 *fen*. In March 2004, US$100 and £100 bought around Rmb828 and Rmb1,530 respectively.

FOREIGN CURRENCY

There is no limit to the amount of foreign currency you can take into China, but amounts over US$5,000 should be declared. In the major cities, all freely negotiable currencies can be exchanged for Rmb at branches of the Bank of China, in hotels and the large stores. Traveller's cheques are changed at a slightly better rate than cash.

CHEQUES AND CREDIT CARDS

All major European, American and Japanese traveller's cheques are accepted, although there are no facilities to exchange these en route so travellers are advised to change these for cash at major cities. International credit cards are accepted in only the most upmarket shops and hotels, and a limited number of bank machines in major cities. In other places only Chinese Visa and Mastercards may be used. Cash may be drawn with a four per cent service charge at larger branches of the Bank of China in major cities.

TIPPING

Travellers may find that upmarket hotel staff, particularly bell boys, and guides and drivers often expect tips.

BARGAINING

 ith the exception of state-run stores with fixed prices, always bargain in markets, shops and restaurants, and occasionally hotels. Even state-run stores will sometimes give discounts on expensive items like carpets. Bargaining in China can be good-humoured or it can be infuriating; it is a game won by technique and strategy, not by anger or threats. Thus, it should be leisurely and friendly, and not be seen as a one-way process at all, since the Chinese enjoy it. Finally, it is bad manners to continue to bargain after a deal has been struck, a service rendered, or an item purchased. Ask around before you buy to try and determine what the 'correct' price is. When you have offered the highest price you are willing to pay, do not budge, and as a last resort walk away as feigned uninterest may make for a good deal. Your position is strongest when you appear not to care. There is much more incentive for the budget traveller to learn the language than for the more affluent. The traveller can save a lot of money and make friends more easily if he or she knows how to bargain in Chinese (or Uygur in Xinjiang). It can be a challenge to get the same price as the locals, yet coming close is almost as satisfying.

ACCOMMODATION

dyssey Guides offer a small selection of top-end accommodation for those adventurers who like their comforts away from home too. For this we make no apologies—however, for those independent-minded souls with the instinct to enhance their travel experience by experimenting when looking for a place to stay, the following websites will open the door to a wider choice of hotel options.

www.smarttravel.com	www.asiahotels.com	www.orientaltravel.com
www.zuji.com.hk	www.hotel2visit.com	www.sinohotel.com
www.voyagenow.com		

Lodging along the Silk Road ranges from international joint-venture hotels, like the Hyatt in Xi'an and the Holiday Inn in Urumqi, to stark guesthouses where the sheets are rarely changed. The four basic types of accommodation available can be categorized as follows:

lushe/luguan (traveller's hostel)—the smallest, cheapest and probably the dirtiest lodging, patronized by truck drivers and overnighting bus passengers; toilets are communal and there are no showers; many do not have the necessary licence to accept foreigners.

zhaodaisuo (guesthouse)—often the only place for foreigners to stay in the smaller cities and towns; inexpensive dormitory accommodation is available; communal toilets and public showers, but they tend to be cleaner than a *lushe*.

binguan (hotel)—anything from slightly cleaner and more comfortable than *zhaodaisuo* right up to the level of luxury foreign joint-venture establishments; some English may be spoken, and there may be several restaurants; patronized by foreigners, Chinese businessmen, and senior cadres.

fandian (hotel or restaurant)—covers the entire range from *lushe* to *binguan*, usually at the higher end of Chinese accommodation.

Receptionists assume all foreigners are wealthy and require only top-quality rooms. They will explain that the cheaper rooms are unavailable or inadequate, and it may take a little time and patience to get the room you want. Regardless of the type of accommodation, there is the ubiquitous thermos of *kai shui* (boiled water) in every room and every floor has a *fuwuyuan* (attendant) who looks after your needs and holds the keys to your room. Location of accommodation is contained in the Practical Information section for each city. Quoted prices are subject to change and should only be used as reference.

Food and Drink

Food and drink along China's Silk Road varies little from Xi'an to Kashgar—wholesome and tasty, if simple and repetitive. Although most cities and towns have restaurants specializing in Sichuan, Cantonese and Beijing or Shanghai cuisine, travellers immediately become aware of the Islamic influence on eating habits in northwest China—pork, the staple meat of the Han Chinese, is replaced by beef in Gansu and mutton or lamb in Xinjiang.

Night markets (*ye shi*) and small restaurants (*xiao chi*) are by far the tastiest places to eat. Each night around dusk, street vendors set up stalls and tables on prearranged streets throughout the various cities. These lively night markets provide an excellent opportunity to stroll and sample from the various cauldrons, woks and grills that line the street. Small restaurants are best for authentic local dishes and distant regional flavours. The best way to order is by pointing to what others are having or by going into the kitchen and picking out various meat and vegetable combinations. With few exceptions, hotel restaurants offer expensive and unexciting meals, a last resort when deciding where to eat. The Practical Information section for each city contains useful information on night markets, small restaurants and local specialities.

he most popular of all foods in the northwest is barbecued mutton on skewers (*kao yangrou*), which tends to be less spicy the further west you go and is eaten with a wide variety of flatbreads (*bing*) that can be sweet, salty or plain. In Gansu, hot pot (*huoguo*), a cross between the spicy Sichuan and more functional Mongolian styles, is a common way of cooking and eating skewers of vegetables and meat as well as other favourites such as liver, coagulated blood and skewered entrails. Boiled mutton dumplings (*yangrou shuijiao*) are served either in soup or with a spicy soy/vinegar sauce. In Xinjiang, most meals consist of noodles or bread served with mutton in one form or another. The most common dish is *lamian*—fresh noodles served with sautéed lamb, tomatoes, aubergine and hot green peppers. A more detailed description of Uygur cuisine is contained in Uygur Food, Drink and a Few Words (see page 188). Both Xinjiang and Gansu produce a wide variety of fruit (*shuiguo*), which is in season in summer months—apricots (*xingzi*), plums (*meizi*) and mulberries (*sangshu*) in June; melons (*gua*) in July; peaches (*taozi*), figs (*wuhuaguo*) and grapes (*putao*) in August; pomegranates (*shiliu*), apples (*pingguo*) and pears (*lizi*) in September. There are over 50 types of Hami melons and many different species of watermelon (*xigua*, or western melon), which first came to China from Africa via the Silk Road.

Tea (*cha*) is taken with meals or just bread. In Xi'an and Gansu, the most common variety is a smooth green tea, whereas in Xinjiang people drink a rough black tea resembling sticks and twigs. Beer (*pijiu*) and rice wine (*baijiu*) are popular, particularly among the Hans, and often accompany meals. Each province and city tends to have its own beer, none of which tastes as good as those of east and southwest China, but can still be satisfying when it is cold and you are hot. Most types of refreshments that you may desire in the desert heat—from Coca-Cola to flavoured water, thick fresh yoghurt to fruit juice as well as ice cream, frozen yoghurt and popsicles—are available from vendors with refrigerators on almost every street corner.

HABITS, CUSTOMS, AND CULTURE

China is probably one of the safest countries to visit, although you should still travel wisely, keeping your money close to you at all times. Be cautious in crowded public areas like bazaars, bus and train stations, since razor slashers and theft from pockets and day packs are not uncommon. The best prevention against theft is a money belt worn inside your clothing.

 s few Chinese are able to leave the country, they travel extensively and in great numbers within China. Contact with the local tourists can be rewarding as they are friendly and interested in meeting foreigners. Men are constantly offered cigarettes, beer and rice wine as a token of their friendship or merely as a standard act of courtesy. Spoken English is generally poor, but you will find that a few words of Mandarin go a long way and are greatly appreciated. Chinese women are less outgoing than the men and more hesitant in approaching foreigners. While the Uygurs are interested in your religion and whether you are Muslim, the Han Chinese will ask where you are from and how much money you make. Questions considered personal in the West are fair game for the Chinese.

Standards of hygiene in China are not perceived in the same way as in the West. Although the Chinese as individuals are clean, their public habits may lead you to think otherwise. Most significant is the habit of hawking and spitting regardless of whether in a restaurant, train, bus, waiting room or on a crowded street corner. Spitting has been a recent government hygiene issue, resulting in many ineffective public signs banning the habit. Hygiene in most restaurants is not up to Western standards but most are safe and offer disposable chopsticks, the result of another government hygiene campaign.

As in most Asian countries, 'squat' toilets are the norm (with the exception of luxury-class hotels) and you will need to get used to them. Public toilets consist of long rows of holes in the ground, which are sometimes separated by low walls. They are found in numerous locations throughout the city as the Chinese often do not have toilets in their own homes. Buy your own toilet paper and carry it around with you. Most Western health and sanitary products should be brought with you; items such as tampons are expensive and often hard to find. Chinese pharmacies carry Eastern and Western medicines and are the best places to go for basic stomach disorders, colds and headaches.

TIME AND COMMUNICATIONS

 hina is eight hours ahead of Greenwich Mean Time (London) and 13 hours ahead of Eastern Standard Time (New York). Since time is standardized throughout China, Xinjiang finds itself with dawn at 7.30 or 8 am and dusk around 10.30 or 11 pm (even later in the summer). Though air and rail timetables and bus schedules use Beijing standard time, locals often refer to the unofficial Xinjiang time, which is two hours behind. So it is essential to determine whether departure times are Beijing or Xinjiang time. Office hours in Xinjiang are 10 am–2 pm and 4–8 pm, Beijing time, but this can vary from city to city; the further south and west you go the more lax the adherence to official hours becomes. Beijing time is three hours ahead of Pakistani standard time.

International telephone calls can be made from most cities along the Silk Road, at hotels, post offices and telecommunication centres. Most hotels have International Direct Dial (IDD), collect calls are easy to make and the connection is reasonably good. The cheapest way to make international call is with a phone card, which can now be bought and bargained for. Calls to the US and Europe cost approximately US$0.30 per minute. Post offices are easily accessible, yet foreigners may find it easier to use the ones located in the hotels, where you can send domestic and international mail and packages. It is advisable to get someone to write out the name of the foreign country in Chinese characters. Officials usually check the contents of packages. International express mail service (such as DHL) is available in Xi'an, Lanzhou and Urumqi. Friendship Stores will mail items purchased in the store. Receiving mail in China at various Postes Restantes (located at the main post offices) or hotels is fairly hit-and-miss. Faxes and emails can be sent from or received at business centres, which are becoming more common in hotels, and at cafés in the larger towns.

HOLIDAYS

In contrast to the long calendar of traditional Chinese festivals, the modern Chinese calendar now has only four official holidays: January 1, New Year's Day; May 1, Labour Day; October 1, National Day commemorating the founding of the

People's Republic of China (PRC); and Chinese New Year, also called the Spring Festival, a three-day holiday in late January or early February celebrating the Lunar New Year. As offices usually close for several days around major holidays it is essential to book travel arrangements well in advance, especially as this is a popular time for the Chinese themselves to travel. In the Muslim areas of Gansu and Xinjiang, Islamic festivals are celebrated, though not officially classified as national holidays. These include the *Bairam* or 'Minor' festival and *Korban* or 'Major' festival. The month-long Ramadan fast is also observed. Travellers should avoid travelling during public holidays, when, it seems, the whole population of China is on the move.

RED TAPE

here are numerous and seemingly absurd rules and regulations governing foreign travel in China that can be extremely frustrating, especially when enforced by power-starved minor officials. With decades of whimsical official policy, the Chinese are reluctant to take matters into their own hands: 'never take the initiative in making decisions—you may be held responsible for the consequences' reads a maxim from an old civil-service manual. When stumbling upon these various regulations, do not raise your voice or become visibly upset, and above all never give the person you are dealing with a reason to refuse you. In most cases a compromise is usually possible with neither party losing face.

THE CHINESE LANGUAGE

EXPLANATION OF PINYIN

In 1958, the Chinese government adopted pinyin as the official system for romanizing Chinese characters, now used by the Western press and most phrase books. Previously the Wade-Giles system was the most common way for English speakers to phoneticize Chinese, and can still be found in many old history and art books on China. Throughout this book, the spellings of people, places and things follow the pinyin transliteration. In the Xinjiang section the pinyin is used, with the historical or Uygur names following in parenthesis. Mandarin (*putonghua*, or common speech) is the official language of China; in Beijing the most standard form of *putonghua* is spoken, and pinyin follows that pronunciation. Signboards and restaurant names are often written in pinyin, mostly for a foreign look, which many Chinese themselves have difficulty reading. Nowadays, however, Chinese schoolchildren begin learning pinyin from the age of seven. Letters in pinyin correspond closely to standard English pronunciation, although some letters have different sounds.

Initials (Word Beginnings)

c	like the *ts* in 'fi*ts*'
q	like the *ch* in '*ch*eese'
x	somewhere between *sh* and *s*, an aspirated sound
z	like the *ds* in 'la*ds*'
zh	like the *j* in 'judge'

Finals (Word Endings)

a	like *ah* in 'cheet*ah*'
ai	like the *ie* in 'tie'
e	like 'her' without the *r*
ei	like the *ay* in 'ray'
i	like *ee* in 'wh*eeze*' except after c, ch, r, sh, z and zh when it becomes a short sound, like the *i* in 'sir'
ian	like 'yen', or the *ien* in Vie*n*na
ie	sounds like ieh, or the *ye* in 'yes'
o	like 'oh', slightly drawn out
ou	like *o* in 'm*ow*'
u	like the French '*tu*' or the German '*ü*'
uai	sounds like 'why'
uan	like *uan* in 'ig*uan*a', sounds like 'wan'
ue	like the *ue* in the Spanish 'f*ue*go'
ui	like *ey* in 'h*ey*'

Every Chinese character has only one syllable with its own tone and meaning; words consisting of several characters will take on a variety of different meanings (each syllable retains its own tone and pronunciation):

Pinyin		English Approximation
Beijing	=	Bay-Jhing (not zhing)
Cixi	=	Ts-shee
Mao Zedong	=	Mao Ds-dong
Qianlong	=	Chien-lohng
Xi'an	=	Shee-Ahn
Zhou Enlai	=	Jho En-lie

Chinese has four tones, which are marked above the word and used primarily in language texts. The tone of a word corresponds with its meaning; the same word pronounced with a different tone takes on an entirely different meaning. The four tones are: flat (¯), rising (ˊ), falling-rising (ˇ) and falling (ˋ). Although difficult to learn at first, they are essential to being understood in China. If you ask for something as simple as tea (*cha*) in a restaurant, using the wrong tone, the waiter will either give you a blank look or a fork.

VOCABULARY

ne of the best ways to learn 'street Chinese' or basic 'market Mandarin' is by listening and repeating. When making a purchase, ask the name of the item (*zhèige jiào shénme míngzi?* 这个叫甚么名子？) before asking how much it is (*duoshao qián?* 多少钱), and if five *kùai* is too expensive offer him two (*Wu kuài tài guì le! Liang kuài hao bù hao?* 五块太贵！两块好不好？). Within a few weeks, with a keen ear, you can pick up a surprising amount, which is particularly satisfying if you plan to spend several months in China. There are many dialects spoken in China, which vary widely in their proximity to *putonghua*. In the northwest, spoken Chinese is fairly standard with some local flavour and regional variation. In order to make something a question add '*ma*' to the end of the sentence. The following is a relatively simple list of phrases and words broken down into four sections: basics, getting around, food and drink and numbers.

BASICS

Hello, how are you?:	*Nǐ hǎo ma?*	你好吗?
Very good, thank you:	*Hěn hǎo, xièxiè nǐ*	很好，谢谢你
Yes/no:	*Dùi / Bù*	对 ／ 不
Goodbye:	*Zàijiàn*	再见
I do not speak Chinese:	*Wǒ bù huì shuō Zhōngwén*	我不会说中文
Can you speak English?:	*Nǐ huì shuō Yīng yǔ ma?*	你会说英语吗？
I understand / don't understand:	*Wǒ dǒng / bùdǒng*	我懂 ／ 不懂
I know / don't know:	*Wǒ zhīdào / bù zhīdào*	我知道 ／ 不知道
OK?:	*Xíng bù xíng / hǎo bù hǎo?*	行不行 ／ 好不好？
Is it possible? / Not possible:	*Kěyǐ ma? / Bù kěyǐ*	可以吗？／ 不可以
Sorry / Excuse me:	*Dùibùqǐ*	对不起
What's the problem?:	*Yǒu shénme wèntí?*	你有甚么问题？
No problem:	*Méi yǒu wèntí*	没有问题
Big problem:	*Dà wèntí*	大问题

It doesn't matter / Forget it:	*Méi guānxi / Suàn le*	没关系／算了
Are you crazy?:	*Nǐ húlihútu ma?*	你糊理糊涂吗？
Was it fun?:	*Hǎo wánr ma?*	好玩吗？
It was very interesting:	*Hěn yǒu yìsi*	很有意思
OK, so-so:	*Mǎmǎhūhū* (horse horse tiger tiger)	马马虎虎
What does this mean?:	*Yǒu shénme yìsi?*	有甚么意思？
I am a student:	*Wǒ shì xuéshēng*	我是学生
What is your name?:	*Nǐ jiào shénme míngzi?*	你叫甚么名字？
How old are you?:	*Nǐ jǐ suì?*	你几岁？
Where are you from?:	*Nǐ shì cóng nǎlǐ lái de?*	你是从那里来的？
I am (American):	*Wǒ shì (Měi guó rén)*	我是（美国人）
British:	*Yīng guó rén*	英国人
Australian:	*Aò dà lì yà rén*	奥大利亚人
Canadian:	*Jiā ná dà rén*	加拿大人
Chinese:	*Zhōng guó rén*	中国人
Uygur:	*Wéizú* (Uygur minority)	维族
What is your monthly salary?:	*Nǐ de gōngzī yī ge yuè duōshao qián?*	你的工资一个月多少钱？
I don't smoke:	*Wǒ bù chōuyan*	我不抽烟
Let's go:	*Zǒu ba*	走吧

GETTING AROUND

Where is the (toilet)?:	*(Cè suǒ) zài nǎr?*	（厕所）在哪儿？
Do you have (a double room)?:	*Nǐmén yǒu méi yǒu (shuāngrén jiān)?*	你们有没有（双人间）？
Single room:	*Dānrénjiān*	单人间
Dormitory:	*Sùshè/duōrénjiān*	宿舍／多人间
I want/don't want (a bed):	*Wǒ yào/bù yào (yī gè chuáng wèi)*	我要／不要（一个床位）
Too expensive!:	*Tài guì le!*	太贵了！
Do you have something cheaper?:	*Yǒu méi yǒu piányi yī diǎn?*	有没有便宜一点的？
Hot water:	*rè shuǐ*	热水
Shower:	*línyù*	淋浴
Where is the bus station?:	*Qìchē zhàn zài nǎr?*	汽车站在哪儿？
How much is a ticket to (Kashgar):	*Dào (Kāshí) de piào duō shǎo qián?*	到（喀什）的票多少钱？

I want two tickets to Hami:	*Wǒ yào liǎng zhāng dào Hāmì de piào*	我要两张到哈蜜的票
Now, what time is it?:	*Xiànzài, jǐ diǎn zhōng?*	现在几点钟？
What time is the next (bus)?:	*Xià tàng (qìchē) jǐ diǎn zǒu?*	下趟 (汽车) 几点 走？
Bus Station:	*qìchē zhàn*	汽车站
Train Station:	*huǒchē zhàn*	火车站
Airport:	*fēi jǐ chǎng*	飞机场
I want to leave at (6 o'clock):	*Wǒ yào (liù diǎn) zǒu*	我要六点走
one hour:	*yīge xiǎoshí*	一个小时
one minute:	*yī fēnzhōng*	一分钟
half an hour:	*bànge xiǎoshí*	半个小时
I want a hard sleeper:	*Wǒ yào yìngwò*	我要硬卧
soft sleeper:	*ruǎnwò*	软卧
hard seat:	*yìngzuò*	硬座
Excuse me, can you please buy a ticket for me?:	*Máfan nǐ, nǐ kěyǐ tì wǒ mǎi yìzhāngpiào ma?*	麻烦你，你可以替我买一张票吗？

East:	*dōngbiān*	东边;	West:	*xībiān*	西边
North:	*běibiān*	北边	South:	*nánbiān*	南边
left:	*zuǒbiān*	左边	right:	*yòubiān*	右边
Yesterday:	*zuótiān*	昨天	Today:	*jīntiān*	今天
Tomorrow:	*míngtiān*	明天			

Museum:	*bówùguǎn*	博物馆
Post office:	*yóudiànjú*	邮电局
Stamp:	*yóupiào*	邮票
Post card:	*míng xìn piàn*	明信片
I'd like to make a phone call:	*Wǒ yào dǎ diànhùa*	我要打电话
Collect call:	*duìfāng fùqián*	对方付钱
Public Security:	*gōngānjú*	公安局
Bank of China:	*Zhōngguó yínháng*	中国银行
Change money:	*huàn qián*	换钱
Travel agency:	*lǚxíngshè*	旅行社
CAAC:	*Zhōngguó Mínháng*	中国民航
Bookstore:	*Shūdiàn*	书店

FOOD AND DRINK

| I don't eat meat: | *Wǒ bù chī ròu* | 我不吃肉 |

Bronze 'you' with loop handle (Shang Dynasty, 13th–11th century BC), unearthed in 1971 at Jingyang County, Shaanxi Province

I like/don't like spicy food:	Wǒ xǐhuan / bù xǐhuan chī làde		我喜欢／ 不喜欢吃辣的	
I'm full:	Wǒ chībǎole		我吃饱了	
Do you have (vegetables)?:	Nǐmén yǒu méiyǒu (shūcài)?		你们有没有 （蔬菜）？	
I would like egg fried rice:	Wǒ yào dàn chǎofàn		我要鸡蛋炒饭	

aubergine:	qiézi	茄子	bean curd (tofu):	dòufu	豆付
bean sprouts:	dòuyá	豆芽	beef:	niú ròu	牛肉
chicken:	jī ròu	鸡肉	Chinese cabbage:	báicài	白菜
chopsticks:	kuàizi	筷子	cold beer:	bīng píjiǔ	冰啤酒
eggs:	jīdàn	鸡蛋	fish:	yú	鱼
fried noodles:	chǎo miàn	炒面	fried rice:	chǎofàn	炒饭
garlic:	dà suàn	大蒜	ginger:	jiāng	姜
hot peppers:	làjiāo	辣椒	mushrooms:	mógu	蘑菇
mutton:	yáng ròu	羊肉	noodles:	miàntiáo	面条
oil:	yóu	油	peanuts:	huā shēng	花生
pork:	zhū ròu	猪肉	raisins:	pútáo gān	葡萄乾
rice:	mǐfàn	米饭	soda:	qì shuǐ	汽水
soup:	tāng	汤	stir fried:	chǎo de	炒的
string beans:	jiāngdòu	江豆	tomatoes:	fān qié	番茄
wine:	pútáo jiǔ	葡萄酒	yogurt:	suān nǎi	酸奶
a little bit:	yī diǎndiǎn	一点点儿	a little more:	duō yìdiǎn	多一点儿
one bowl:	yi wǎn	一碗	cup:	bēizi	杯子
small:	xiǎode	小的	big:	dàde	大的

tea:	chá	茶;	black tea:	hóng chá 红茶;	green tea: lù chá 绿茶
coffee:	kāfei	咖啡	boiled water:	kāishuǐ	开水
ice cream:	bīng qílín	冰淇淋	popsicle:	bīnggùnr	冰棍儿

waitress:	(fúwùyuán) xiǎojiě	（服务员）小姐
waiter:	fúwùyuán	服务员
the check:	jié zhàng	结账
great food / delicious:	hěn hǎo chī	很好吃
terrible food:	fēicháng bù hǎo chī	非常不好吃
I am uncomfortable / unwell:	Wǒ bù shūfu	我不舒服
headache:	tóu tòng	头痛
cold:	gǎnmào	感冒
diarrhoea:	lǎ dùzi	拉肚子

doctor: *yī shēng*   医生
hospital: *yī yuàn*   医院
rest: *xiūxi*   休息

NUMBERS

1	*yī*	一	one kilo:	*yī gōng jīn*	一公斤
2	*èr*	二	half a kilo:	*yī jīn*	一斤
3	*sān*	三	quarter kilo:	*bàn jīn*	半斤
4	*sì*	四			
5	*wǔ*	五			
6	*liù*	六	Monday:	*xīngqī yī*	星期一
7	*qī*	七	Tuesday:	*xīngqīèr*	星期二
8	*bā*	八	Wednesday:	*xīngqī sān*	星期三
9	*jiǔ*	九	Thursday:	*xīngqī sì*	星期四
10	*shí*	十	Friday:	*xīngqīwǔ*	星期五
11	*shí yī*	十一	Saturday:	*xīngqīliù*	星期六
12	*shí èr*	十二	Sunday:	*xīngqītiān*	星期天
19	*shí jiǔ*	十九	January:	*yī yuè*	一月
20	*èr shí*	二十	February:	*èr yuè*	二月
21	*èr shí yī*	二十一	March:	*sān yuè*	三月
22	*èr shí èr*	二十二	April:	*sì yuè*	四月
29	*èr shí jiǔ*	二十九	May:	*wǔ yuè*	五月
30	*sān shí*	三十	June:	*liù yuè*	六月
50	*wǔ shí*	五十	July:	*qī yuè*	七月
100	*yī bǎi*	一百	August:	*bā yuè*	八月
101	*yī bǎi líng yi*	一百零一	September:	*jiǔ yuè*	九月
125	*yī bǎi èr shí wǔ*	一百二十五	October:	*shí yuè*	十月
500	*wǔ bǎi*	五百	November:	*shíyī yuè*	十一月
1000	*yī qiān*	一千	December:	*shíèr yuè*	十二月

SHAANXI PROVINCE

XI'AN

Xi'an has been the capital of the Chinese Empire at various times in history for a total of some 1,100 years. It was the starting point for the great trade caravans of the Silk Road. Fabulous archaeological discoveries in and around the city tell of Xi'an's past glories, never greater than during the seventh to tenth centuries, when the Tang court opened its doors to the widely varied cultural and economic influences of Byzantium, Arabia, Persia, the Kingdoms of Central Asia, Tibet, Burma, India, Korea and Japan.

The development of the region began long ago; the fertile valleys of the Wei and Yellow rivers that run through Shaanxi Province are known as the 'cradle of Chinese civilization'. In 1963, the skull and jaw bone of Paleolithic Lantian Man were discovered 27 kilometres southeast of Xi'an, placing the earliest occupation of the area by *homo sapiens* at 800,000 BC. In the early Neolithic era, around 5000 BC, a rich, settled agricultural society developed, growing millet and vegetables, domesticating animals and firing pottery. This was the Yangshao or Painted Pottery Culture, followed by the Black Pottery or Longshan Culture, which lasted until around 3000 BC. A typical Yangshao community has been excavated at Banpo, east of Xi'an, where there is now a museum.

During the Bronze Age, the Western Zhou dynasty (1027–771 BC) established its capital in the region of Fenghao, about 16 kilometres southwest of present-day Xi'an. The Zhou emperors were mostly ineffective in governing the region and China was soon divided into over a hundred small principalities, whose expanding independent power gradually forced the Zhou to move their capital to Luoyang, in present-day Henan. In the Spring and Autumn periods (770–476 BC), the Zhou rulers lost the allegiance of their vassal states and the tumultuous Warring States period began. This chaotic period was known as the Golden Age of Chinese philosophy: the 'One Hundred Schools of Thought' contended with one another while Confucianism and legalism vied for political power. The state of Qin rose to dominance during the Warring States period and in 246 BC Emperor Zheng came to the throne at the tender age of 13. Between 230 and 221 BC, he established the superiority of the Qin dynasty by annexing six other states and unifying China. He took the title of Shihuangdi, the

(above) A plum blossom in gold leaf, once used by women as a forehead decoration. It would have been stuck to the centre of the brow with glue. (Right) The 'just fallen off a horse look' hairstyle, on a painted pottery model of a woman with a fashionably plump figure. Both from the Tang dynasty (618–907 AD)

First Emperor of Qin (reigned 221–206 BC), and a magnificent capital was established in Xianyang, east of Xi'an on the north bank of the Wei River.

Qin Shihuangdi standardized coinage, wagon axle lengths, weights and measures, styles of literary composition and a code of law; he introduced an administrative system that all succeeding Chinese dynasties would follow in one form or another. But he was also cruel and tyrannical. So that no moral code would challenge his rule of law, he ordered the burning of Confucian books and classics that 'discredited the present in favour of the past', and executed hundreds of intellectuals and advocates of Confucianism by burying them alive.

 he Han dynasty ruled a state almost as large as the territory of modern-day China, and existed concurrently with the Roman Empire. In 194 BC, the Emperor Han Huidi built a magnificent imperial city called Chang'an (Everlasting Peace), just northwest of present-day Xi'an, protected by a wall 22 kilometres in circumference. In the first century AD, the historian, Ban Gu, composed an ode to the glory of the extravagant Han capital:

> The walls were as of iron, a myriad spans in extent; the encircling moat dug deep as an abyss. Three stretches of highway were laid out, twelve gates of ingress and egress were erected. Within were the streets and cross-streets, the ward gates numbered a thousand. Nine market places were opened, the merchandise displayed, kind by kind in ordered rows.

Caravans of traders from the Western Regions began arriving soon after the discovery of the Silk Road. The official market places, crowded with goods and merchants, were also used for public executions and divination. Imperial gardens were stocked with rare plants and animals, tribute gifts from the distant Western kingdoms. Palaces and the multi-storeyed houses of the rich and noble, although mostly of plastered wattle and clay, were brightly decorated and hung with lavish embroideries. Silks were widely worn, carriages were embossed with gold, silver or lacquer, and horses were caparisoned with semi-precious stones. Funerary clay models unearthed from tombs show the high level of sophistication the society had reached. Chang'an had a population of 246,000 at the time.

The capital was moved back to Luoyang in AD 25, after the fall of the Western Han dynasty and the destruction of Chang'an. It was not until AD 589 that the Sui-dynasty Emperor Wendi reunified China and established a magnificent new capital, southeast of the former Han capital, called Da Xing Cheng (Great Prosperity). Sui Wendi's ambitious son, Sui Yangdi, developed and organized the empire; he reformed the bureaucracy, completed the restoration of the Great Wall, and commissioned the building of the 2,000-kilometre-long Grand Canal, which improved communication and transportation between Da Xing Cheng and other strategic cities within the empire; roads were built linking the city with seaports and opening up trade with the outside world.

ith the ascendancy of the Tang dynasty in 618, Chang'an regained its prominence. The Tang created and reigned over the Golden Age of China, considered the most sophisticated period in Chinese civilization. Chang'an was the biggest and most cosmopolitan city in the world; its grid layout was copied in miniature by the Silla kings of Korea for their capital Kyongju, and by the Japanese, who built Nara and Kyoto along the same lines.

The great Tang capital attracted foreigners from all parts of Asia and beyond. Merchants, envoys, soldiers, pilgrims, entertainers and sages thronged the great metropolis. A Persian Sassanid prince took up residence-in-exile, while the sons of many tribute kings could be found at the capital—ostensibly for education, but in fact as hostages ensuring their fathers' good behaviour.

Religions flourished in this cosmopolitan atmosphere. A Zoroastrian temple was built in 631, two Nestorian churches in 638 and 677, while the famous Nestorian Stele standing in the Shaanxi Museum was consecrated in 781. Islam, Judaism and Manicheanism were also introduced. But it was Buddhism, introduced along the Silk Road, that flourished, making Chang'an the centre of Buddhist learning in East Asia.

At court, Turkish costumes were the vogue. Chinese women rode horses, polo was a popular sport, and many foreigners held official posts. But anti-foreign resentment was to flare up in the city, especially against the Turks, who were said to number 10, 000 by the mid-seventh century. The later hostility in the ninth century led to the repression of all foreign religions in favour of Taoism, which was indigenous to China.

In the latter half of the seventh century, imperial power lay in the hands of the viciously ambitious Empress Wu Zetian (627–705), who had been a concubine of the Emperor Taizong. After Taizong's death she married his son, Gaozong, and gradually gained power and control, becoming the first and only female ruler of China in 690. She favoured the capital at Luoyang, and Chang'an was once again neglected.

pon Empress Wu's death her grandson Xuanzong, also known as Minghuang, 'the Brilliant Emperor', returned the capital to Chang'an and raised the city to an unprecedented level of sophistication. He reigned for 40 years over what was to prove the artistic and cultural apex of Tang China, known as the High Tang. Two of China's most famous poets, Li Bai and Du Fu, lived during this period. By the mid-eighth century, China had a population of over 53 million, with two million in Chang'an. Emperor Xuanzong is best known for his love for the beautiful concubine Yang Guifei (originally his 18th son's wife). But his growing neglect of his duties in favour of his plump paramour led to court intrigue, corruption and instability, and the rise of General An Lushan, who was half-Turk, half-Sogdian. The general led a rebellion that lasted from 755 to 763, causing the death of millions and a migration south to the Yangzi River Valley for millions more. Order was restored only with military assistance from the Uygurs and an army of mercenary Arabs, but not before the Tibetans briefly occupied the city.

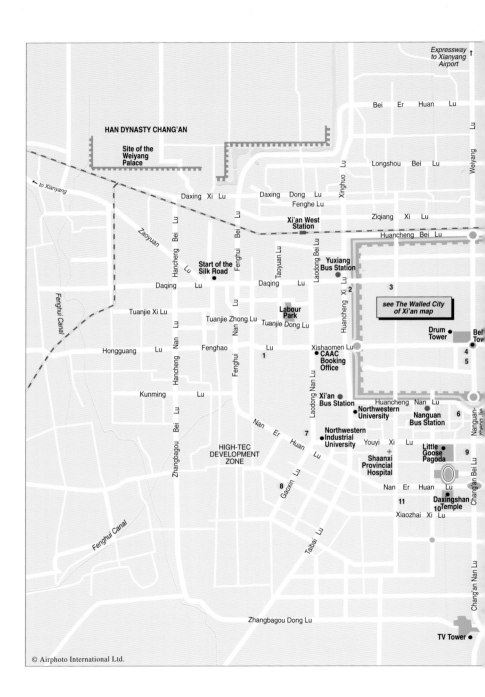

© Airphoto International Ltd.

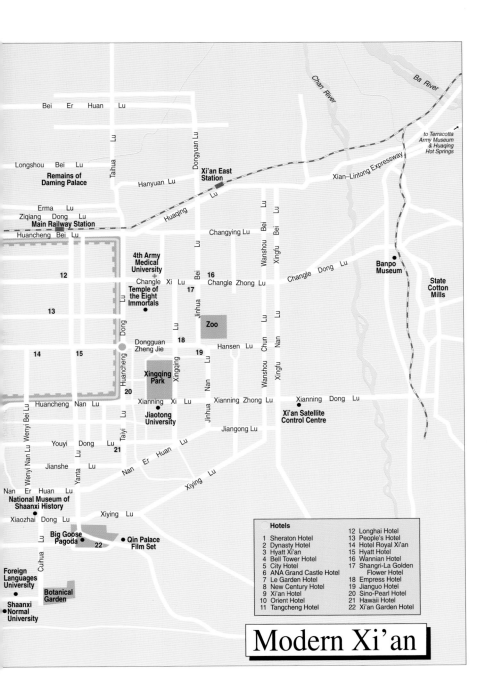

Bei Er Huan Lu

Longshou Bei Lu
Remains of Daming Palace

Taihua Lu

Dongyuan Lu

Hanyuan Lu

Xi'an East Station

Chan River

Ba River

to Terracotta Army Museum & Huaqing Hot Springs

Xian–Lintong Expressway

Erma Lu
Ziqiang Dong Lu
Main Railway Station
Huancheng Bei Lu

Huaqing Lu

Changying Lu

Wanshou Bei Lu

Xingfu Bei Lu

Changle Dong Lu

Banpo Museum

State Cotton Mills

12

Changle Xi Lu
Temple of the Eight Immortals

16
Changle Zhong Lu

17

4th Army Medical University

13

Dong Lu

Jinhua Bei Lu

18
Zoo

Hansen Lu

Chun Nan Lu

14

15

Huancheng Dong Lu

Dongguan Zheng Jie

19

20

Xingqing Park

Xingqing Lu

Jinhua Nan Lu

Wanshou Nan Lu

Xingfu Nan Lu

Huancheng Nan Lu

Xianning Xi Lu

Xianning Zhong Lu

Xianning Dong Lu

Jiaotong University

Jiangong Lu

Xi'an Satellite Control Centre

Wenyi Nan Lu

Wenyi Bei Lu

Youyi Dong Lu

Taiyi Lu

21

Jianshe Lu

Yanta Lu

Nan Er Huan Lu

Xiying Lu

Nan Er Huan Lu
National Museum of Shaanxi History

Xiaozhai Dong Lu

Xiying Lu

Cuihua Lu

Big Goose Pagoda

22

Qin Palace Film Set

Foreign Languages University

Botanical Garden

Shaanxi Normal University

Modern Xi'an

rom 775, provincial warlords along with Tibetan and Turkish invaders plagued the empire, and the government eventually lost control of transportation networks and the tax collection system, their primary source of power and revenue. The increasing wealth and power of Buddhist monasteries contributed to the government's xenophobia between 843 and 845, when Buddhist monasteries, Christian churches and Zoroastrian and Manichean temples were destroyed, and non-Chinese monks and clerics expelled. In 880, the emperor was forced to abandon Chang'an to an army of rebellious peasants who sacked it. Although the dynasty continued for another 27 years, it never regained control and in 907 it fell, together with Chang'an. Chang'an was renamed Daanfu and China once again split up into warring states.

The rich agricultural region of the Yangzi in southern China became the next economic centre of China. Famines, floods, droughts and peasant uprisings impoverished Shaanxi Province, and Chang'an was never again more than a provincial capital. The city was renamed Xi'an in 1368, meaning 'Western Peace'. It was rebuilt in 1370 by the Ming Emperor Zhu Yuanzhang as a gift to his son. But in the 1911 revolution against the Manchu Qing dynasty, the Manchus in Xi'an were massacred and their section of town destroyed. Xi'an remained relatively isolated from the rest of China until the completion of the Zhengzhou (Shanghai–Lanzhou) railway in 1930, linking the city with the industry and commerce of modern China.

i'an came to world attention in 1936, when Generalissimo Chiang Kai-shek was kidnapped at the Huaqing Hot Springs, an event that came to be called the Xi'an Incident. Today, metropolitan Xi'an, the capital of Shaanxi Province, has a population of four million. It has been quite intensively industrialized in recent decades, with the emphasis on machinery, textiles and light industrial products, and is the site of many institutes of higher education. The discovery of the terracotta warriors in 1974 and the ensuing migration of tourists have contributed significantly to Xi'an's economic development.

CITY SIGHTS

CITY WALLS AND GATES (CHENGMEN)

The top of the restored Ming-dynasty wall and its four gates provide an historic contrast to the modern city. Much of the wall, which dates back to the 14th century, is still intact. The circumference is 13.7 kilometres, and the wall is 12 metres high, surrounded by a moat. In keeping with traditional Chinese design, the city gates face the four cardinal points. Originally each gate had two structures: a gate tower, and the archers' tower on top of the wall itself. The archers' tower had 48 openings on the outer face, from which projectiles could be fired on an advancing enemy. The renovated West Gate tower is now a museum. You can walk around the city atop the wall; entrances are by the South, East and West gates. Some of the reconstructed watchtowers are now shops. Long stretches of the city wall that once encircled the much bigger Tang capital of Chang'an survive on the outskirts of the city.

BELL TOWER (ZHONG LOU)

Built in 1384, the Bell Tower, in which a great bell once rang at dawn, is a classic example of Ming architecture. Originally the tower was located in the centre of the old Tang imperial city, but it was moved and rebuilt in 1582 at its present location in the southern section of the walled city. It was restored in 1740 and now consists of a triple-eaved, two-storey wooden pavilion resting on a square brick platform nine metres high, pierced by four archways. There is an excellent view of the city from the second floor parapet. Open 8.30 am–5.30 pm.

DRUM TOWER (GU LOU)

Across the square from the Bell Tower, and of a similar style, is the rectangular Drum Tower, first erected during the Ming dynasty in 1380 and restored in 1669, 1739 and 1953. A road goes through the tower under a vaulted archway where a drum was beaten daily at sundown. The second-storey balcony offers a good view of the old Muslim quarter. Open 8.30 am–5.30 pm. During construction work in 1995 on the new Bell-Drum Tower Square, some 200 official copper seals from the Jin dynasty (1115–1234) were discovered in a 13-metre deep well. Most are square, measuring between five and seven square centimetres. Characters on the seals date them to 1224–1232, and archaeologists believe they were hidden in the well during a rebellion.

GREAT MOSQUE (QING ZHEN SI)

Founded in 742, the Great Mosque on Huajue Xiang is the focus of the more than 30,000 Chinese Muslims (Hui) of Xi'an, whose beards and white caps distinguish them from Han Chinese. The buildings of the mosque, which miraculously escaped damage during the Cultural Revolution, stand in four beautiful courtyards of ancient trees, ornate arches and stone steles, all contributing to an atmosphere of serenity.

The present layout dates from the 14th century and was restored repeatedly in 1527, 1660, 1768 and again in 1987. The architecture is pure Chinese, with eaved roofs of turquoise tiles and walls of decoratively carved bricks. The Phoenix Pavilion is preceded by a minaret, and beyond it are two fountains and a raised stone terrace used for worship. In a Stele Hall in the third courtyard stand stone tablets inscribed in Arabic, Persian and Chinese, as well as a Qing-dynasty map of the Islamic world with the black cube of the Kaaba at Mecca in the centre. The larger prayer hall in the fourth courtyard has an inset panelled ceiling decorated with elegant Arabic calligraphy.

s many as 500 worshippers attend daily prayers, and on Fridays as many as 2,000. The mosque is closed to non-Muslims during prayer periods. The mosque is located just northwest of the Drum Tower (there is a signpost in English); take the first lane on the left (west) after passing north through the tower. The old neighbourhood is quite delightful to wander about in; many of the wooden facades of the two-storey buildings have been renovated. Open 9 am–6 pm daily.

SHAANXI MUSEUM (SHAANXI BOWUGUAN OR BEILIN)

Housed in the former Confucius Temple on Baishulin Lu, this museum is one of the best in China, displaying some 2,600 items, all of which were found in Shaanxi Province. Of particular interest are the bronzes from the Zhou dynasty, sculptures from the Sui and Tang dynasties and the famous Forest of Stelae—the largest collection of inscribed stone tablets in China. Unfortunately, like many museums in China, the exhibit cases are dusty and dirty, few captions are in English, and maps and diagrams are frequently covered in an almost opaque plastic.

The Forest of Stelae, occupying several halls, is an impressive collection of over 1,000 inscribed stone tablets. It was started in 1090 and steadily expanded until the 18th century, when it was given its name. The stelae can be divided into four categories: classic works of literature and philosophy, historical records, calligraphy and pictorial stones by famous scholars of their time; the best are from the Tang dynasty, and some from the Song which are engraved with early maps of China. Each tablet stands on the back of a giant tortoise. The Nestorian Stele, cut in 781 in Chinese and Syrian, surmounted by a cross, records the history of the Nestorian Christian community in Chang'an from its founding between 635 and 638 by the Syriac missionary named Alopen.

The top section of Xi'an's Nestorian Stele, dated AD 781. The nine Chinese signs declare: 'Stele for the propagation of the Luminous Religion of Da Qin in the Kingdom of the Middle'. Above the text the Nestorian Cross of Resurrection is engraved standing between clouds and branches on a lotus flower. While the lotus symbolises purity of mind in Buddhism, and the clouds are associated with Daoism, the arrangement with the Cross in the centre implies that the fulfilment of Chinese religiosity is to be found in Nestorian Christianity.

The Walled City of Xi'an

© Airphoto International Ltd.

Railway Station

Beimen (North gate)

Dongmen (East gate)

Ximen (West gate)

Nanmen (South gate)

Heping Gate

Jianguomen

Hongguang Gate

Jiefang Hotel
Bank of China
Long Distance Bus Station
Eighth Route Army Office Museum
Revolution Park
People's Stadium
People's Hotel
Provincial Government Building
Hyatt Hotel
Royal Hotel
Temple of the Recumbent Dragon
Forest of Steles Museum
Telegraph & Telephone Building
Main Post Office
Train Ticket Advance Booking
Lianhu Park
Drum Tower
Drum Tower Square
Bell Tower
Bell Tower Hotel
Great Mosque
Temple of the Town God
Grand New World Hotel
Children's Park
Guangren Temple
Night Market

Dongshunchengjie Beiduan
Dongshunchengjie Nanduan

Dong 8-Lu
Dong 7-Lu
Dong 6-Lu
Shangjie
Dong 5-Lu
Dong 4-Lu
Dong 3-Lu
Dong 2-Lu
Dong 1-Lu
Shangjin Shangjian
Shangjian Lu
Jiang Lu
Jiefang Lu
Heping Lu
Dajie
Dongcangmen
Machangzi
Xiamaling
Kaitong Xiang
Sanxue Jie
Culture Street
Juhuayuan
Dongtingmen
Duanlumen
Dongmutou Shi
Luoma Shi
Naxmin Jie
Xi 1-Lu
Xi 2-Lu
Xi 3-Lu
Xi 4-Lu
Shangde Lu
Xi 9-Lu
Xi 8-Lu
Shangde Lu
Bei Xin jie
Xi 7-Lu
Xi 5-Lu
Xi
Beishunchengjie Dongduan
Beishunchengjie Xiduan
Tangfang Jie
Weimin Xiang
Bayi Jie
Qingnian Lu
Lianhu Lu
Hongbu Jie
Erfu Jie
Xihuamen
Beiyuanmen
Xiyangshi Jie
Huajue Xiang
Beiguangin Jie
Guangming Xiang
Xiaopiyuan Jie
Miaohou Jie
Daxuexi Xiang
Dajie
Damaishi Jie
Sajingiao
Beimadao Xiang
Nanmadao Xiang
Shuanginrenlu
Yandian Jie
Wuxing Jie
Nanyuanmen
Nanguang Jie
Fen Xiang
Zhuba Shi
Delu Xiang
Dacheja Xiang
Dabaqi Xiang
Dongsheng Jie
Nan Dajie
Bei Dajie
Xixin Jie
Xinmin Jie
Dongcangmen
Xibei 3-Lu
Xibei 2-Lu
Xibei 1-Lu
Xiwuyuan
Dongmeng Xiang

Relics from the Silk Road are found in the Sui and Tang Gallery and include excellent Tang pottery exhibits, engraved silver and gold utensils, bronze mirrors, Persian, Arab and Byzantine coins, a stone square commemorating the founding of a polo ground, passes to the different gates of the palace (shaped like a fish and a tortoise), and fragments of coloured silk. In the Third Annex Hall there is a collection of statues: Han-dynasty generals, Tang rhinoceroses, camels, ostriches and horses. Open 8 am–5.30 pm.

SHAANXI PROVINCIAL MUSEUM (SHAANXI LISHI BOWUGUAN)

 he museum, built in Tang style, was opened in June 1991, 18 years after the late Premier Zhou Enlai first suggested that such an establishment was needed to exhibit the wealth of Shaanxi's archaeological treasures. Occupying a large site in the southern suburbs of Xi'an about 3 km from the Big Goose Pagoda, the museum is a must for every visitor to Xi'an.

The permanent collection is housed on the ground and first floors, while exhibitions are staged in the basement. Visitors need at least three hours to do justice to a walk here through China's history. They should spend most of their time examining relics relating to times when Xi'an was the capital of China, especially during the Qin, Han and Tang dynasties.

In the first hall, **Prehistory to 2,000 BC**, relics highlight the importance of the Yellow River and its tributaries which watered the birth and fluorescence of Chinese culture. Artefacts from three prehistoric sites around Xi'an—Lantian, Dali and Banpo—are displayed. Some of the earliest decorated pottery is particularly striking with its bold lines depicting images of fish.

The second gallery of the **Xia**, **Shang**, **Western** and **Eastern Zhou dynasties** covers a 13-centuries-long epoch between the 21st century BC and 770 BC which witnessed the transition from the Stone to the Bronze age. By the Shang and Zhou dynasties, metalworking techniques had become highly sophisticated, with many bronze ritual vessels being cast. The metal and its manufacture was monopolized by powerful leaders who had shamans use the elaborate vessels during rituals and sacrifices. By claiming to contact the spirits and appease the gods they promoted their heavenly mandate to rule. At the time, bronze was only rarely used for weapons. Particularly striking are cooking tripods, called *ding*.

During the succeeding Zhou period, bronze was used for an array of elaborate utensils and vessels. The *bianzhong*, or chime bells, in a set of eight are extremely striking and would have been used in a court setting for entertaining nobles.

The third gallery exhibits relics from the **Spring and Autumn Period**, the **Warring States** and the **Qin dynasty** (770–206 BC). Most interesting are exhibits concerned with advancements in construction, plumbing, metallurgy, agriculture and irrigation which include decorated tile ends to stop infiltration of water into roof timbers; copper sleeves to join ceiling and roof beams together; and water pipes. The period also saw the dawn of the Iron Age which spurned increased production of iron weapons and tools. Terracotta warriors from the tomb of Emperor Qin Shihuangdi are on display, but most visitors will see the ranks of warriors in situ at Lintong. Instead look out for a tiger tally which was a symbol of imperial authority used in war, and the exhibition of coinage. Different shapes of currency using by the Warring States were standardized into the round form with a square hole in the middle by reforms implemented by the first emperor.

The first gallery upstairs houses relics from the **Han dynasty** (202 BC–AD 220). The contents of the cabinets are particularly fascinating to those who may have visited Han tombs to the northwest of Xi'an. An array of funerary relics are displayed here. There are a few hundred miniature warriors and cavalrymen from a Han noble's tomb, and small-scale models depicting daily life, including farmyards with wells, domestic animals. Ferocious tomb-guarding animals were placed at tomb entrances to scare off would-be tomb robbers. Important inventions during the Han were those of paper and silk. The wooden map in the gallery shows how the Han expanded their empire into central Asia by forging the Silk Road. Other less well-known inventions include gear-cogs, hinges and bolts.

 he next gallery, housing **Wei, Jin, Northern and Southern dynasty** (AD 220–581) artefacts is less important as Xi'an had by then lost its capital status. Instead, visitors may instead wish to move on to the gallery exhibiting **Sui and Tang** (AD 581–907) relics during which time Xi'an had regained its importance and was restored as the capital. Most notable relics here are the tri-coloured glazed pottery figurines (see pictures on pages 160 and 204). Many depict women, who were highly liberated during the Tang (see pictures on pages 53, 72 and 311). Examples of their jewellery and other adornments are on display, as are gold and silver artefacts concerned with tea drinking and the refining of medicines. Some articles are made from solid gold. The backdrops to many of the displays are murals reproduced from tombs in the northwest. Most of the originals are stored in the museum's basement and may be viewed by special arrangement.

The final gallery, dedicated to the **Song, Yuan, Ming** and **Qing** dynasties concerns an era during which Xi'an's importance was on the wane, eclipsed primarily by Hangzhou, Nanjing and finally Beijing.

LITTLE GOOSE PAGODA (XIAO YAN TA) AND DA JIANFU TEMPLE
The Little Goose Pagoda is all that remains of the Da Jianfu Temple, built in 684 by Empress Wu Zetian in honour of Emperor Gaozong. In the eighth century, the temple became a centre for the translation of Buddhist texts brought back from

(following pages) Qin Shihuangdi burial mound, marking the position of his tomb at Lintong, east of Xi'an

India by the monk Yiqing. The 15-storey brick pagoda, added in 707, was all that survived the anti-Buddhist movement of the years 843–45, apart from a resilient locust tree. It was said that in 1487 a violent earthquake split the pagoda from top to bottom, but another in 1556 brought the two sides back together; the top two storeys were lost, leaving 13. In all, the pagoda has miraculously survived more than 70 earthquakes. There are some Tang engravings of bodhisattvas on the stone base; in the courtyard stands a 12th-century bell that once rang out across the city. The exhibition room has Buddhist statues from the Tang and later dynasties, Buddhist scriptures and a series of drawings and photographs of the pagoda. The pagoda is less than one kilometre from the south gate; take city bus number 3 from the railway station.

BIG GOOSE PAGODA (DA YAN TA) AND THE DA CI'EN TEMPLE

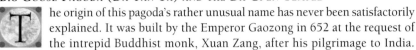

The origin of this pagoda's rather unusual name has never been satisfactorily explained. It was built by the Emperor Gaozong in 652 at the request of the intrepid Buddhist monk, Xuan Zang, after his pilgrimage to India. Xuan requested a large stone stupa, like he had seen on his journey to the West, but instead the emperor offered him a stone and wood pagoda, originally called the Scripture Pagoda. It was here that Xuan translated into Chinese the Sanskrit Buddhist texts, or sutras, which he had brought back with him. Ming-dynasty tablets recount the history of his life. The pagoda was originally five storeys; another five were added in 703 but burned down to the existing seven storeys. Each storey has openings that look out on four directions and can be accessed by a vaulted passageway. The base of the pagoda is square, with four arched doors on each side. The inscriptions are from the Tang period and are adorned with coiling dragons and singing angels at the top. Above the western entrance is an engraving of Sakyamuni preaching the Law. A sweeping view of the city rewards those who climb the wooden stairway inside the pagoda.

Da Ci'en Temple, in which the Big Goose Pagoda stands, was established in 647 by Emperor Gaozong in honour of his mother. At the height of its importance, some 300 monks resided in the gardened courtyards decorated by the works of contemporary artists. After the religious persecution of the mid-ninth century, the temple was neglected and in spite of several restorations never achieved the same stature again. Outside the entrance on the south side is a stone lamp from the Japanese city of Kyoto; inside are the bell and drum towers, and a path leading to the Great Hall, which contains statues of the Buddha and his disciples. The existing halls and statuary date from 1466. The temple and pagoda are several kilometres south of Xi'an; take city bus number 5 from the railway station. Open 8.30 am–6 pm daily.

SIGHTS AROUND XI'AN

Day tours to the sites outside Xi'an are broken up into those east and west of the city. CITS, OTC and other travel services located in the various hotels offer tours that range from the all-inclusive luxury-class bus with guide and interpreter to the standard Chinese tour consisting solely of transportation.

EAST OF XI'AN

BANPO MUSEUM (BANPO BOWUGUAN)

The remains of this Neolithic community lie seven kilometres east of Xi'an and were discovered in 1953 by workers laying foundations for a factory. It is one of the largest and most complete Neolithic sites in the world, belonging to the Yangshao Culture (5000–4000 BC). The Banpo community of 200–300 people was engaged in slash-and-burn agriculture, hunting, fishing and the domestication of dogs, pigs and chickens. It also planted hemp from which clothing was made. The pottery displayed non-abstract as well as abstract themes; earlier pieces were designed with fish, fishnets and deer, and later ones with geometric patterns. The Chinese believe the community was an ancient communist matriarchal settlement; women's graves, kept separate from the men's, contained a greater number of funerary objects.

The covered site is 4,000 square metres with a raised walkway around the area and explanatory notes in Chinese and English are provided. It contains the foundations of 45 round and square dwellings, a communal meeting-place, 200 storage pots, five pottery kilns and more than 200 graves. Artefacts and pottery shards are on exhibit in the display halls on either side of the excavation site. To visit the museum on your own, take city bus number 8 from the Bell Tower. Open 9 am–5.30 pm daily.

HUAQING HOT SPRINGS (HUAQING CHI)

 hirty kilometres (18 miles) east of Xi'an in the northern foothills of Li Shan (Black Horse Hill), is the popular scenic park known as Huaqing Hot Springs, which have been the site of imperial pleasures since the Zhou rulers of the eighth century BC. Qin Shihuangdi had a residence here, as did the rulers of the Han and Sui dynasties who enlarged the site, building new bathhouses, pagodas, walkways and gardens. The Tang resorts are the best known. In 644, Emperor Taizong built a palace at Huaqing, later enlarged by Emperor Xuanzong who spent winters here between 745 and 755 with his concubine, Yang Guifei. The Tang buildings were destroyed, except for the pool where the delicate Yang used to bathe. In 936, a Taoist community built a monastery from the ruins; small temples on the slopes and at the foot of the hill remain.

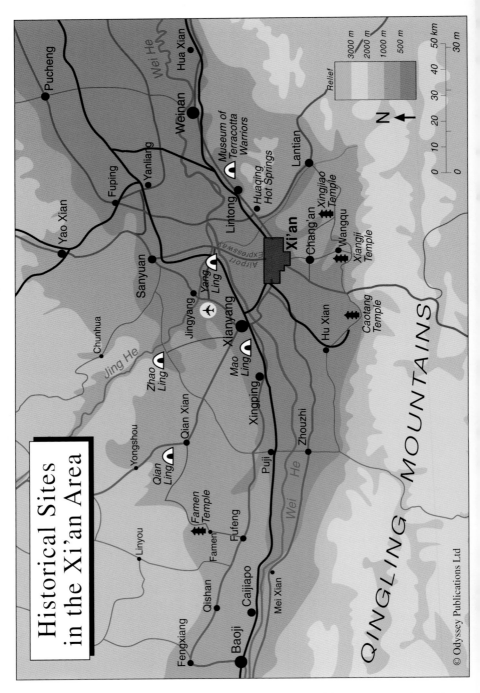

Historical Sites
in the Xi'an Area

QINGLING MOUNTAINS

© Odyssey Publications Ltd

(right) *Terracotta charioteer excavated from Pit One of the Qin Terracotta Army Museum*

The famous Xi'an Incident, in which Generalissimo Chiang Kai-shek was kidnapped, occurred here in 1936. The 'Young Marshal' Zhang Xueliang, son of the Manchurian dictator Zhang Zuolin (who had been assassinated by the Japanese) and a subordinate of Chiang's, acted out of frustration with the Nationalist Party leader's preoccupation with fighting the Communists instead of the Japanese. Collaborating with the Communists, Zhang captured his leader at the Huaqing Palace after a brief chase in the woods of Li Shan. After almost two weeks, Zhang was ordered by Stalin to release Chiang and was later taken into exile in Taiwan. Zhang inspired a measure of co-operation between the Kuomintang (Nationalists) and the Communists for the next nine years of war against the Japanese, but open civil war broke out again in 1946. The rooms where Chiang lived in the palace are marked, as well as the spot up the hill where he was eventually caught.

ost of the halls and pavilions in the park date from the turn of the century, when the resort was partially rebuilt at the end of the Qing dynasty (1644–1911). The temperature of the mineral water in the public baths (which are open to the public) is a constant 43°C (109°F). Outside the park there are vendors offering a wide variety of antique embroidery and handicrafts as well as numerous food stalls and restaurants.

QIN TERRACOTTA ARMY MUSEUM (QIN BING MA YONG BOWUGUAN)

The amazing 'Terracotta Army', 36 kilometres (22 miles) east of the city (just beyond Huaqing Hot Springs), transformed Xi'an from a provincial capital to a world-famous tourist destination and archaeological site. The site was discovered in 1974 by local farmers digging a well. Although there is no historical record of the thousands of life-size armoured soldiers and horses, it is believed they were intended to serve as bodyguards for the ghost of Qin Shihuangdi (reigned 221–210 BC). The figures were discovered five metres below the surface in vaults originally built with walls of pounded earth and a wooden roof. In 206 BC, the vaults were opened by General Xiang Yu who set fire to the roof, which then collapsed, damaging the figures below.

The museum comprises three buildings each spanning a vault (or pit), plus two exhibition halls, one for the two bronze chariots and the other for various relics found around the vast mausoleum. **Pit One**, discovered in May 1974, is expected to yield 6,000 warriors. To date, 1,087 warriors, mainly infantry, the traces of eight wooden chariots and 32 terracotta horses have been unearthed and repaired. The spot where the initial discovery took place, as peasants sank a new well for groundwater, is clearly marked. Excavations are continuing and renovation work can be seen progressing towards the back end of the massive pit, roofed by an aircraft hangar-like structure.

Pit Two, discovered in May 1976, is thought to contain around 1,000 warriors, many of them in active archery positions, both upright and kneeling. Prime exhibits are displayed in glass cases within the pit building, including a cavalryman leading his horse and a general. As with Pit One, archaeological work is continuing.

Pit Three, discovered in June 1976, is thought to be the command headquarters. It is the smallest pit and completed excavation work has yielded 69 warriors and four horses. Traces of burnt deer horn and animal bones were found here, and archaeologists say that they evidence sacrificial rites having been symbolically carried out by 'commanders' before going to battle.

Between pits two and three a perspex roof covers what is termed 'Pit Four'— however it was found to be totally empty. One theory is that this pit was earmarked for a live burial of Qin Shihuangdi's own soldiers, in keeping with burial practices for royals during the Warring States period which preceded the establishment of the Qin dynasty. Ritual demanded that actual living soldiers, not clay figurines, were entombed to act as tomb guards. Some scholars believe that maintaining such a practice was impractical as a result of unrest which broke out in the wake of a struggle for succession after the emperor's death. Real soldiers probably could not be spared for a live burial at a time when the dynasty was at stake and the defence of the empire was paramount.

Each of the soldiers has distinctive facial features, and there is a wide range of hairstyles, beards and moustaches. They range in height from 1.80 to 2.03 metres, and average 150 kg in weight. Hollow from the waist up, they were originally painted, although the colour has now almost completely faded. The ranks of soldiers are divided into archers, cavalry, charioteers and infantry armed with swords and spears. Many genuine bronze weapons have been discovered, including swords, daggers, crossbow triggers and spears, but the wooden weapon shafts have completely decayed and the chariots, which were also probably wood, no longer exist. The horses stand 1.5 metres (5 feet) tall, and the metal parts of replica chariots have been found.

 n 1981, two bronze chariots were found west of the museum, each drawn by four horses 72 centimetres high and one metre long. Originally painted white, they have now faded to grey, but the harnesses are still inlaid with gold and silver. Each chariot has a carriage with an awning of thin bronze painted with clouds and geometric patterns. These are excellent examples of the Qin dynasty's metallurgical skills.

The bronze chariots, and other detailed exhibits of artefacts, are located in the display halls on either side of the museum. Outside the museum is a peasant market with antique embroideries, handicrafts and imitation clay warriors and horses. Admission to the museum is now Rmb90.

TOMB OF QIN SHIHUANGDI (QIN SHIHUANGDI LINGMU)

The museum site is only part of the vast mausoleum that the emperor built for himself. The actual tomb—buried beneath an artificial tumulus of earth—is located 1,500 metres (one mile) from the terracotta army museum. The tumulus is 260 feet high and covered with pomegranate trees. There is a terrace at the top of a long flight of steps overlooking the surrounding fields (see picture on pages 64 and 65).

According to the first-century Chinese historian, Sima Qian, the tomb took 700,000 workers 36 years to build. There is, according to records, an Imperial City below the burial mound containing a throne room, treasure house, and a huge stone relief map of China covered by a copper dome representing the sky, inlaid with precious stones as celestial bodies. Model palaces and gardens line a hundred rivers flowing with mercury. Traces of mercury have been found in the walls of the underground palace. The mind boggles at the treasure that may still be awaiting excavation. The tomb is supposedly guarded by Indiana Jones-style booby traps. Apparently artisans were ordered to make automatic crossbows and arrows; if anyone had tried to make a hole and enter the tomb, they would immediately have been fired on. The tomb was plundered in 206 BC by the rapacious General Xiang Yu after the fall of the Qin dynasty, and probably hundreds of times since then, but there are still thought to be built-in defences inhibiting further excavations.

(left) Tang dynasty painted pottery figurine displaying a 'wild bird' coiffure, with a central roll of hair hanging low over the brow. (top) The back of a gilt bronze mirror, inlaid with images of four phoenixes trailing ribbons, a design symbolizing eternal love. (bottom) Part of a gold comb. Tang women often tucked combs in their hair to hold it in place

WEST OF XI'AN

YANG LING MUSEUM AND FAMEN TEMPLE

Detailed descriptions of the new purpose-built museum displaying artefacts excavated from the Han Yang Mausoleum, tomb of Liu Qi the fouth Han emperor Jingdi, and the Famen Temple, can be found in the Odyssey guide to Xi'an (*see* Recommended Reading on page 340).

TOMB OF EMPEROR HAN WUDI (MAO LING)

The 'Martial Emperor' Han Wudi (reigned 141–87 BC) set about expanding his empire's sphere of influence: south to Vietnam, north to Korea and west to Central Asia. He sent his emissary Zhang Qian on the first of several ambassadorial and exploratory missions along the then-undocumented Silk Road. The emperor's tomb, 40 kilometres (25 miles) west of Xi'an, has not been excavated, but a commemorative monument marks the tumulus.

TOMB OF HUO QUBING (HUO QUBING MU)

 ixteen remarkable stone figures of beasts and demons adorn the burial ground of the Han-dynasty General Huo Qubing (140–117 BC), also known as the 'Swift Cavalry General'. He spent his short life fighting the encroaching Xiongnu (Hsiung-nu) in the service of Emperor Han Wudi, first under the command of his uncle when he was 18, and in 121 BC when he led a cavalry army, driving them out of the Hexi Corridor of Gansu. When Huo died at the age of 24, Emperor Wudi decreed that his tomb be built in the shape of the Qilian Mountains of Gansu, where the general had achieved his first victory. There is a small museum at the tomb with exhibits of bronze artefacts and money. It is located one and a half kilometres (a mile) east of Mao Ling.

IMPERIAL TOMBS OF THE TANG DYNASTY (TANGDAI DIHUANG LINGMU)

The 18 Tang-dynasty tombs in the hills northwest of Xi'an are spread out in a line 120 kilometres long. They remain mostly unexcavated,except for the Qian Ling and Zhao Ling sites. Each tomb had its own avenue of stone figures forming a 'spirit way'. Qian Ling (85 kilometres from Xi'an) contains the mausoleums of Emperor Gaozong (reigned 650–684) and his stepmother, the all-powerful Empress Wu Zetian who usurped the throne for 20 years. Their long spirit ways, with their winged horses, giant birds, war-horses and guardians, are stunning. A tall stele on the left stands in honour of Gaozong; opposite is the uninscribed 'Wordless Stele', erected by the empress to mark the supreme power that no words could express.

Near Qian Ling are the tombs of Princess Yongtai and Prince Zhanghuai, children of Gaozong and Wu Zetian, containing painted murals depicting various aspects of court life; many reflect the strong influences of the Silk Road cultures in clothing, sports and entertainment.

The Zhao Ling site contains 19 tombs, including the tomb of Emperor Taizong (reigned 627–650), 60 kilometres (37 miles) northwest of Xi'an on the peak of Mount Jiuzong. The frescoes in the vault include scenes of the court welcoming foreigners, and polo games. The stone carvings of the emperor's beloved war-horses, which graced the tomb entrance, are now housed at the **Shaanxi Provincial Museum**. Within the tomb are 167 lesser tombs of imperial relatives and high-ranking officials. A museum on the site has a fine collection of funerary objects, including glazed-pottery figures (many with Central Asian features), pottery camels and horses, and wall paintings.

NESTORIAN DA QIN PAGODA AND TAOIST LOU GUAN TAI TEMPLE

About 70 km west of Xi'an and 25 km south of Zhouzhi stands a 31 m high pagoda of octagonal design. It was originally part of a Nestorian monastery built after 650 and it is the only large, standing architectural Nestorian monument in China. The monastery was heavily damaged by an earthquake in the middle of the eighth century and was restored in 963 as a Buddhist temple. A replica of the Nestorian Stele from 781 stands next to the pagoda, but nothing remains of the church or any other Christian buildings. Only 2 km east of the Da Qin Pagoda stands the large Taoist temple complex of Lou Guan Tai. According to tradition, it was here that Laozi wrote the *Tao Teh Ching* in the sixth century BC. Several emperors from the Tang Dynasty made large donations to the temples.

SOUTH OF XI'AN

Two Buddhist temples associated with early Silk Road travellers are located south of the city; buses to both sites depart from the Short Distance Bus Station at the South Gate.

TEMPLE OF FLOURISHING TEACHING (XINGJIAO SI)

This lies 20 kilometres (12 miles) to the southwest of Xi'an. It was dedicated in 669 to the memory of Xuan Zang, whose ashes lie beneath an elegant five-storey brick pagoda, and the three-storey pagodas on either side are dedicated to two of Xuan Zang's disciples; the pagodas are all that remain of the original temple complex. They are located in a walled enclosure called the Ci'en Pagoda Courtyard. The bell and drum towers, the Great Hall of the Buddha, the Preaching Hall and the library were all built in the 1920s and 1930s, but some of the Buddha statues date from the Ming dynasty. The library contains some early Buddhist sutras in Sanskrit and editions of translated works, including those of Xuan Zang. The main hall contains a white jade Buddha from Burma.

STRAW HUT TEMPLE (CAOTANG SI)

This lies surrounded by fields 55 kilometres (34 miles) southwest of Xi'an. In the fourth century, there was a palace here where the Indian monk Kumarajiva, the first great translator of Buddhist texts from Sanskrit to Chinese, lived and worked. Prior to accurate translations, the Chinese believed Buddhism to be a foreign form of Taoism. The temple was constructed during the Tang dynasty on the remains of the palace. In the complex stands a small stone stupa marking Kumarajiva's ashes.

XI'AN PRACTICAL INFORMATION

Streets and avenues are laid out in a grid pattern; walking is convenient and easy; modern shopping areas along Jiefang Lu and Dong Dajie; bus routes are outlined on the map; taxis are available throughout the city; business, museum and site hours are generally 8 am–12 pm and 3 pm–6 pm, Beijing time.

TRANSPORTATION

Daily flights and trains link Xi'an to most major cities in China (and points in between), including Beijing, Shanghai, Guangzhou, Kunming, Chengdu, Lanzhou and Urumqi (flights to/from Beijing four times a day; flights to/from Urumqi four times a week, twice in winter; three times a week to/from Dunhuang, except in winter); scheduled flights to/from Hong Kong fly daily. Daily buses to/from Tianshui and Lanzhou at the

(top) Octagonal, petal-shaped gold cup decorated with musicians and dancers. The shape of the cup comes from the New East–it was probably made by a Persian or Sogdian silversmith living in Xi'an. (above) Gold bowl decorated with lotus petals and mandarin ducks (height 5.5cm, diameter at mouth 13.7cm). Both date from the Tang dynasty and were excavated from Hejia Village, Xi'an, in 1970. (right) Tang-dynasty ox-head agate drinking horn, unearthed at Hejia Village, Xi'an. It was probably imported from Central Asia or Sassanian Iran

Long Distance Bus Station just opposite the main train station. The main CAAC booking office is just west of the West Gate on Xishaomen Lu; for trains, there is a foreigner ticket window in the main station or try the advance booking office on Lianhu Lu. A pleasant way to travel from Beijing is to take the train to Taiyuan, overnight there and then continue next day to Xi'an. It is also cheaper to fly to Shenzhen than to Hong Kong and there is a daily service on this route. For flight schedules visit www.linktrip.com/silkroad/shaanxi/fs_xian.htm, for trains check out www.linktrip.com/silkroad/shaanxi/ts_xian.htm.

ACCOMMODATION

Most of the following hotels offer a wide variety of services beyond what is listed below, including laundry, international telephone calls, post office, foreign exchange, gift shop, massage, hairdressing, etc.

Sheraton Xi'an Hotel (Xi'an Xi Lai Deng Jiudian)

262 Feng Hao East Rd. Tel: (029) 8426 1888; fax: (029) 8426 2188; email: sheraton.xian@sheraton.com; website: www.sheraton.com/xian

西安喜来登大酒店　丰镐路 12 号

Five-star, 438-room luxury hotel conveniently located near Xi'an City wall, adjacent to the West Second Ring Road; only minutes away from the city centre and near the new Xian Developing Zone of High Technology Industries.

Paradise Resort Xi'an (Qujiang huibinyuan binguan)
South Section, Yanta South Road. Tel: (029) 8766 3333; fax: (029) 8766 3388;
email: sales@xianparadiseresort.com; website: www.xianparadiseresort.com
曲江惠宾苑宾馆 雁塔南路南段
Garden-style, five-star hotel located close to the Big Goose Pagoda.

Hyatt Regency Hotel (Kaiyue Fandian)
158 Dongda Jie. Tel: (029) 769 1234; fax: (029) 769 6799;
email: reservation@hyatt.com.cn; website: www.xian.regency.hyatt.com
西安凯悦（阿房宫）饭店 东大街 158 号
Luxury hotel located within the ancient walls of historic Xi'an; international-style
facilities (including health spa and business centre); Chinese and Western restaurants;
cars for hire and tours to the sights.

Shangri-La Golden Flower Hotel (Xiang Ge Li La Jinhua Fandian)
8 Chang Le Road West. Tel: (029) 8323 2981; fax: (029) 8323 5477;
email: slx@shangri-la.com; website: www.shangri-la.com
西安香格里拉金花大酒店 长东西路 8 号
Five-star hotel with convenient location providing easy access to city centre (10
mins), international airport (40 mins) and the Terracotta Warriors site (30 mins).

ANA Grand Castle Hotel (Chang'an Chengbao Da Jiudian)
12 Xi Duan Huan Cheng Nan Lu. Tel: (029) 8760 8888; fax: 8723-1500;
email: sales@anahotelxian.com; website: www.anahotelxian.com
长安城堡大酒店 环城南路西段 12 号
This modern five-star re-creation of a Tang dynasty castle has space, elegance and
excellent service. It is ideally located just beyond the South Gate of the city's Ming
Dynasty wall.

Bell Tower Hotel (Zhonglou Fandian)
110 Nan Da Jie. Tel: (029) 8760 0000; fax: (029) 8727 1217
钟楼饭店 钟楼西南角
Good central location overlooking the Bell Tower and a short walk from the Drum
Tower and Great Mosque. Chinese and Western restaurants.

Dynasty Hotel Xi'an (Qindu Jiudian)
55 Huan Cheng Xi Lu (northern section). Tel: (029) 8862-6262;
fax: (029) 8862-7728; email: dynasty@pub.xaonline.com
秦都酒店 环城西路 55 号
Four-star joint-venture hotel. Western, Cantonese and Korean restaurants.

Grand New World Hotel (Gudu Xin Shijie Jiudian)
48 Lian Hu Lu. Tel: (029) 8721-6868; fax: 8721-0708;
email: gnwhbcatub@xaonline.com
古都新世界大酒店   莲湖路 48 号
This hotel, in the old walled city, is famous for its restaurants and the massive bas-relief of Emperor Qin. Approximately ten minutes' walk to the city wall, Great Mosque and the local Peoples Market.

FOOD AND DRINK

 lthough there is no distinctive local cuisine, Xi'an does offer a wide variety of small restaurants that specialize in Sichuan, Cantonese and Beijing/Shanghai flavours as well as a number of Hui restaurants that serve Muslim food. There are several Chinese restaurants with English menus on Jiefang Lu just north of the Heping Gate; also try the smaller streets in the northeast corner and southern portions of the walled city. For a Chinese banquet-style dinner, try the Wuyi Fandian on Dong Dajie. Street stalls and night markets offer the best food in Xi'an; the biggest of which is located on Dongxin Jie east of Jiefang Lu. Other smaller ones are located just inside the Heping Gate on Xiamaling Jie, southeast of the Bell Tower within the Jiefang market area, and around the Drum Tower. Grilled mutton skewers and dumplings are most common, hot pot (Mongolian-style), goat's head soup, cold noodles, and spring rolls filled with pickled vegetables are also found. One popular local dish is the hearty *yangrou paomo*—a spicy mutton and vegetable soup poured over broken pieces of flatbread. Local drink includes *Xifeng Jiu*, a colourless spirit, and *Huanggui Choujiu* (Yellow Osmanthus Thick Wine), a milky rice wine developed during the Tang period. *Baoji Pijiu* is the best of the local brews.

XI'AN TO BAOJI

The 720-kilometre (450-mile) mule track between Xi'an and Lanzhou was travelled by Silk Road traders in roughly 18 stages. A motor road built during the early 1930s by thousands of famine refugees with US$400,000 provided by the China International Famine Relief Commission USA shortened the journey to four days. In 1954, the railway link was completed.

Harry Franck, an American who travelled extensively in China in the 1920s, made the journey with pack mules and two carts. 'Beyond Xianyang the whole dust-hazy landscape was covered as far as the eye could see with graves . . . [he wrote] and nowhere a touch of any colour but the yellow brown of rainless autumn . . . Cave dwellings had become almost universal, and were to remain so for many days to come; villages, whole towns of caves, stretched in row after row up the face of great

© Airphoto International Ltd.

Eastern Silk Road (Within Jade Gate)

N

0   100   200   300 kms
0   100   200 miles

loess cliffs . . . The smaller towns and hamlets that lay scattered along the way, and often thickly over the surrounding country, were also monotonously alike, always filthy and miserable.' Cave dwellings are still common throughout the Yellow River loess regions of Shaanxi, Henan and Gansu.

This area saw the rise to power of the Zhou tribe of the Western Zhou Kingdom (1027–771 BC). Although the period's history is semi-legendary, its cultural relics are not. In Qishan County lie ruins of a Western-Zhou palace, and the nearby Zhou Yuan Cultural Relics Exhibition Hall houses the fine bronzes that were found there.

Baoji is at the junction of the Xi'an–Lanzhou rail line and the 669-kilometre (415-mile) Baocheng line, which links Shaanxi Province with Chengdu, the capital of Sichuan Province, to the south. (This latter line follows the old southwest trade route from Xi'an through Yunnan Province into Burma.) A cultural centre during the Zhou and Qin dynasties, the Baoji area was the battleground for wars between the states of Wei, Shu and Wu during the Three Kingdoms period (220–265). On a nearby hillside is **Jintai Monastery**, built in the Ming dynasty (1368–1644) and home to the founder of the Taoist kung fu sect, Zhang Sanfeng. At **Beishouling** is an exhibition hall on a Neolithic site. A funicular tram runs to a scenic summit in the nearby Qinling Mountains.

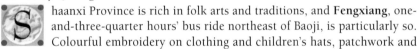 haanxi Province is rich in folk arts and traditions, and **Fengxiang**, one-and-three-quarter hours' bus ride northeast of Baoji, is particularly so. Colourful embroidery on clothing and children's hats, patchwork and good luck toys for children and newly-weds, and artistic New Year woodcut pictures are created here. The best known of the crafts are the clay figures and masks of folk heroes, gaudily painted yellow, red, green and black. Tiger masks, decorated with butterflies and flowers, are said to have been first made in the Ming dynasty by a soldier whiling away his long hours on guard duty. One night, enemy soldiers surrounded Fengxiang, and the commanding officer ordered the soldiers to don the tiger masks and stand, sword in hand, on the ramparts of the city wall. The terrified enemy rode off in a hurried retreat. The tiger motif may, however, date as far back as the Zhou dynasty.

(previous page) Chinese Muslims at prayer in Lanzhou

GANSU PROVINCE

natural corridor linking China with Xinjiang and Central Asia, the province of Gansu was historically the last frontier in Chinese territory. It was a passageway through which the ancient trade routes slipped between the high Tibetan plateau to the west and the rolling Mongolian expanses to the north. In the northwest, the Gobi Desert is bordered by the Mongolian plateau on one side and Qilian Mountains of Qinghai Province on the other, forming the Hexi Corridor. Caravans of traders, pilgrims and missionaries navigated through this desolate strip before entering the eastern hinterlands of the Taklamakan. Southeast Gansu contains the expansive Gannan grasslands, where nomadic Tibetans practise a pastoral economy herding horses, sheep, cattle and camels. Towns in Gansu grew up from the existing oases along the Silk Road, and several Buddhist grottoes were carved along the route, notably at Dunhuang and Maijishan.

The northern Silk Road entered Gansu after leaving Chang'an, continuing over the Liupan Mountains and through the southern part of the present-day **Ningxia Hui Autonomous Region** (formerly part of Gansu) to **Jingyuan**, northeast of Lanzhou. The route then crossed the **Yellow River** and joined the other trade routes in the northern Hexi Corridor. The southern route entered Lanzhou via Tianshui, crossing the Yellow River near Binglingsi Thousand Buddha Caves. After skirting the edge of Qinghai, the route then ascended the Qilian Mountains and joined the Hexi Corridor route at Zhangye. The middle road, which became the main route after the tenth century, passed through Wuwei and followed what is today the Lanzhou–Urumqi railway line. Other caravan routes branched westwards into Tibet and northwards to Mongolia.

Gansu has served as an important military and communications link with the other northwestern provinces since the Han dynasty, when the Chinese were fighting for control of this inhospitable region, and the lucrative Silk Road trade, with the pugnacious Xiongnu tribes, Tibetans and others. As the Chinese pushed their border west they extended the Great Wall, guarded by watchtowers and garrisons. Jiayuguan was the last garrison in Chinese territory, where a fort and portions of the Great Wall still remain. The Han soldiers relied heavily on horses to patrol the region, many imported from the newly discovered kingdoms of Central Asia. The world-famous 'Flying Horse of Gansu', a small bronze sculpture from the Han dynasty, was discovered in Wuwei, the former political and commercial centre of the Hexi Corridor. When the Xiongnu were finally defeated in the latter part of the Han dynasty, the Chinese set up prefectures in the region. But it was not until the Mongol Yuan dynasty (1279–1368) that Gansu became an official province of China.

Largely barren, Gansu has always been backward and impoverished. Today, the central government has made some efforts to industrialize the region, particularly Lanzhou. Although the province has rich deposits of oil, coal, nickel, platinum, chromium, lead, limestone, gypsum and marble, these resources have not yet been fully exploited, and Gansu remains one of the poorest provinces in China. Scientists at the Desert Research Institute in Lanzhou are developing cost-effective ways to stem soil erosion and protect arable land from the shifting desert sands (known as 'yellow dragons'), including the establishment of greenbelts with ambitious tree-, grass- and shrub-planting campaigns. The open plains in the southern grasslands and the desert region in the Hexi Corridor give Gansu a wild, isolated feeling. The few towns that survive in these regions are worth visiting for their stark beauty as well as for the colourful minority cultures, particularly in the grasslands.

While the majority of the population is Han Chinese, Gansu is also home to nine different minority groups: **Hui**, **Dongxiang**, **Tibetan**, **Tu**, **Yugur**, **Salar**, **Mongolian**, **Baoan** and **Kazakh**, who live in seven autonomous counties. The **Dongxiang** (Mongol Muslims), **Yugur** and **Baoan** people are found only in Gansu. At the National Minorities Institute in Lanzhou, Gansu's minorities can study their own language and culture.

Gansu is considered yet another birthplace of Chinese civilization and several archaeological sites cluster around water sources still used today—the rich oases of the Hexi Corridor and the river valleys south of Lanzhou. The earliest site, Neolithic Dadiwan, is in Qinan (northeast of Tianshui) and dates back 12,000 years. The distinctive black- and red-painted Neolithic pottery of Gansu has been unearthed and extensively categorized in the provincial museum in Lanzhou, and pieces have also appeared on the international market.

TIANSHUI

Tianshui is the first of the Silk Road cities in Gansu Province. The Buddhist grottoes of **Maijishan** (which looks like a pile of wheat, hence the name **Wheat Stack Mountain**) represent the fourth largest Buddhist cave complex in China, after Datong, Luoyang and Dunhuang. Surrounded by beautiful countryside, the caves lie 35 kilometres southeast of Tianshui. The strange circular red hill holds 194 caves housing more than 7,000 clay and stone statues and 1,300 square metres (a third of an acre) of wall paintings. The site is treasured for its rich collection of clay sculpture. Like Dunhuang, the local rock is too soft for carving and the sculpture is of clay or clay with a stone core; the all-stone sculptures were probably brought in from elsewhere. Various natural disasters have destroyed much of the original site: an earthquake in 734 caused a partial collapse of the hillside and many of the cave frescoes have been lost to the moisture.

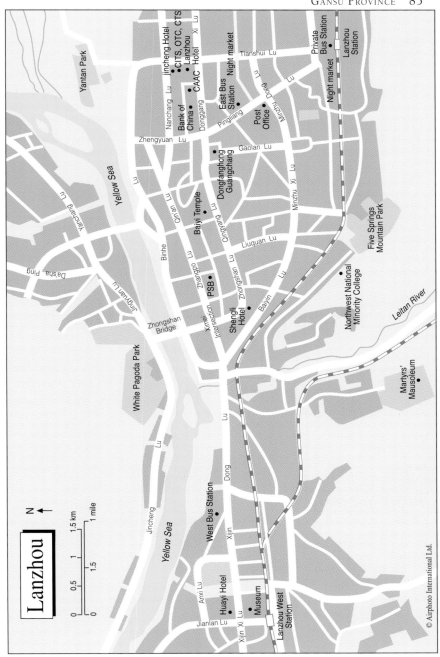

Lanzhou

N

1.5 km
1 mile

Yantan Park

Yellow Sea

Jincheng Hotel
CITS, OTC, CTS
Lanzhou Hotel
CAAC
Night market
Tianshui Lu
Private Bus Station
Lanzhou Station

Nanchang Lu
Bank of China
Donggang
East Bus Station
Pingliang
Post Office
Minzhu Dong Lu
Night market

Zhengyuan Lu
Gaolan Lu

Dongfanghong Guangchang

Qin'an Lu
Baiyi Temple

Minzhu Xi Lu

Binhe

Qingyang
Liuquan Lu

Five Springs Mountain Park

Zhangpo
Baiyin

Northwest National Minority College

Leitan River

PSB

Ximei Intersection
Zhongshan Lu

Shengli Hotel

Zhongshan Bridge

White Pagoda Park

Dasha Ping

Jing Yang Lu

Yanchang Lu

Martyrs' Mausoleum

Lu

Dong

West Bus Station

Jincheng

Yellow Sea

Xijin

Anxi Lu

Huayi Hotel

Museum

Jianlan Lu

Xijin Xi Lu

Lanzhou West Station

© Airphoto International Ltd.

oday, only 194 caves remain. The first caves are thought to have been hewn during the Qin dynasty, but the earliest extant ones date from the Northern Wei (386–534); others were added during the Sui, Tang, and as late as the Qing dynasty. Graceful stone figures from the sixth century reflect the Gandharan (Greco-Indian) artistic influence, while the lively and bold clay statues of the Tang and Song are more traditionally Chinese. A number of huge Buddha images carved on the rock surface dignify the site. The caves are easily accessible via a good system of walkways and spiral steps, but many are only visible through wire netting unless you hire a guide. To visit some caves, extra payment is required, sometimes per person, sometimes per group. Check this before starting the tour.

TIANSHUI PRACTICAL INFORMATION

Local speciality products include carved lacquerware screens and furniture inlaid with semi-precious stones as well as silk carpets. Tianshui is now the second largest city in Gansu after Lanzhou, an industrial and commercial town with little of interest for the modern traveller other than as a stepping stone for visiting Maijishan.

TRANSPORTATION

By road or rail: there are daily trains and buses to/from Lanzhou and Xi'an. Excursions to Maijishan leave several times a day opposite the Tianshui bus station.

ACCOMMODATION

Tianshui Binguan

5 Yingbin Lu. Tel (0938) 821-2611; fax 821-2823

天水宾馆　迎宾路 5 号

LANZHOU

anzhou, the provincial capital of Gansu, hugs the banks of the **Yellow River** for more than 40 kilometres (25 miles), huddled in a narrow valley dominated on either side by bare brown hills. This unusual geographic setting is responsible for Lanzhou's relatively mild climate and also made the city a natural centre for communications and defence between China and the West for over 2,000 years.

The city was a caravan stop along the Silk Road and a transit point for the wool, silk and tea trades linking Mongolia, Sichuan and Tibet. Lanzhou's importance lay in its strategic position at the threshold of the Hexi Corridor, and in facilitating the transhipment of goods along the Yellow River using inflated animal-hide rafts. It was also a central mail station in the vast Chinese pony express system, supplying horses for government envoys, messengers and foreign tribute missions. Lanzhou has continued to serve as an important transportation centre and today is the major railway junction for northwest China.

Beginning in the late 18th century the northwest was plagued by violent Muslim rebellions, and in 1872, General Zuo Zongtang was appointed to subdue the region. He established his governor-generalship in Lanzhou and set up the Lanzhou Arsenal with loans raised in Shanghai from foreign and Chinese investors. Built by skilled Cantonese workers, the arsenal manufactured shells for Zuo's German cannon and other ammunition.

At the end of the 19th century, rights to bituminous coal deposits in the vicinity of Lanzhou became a bone of contention between the British-owned Chinese Engineering and Mining Company, and the Lanzhou Company, a Chinese government enterprise. Litigation dragged on for years before an amalgamation of the two companies resulted in shared—and increased—profits.

riefly in the 1920s, the Christian warlord Feng Yuxiang stationed part of his National People's Army in Lanzhou, creating tension with the Muslim Ma family warlords, who held sway in southern Gansu, eastern Qinghai and Ningxia. The Ma warlords finally surrendered Lanzhou to the People's Liberation Army in August 1949, after six weeks of bitter fighting.

The decision of the Communist Party Central Committee in 1953 to develop Lanzhou into the major industrial centre of the northwest resulted in a population explosion. Since the late 1960s it has been the centre of China's atomic energy industry. The establishment of petro-chemical, non-ferrous metal, machine-building, wool, leather and plastics industries, as well as academic and technical institutes, brought experts and technicians from all over China, boosting the population to 1.3 million. Today this figure has reached over two million, 97 per cent of which are Han Chinese.

Marco Polo stayed in Lanzhou for a full year in the late 13th century, but 'with no experiences worth recording'. In 1925, American botanist-explorer, Joseph Rock, described Lanzhou as 'the dirtiest Chinese capital I've ever seen' and mentioned the plight of White Russian military officers thrown in gaol or executed. Peter Fleming, the British journalist and adventurer who visited Lanzhou ten years later with the young Swiss traveller, Ella Maillart, found the streets of the city 'romantic'.

Today, Lanzhou is a polluted, sprawling Chinese city, most notable for being the first big stop along the Silk Road after Xi'an. There are some beautiful parks, good night markets, and the museum is definitely worth a visit. The Muslim community provides an interesting contrast in cultures and the first glimpse of the darker Turkic features found throughout Chinese Central Asia.

SIGHTS

GANSU PROVINCIAL MUSEUM (GANSU SHENG BOWUGUAN)

 ocated on Xijin Xi Lu opposite the Friendship Hotel, this museum houses a superb collection of the Neolithic pottery for which Gansu is famed. Exhibits are clearly and informatively labelled in English. The storage rooms bulge with more than 432,000 objects. The display is on the second floor and includes primitive agricultural stone tools and red-grey bowls and vessels from the rich Dadiwan site, in central Gansu. The utensils are 6,000 to 12,000 years old. There is also black-and-red pottery from the numerous Neolithic and Chaleolithic cultures of Yangshao (7000–4000 BC), Majiayao (5000–4000 BC), Miaodigou (5000–4000 BC), Qijia (4000–3000 BC), Banshan (2000 BC), Siwa (1100–770 BC) and Xindian (770–476 BC). Displays include a replica of a burial site found at Wuwei (in the Hexi Corridor), thought to belong to the Qijia culture. It contained three skeletons, one male and two female, along with turquoise, ornamental beads and pottery.

Also on the second floor is a Han-dynasty exhibit of bronze vessels, axe heads, riding accoutrements and more than 20,000 documents written in ink on wooden tablets. Discovered in northwestern Gansu, the documents record the history of the region, including military events at the garrisons. On display as well are the oldest paper fragments ever found, dating from the second century BC. Most interesting are the many bronzes found in the **Leitai Han Tomb** in Wuwei, especially the 'Flying Horse of Gansu', an elegant 245-millimetre-high figure of a horse poised with its rear hoof on the back of a small bird. On show is a copy of this magnificent piece, as the original is usually featuring in exhibitions abroad. 220 pieces were discovered, and there is a stunning display of the soldiers of the Eastern Han army shown in processional order behind their chariots and mounted on horses.

 ating from the Wei and Jin dynasties (220–420) is a painted brick tomb transported from Jiayuguan in the Hexi Corridor. Bricks from tomb number five have been reconstructed in their original form in the grounds of the museum. Each brick, about 16 by 35 cm, is faced with a naive portrayal of daily life. More than 1,000 other tombs have been discovered in the Jiuquan-Jiayuguan area. Exhibits may be viewed by appointment only. Museum reception, tel (0931) 232-5049; fax 233-4106.

On the third floor are exhibits relating to the Red Army's 10,000-kilometre Long March in 1935, which ended west of Gansu. There are also fossils from the **Yellow River**, including what is reputed to be the most complete fossilized skeleton in the world, a mammoth (*Stegodon hunghoensis*), found in 1973. On the first floor is a good exhibit of Gansu's flora, fauna, geology, minerals and natural parks.

On Sunday, Monday and occasionally Tuesday, the museum is closed and visitors may find the gates closed on any other day due to a VIP visit—or for no apparent

(preceding pages) 1979 photograph showing the Great Buddha at Binglingsi

reason. The museum is also closed during the winter months. Take city bus number 1 from the train station.

PARKS

The north side of the **Yellow River** is dominated by several large mosques and the multi-peaked **White Pagoda Park (Bai Ta Shan)**, a pleasantly green and shady place tiered with stone steps, and replete with gateways, pavilions, painted corridors and temples. A 500-year-old Yuan-dynasty pagoda (restored during the Ming) seven storeys high is the central architectural monument. Nearby is the five-arched **Zhongshan Bridge**, constructed in 1907 with German and American engineering expertise and grandly dubbed 'the first bridge over the Yellow River'.

ive Springs Mountain Park (Wuquan Shan Gongyuan) lies at the foot of Gaolan Hill southeast of the city. A legend about the origin of its freshwater springs recalls the earliest days of the Silk Road. Emperor Han Wudi, finding his western borders under attack from the Xiongnu in 121 BC, sent General Huo Qubing with a 200,000-strong cavalry force to defend the region. Leaving the capital of Chang'an, the force pushed on for many days to arrive exhausted, thirsty and hungry in Lanzhou at the foot of this hill. Only after pitching camp did they realize that there was no water and General Huo, moved by the sight of his weary army, went to find some himself. Infuriated by his initial failure, he drew his sword in anger and struck a rock, shouting 'I refuse to believe there is no water here!' When he withdrew his sword, pure spring water gushed forth. He repeated this action four more times, until the needs of his troops were satisfied; the five springs flow to this day. Near the park is a zoo.

Among the numerous temples and pavilions that dot the hillside is the **Chongqing Temple**, which houses a 13th-century iron bell and a finely-moulded bronze Buddha from the Ming dynasty.

BINGLINGSI THOUSAND BUDDHA CAVES (BINGLINGSI SHIKU)

Seventy kilometres (43 miles) southwest of Lanzhou in **Yongjing County** (about two hours by road) is one of China's largest hydro-electric power stations, **Liujiaxia Dam**, which generates 5.7 billion kilowatt-hours of electricity annually. Between June (sometimes as late as July) and October, tourist boats depart daily from the dam, travelling upstream on the **Yellow River** for two hours to reach the Thousand Buddha Caves of Binglingsi. During the winter months the water level is too low for boats, and there is no access by road.

The river trip to the caves is striking. Some cultivation lies along the river banks among the otherwise barren, yellow-brown hills and ridges. These jagged contours are eroded into strange shapes coloured occasionally by strata of red-orange earth. The entrance to Binglingsi, at **Dasi Gou (Big Temple Gully)**, is guarded by giant rocks shaped like gnarled fingers.

The caves, which stretch for 200 metres, were carved into the western wall of the inlet over a period of 1,500 years. Excavation work began only in 1952. The caves are mentioned in historical documents as early as the fifth century and they were an important centre of Buddhism for hundreds of years, flourishing under the Song and Ming dynasties. The name is comparatively new; under the Tang the monastery was known as Lingyansi (Supernatural Cliff Monastery). Binglingsi is a Chinese corruption of the Tibetan phrase meaning 'Place of Ten Thousand Buddhas', a common name for Buddhist cave temples. The town of Yongjing was a crossroads for com-merce, and due to the many pilgrims who visited here the artwork was continually restored and expanded. The damaged statues reveal how the pieces were constructed: mud and straw over inner wooden frames, the whole then covered with stucco and paint.

The earliest caves date from the Northern Wei dynasty, the latest from the early Qing dynasty. Some of the niches are Indian-style carved-stone stupas, rarely seen in China. Nearly 700 stone statues and 82 stucco ones have survived. The largest of these is the imposing Maitreya (the coming Buddha), which is 27 metres high and made of straw and stucco, the first sight of the caves from the river. Cave 169 is the oldest cave, containing one Buddha and two bodhisattvas—as shown in photographs in the tourist booklet available at the site. It has a separate substantial entrance fee.

fter the construction of the Liujiaxia Dam, the water level of the river rose more than 20 metres (65 feet), burying in mud all of the 171 large caves on the lower level. The best of the 800 figures they contained were saved, however, and are being placed in other caves.

Time and water levels permitting, it is possible to climb up the sandy gully through the high yellow rock gorges to the Upper Monastery (about 45 minutes). Here there is a small community of Tibetan lamas living in tiny mud huts built against the rock-face, cultivating small plots of corn and a few fruit trees. They tend a small, newly reconstructed temple housing early Qing-dynasty sutras. The temple was destroyed three times, and ruins of the lamas' former quarters are scattered about. Surviving monuments include a fine Song-dynasty incense pagoda carved in red stone and a nearby cave with a large Tang-dynasty Buddha holding the wheel of life.

Excursions to Binglingsi can be arranged by any one of the travel agencies in Lanzhou. Alternatively, there are inexpensive Chinese tour buses that depart from the bus station in front of the Shengli Hotel early in the morning. It is also possible to take a public bus to Yongjing and then catch one of the tour boats. Take along a lunch-box, as facilities at the site are minimal. A permit to photograph the Binglingsi cave interiors costs Rmb800.

LANZHOU PRACTICAL INFORMATION

 here are relatively few sights in Lanzhou; city bus number 1 begins at the main railway station, and makes stops at the Lanzhou Hotel, Shengli Hotel (main shopping area), West Bus Station, and finally the Friendship Hotel and Gansu Provincial Museum; normal business, museum and site hours are 8–12 and 3–6, Beijing time.

TRANSPORTATION

Daily flights to/from Beijing, Dunhuang, and Xi'an; four times a week to/from

Over the centuries travellers and traders along the Silk Road left a legacy of cultural and social influences, which can be seen today in the great variety of faces and costumes of the people in China's northwest

Guangzhou, Shanghai, Jiayuguan and Urumqi; the airport is 75 kilometres from the city (bus from CAAC booking office on Donggang Xi Lu); several trains daily to/from Urumqi, Shanghai and Beijing (and points in between); there is a foreigner ticket window in the main train station; daily buses to/from Xi'an, Wuwei, and Tianshui (East Bus Station), to/from Linxia, Xiahe and Hezuo (West Bus Station). For flight schedules visit www.linktrip.com/silkroad/gansu/fs_gasu.htm, for trains check out www. linktrip.com/silkroad/gansu/ts_gasu.htm.

ACCOMMODATION
Lanzhou Sunshine Plaza
428 Qing Yang Road, Chengguan District. Tel: (0931) 460 8888;
fax: (0931) 460 8889; e-mail: tsygds@sohu.com
阳光大厦 城关区庆阳路 428 号
A five-star international commercial hotel centrally located. Night Club. Karaoke Bar. Chinese and Western restaurant facilities.

Hotel Savoy (Lanzhou Sifang Jiudian)
788 Xijin Xi Road. Tel: (0931) 2566868; fax: (0931) 258 0668
兰州四方酒店 七里河区西津西路 788 号
Five-star hotel located in the Qilihe District.

Lanzhou Legend Hotel (Lanzhou Feitian Dajiudian)
599 Tianshui Lu. Tel: (0931) 853 2888; fax: (0931) 853 2333
兰州飞天大酒店   天水路399号
Four-star hotel with a health centre and Chinese and Western restaurants. Located in the heart of the city, it is about 76 km from the airport and 2 km from the railway station.

JJ Sun Hotel
481 Donggang Xi Lu. Tel: (0931) 880 5511; fax: (0931) 885 4700
兰州锦江阳光酒店   东岗西路 481 号
Four-star hotel situated in the commercial centre of Lanzhou, overlooking the 'Red East' Square and Lanzhou University.

Xi Lan International Hotel (Xilan Guoji Dajiudian)
133 Dingxi Road,Chengguan District. Tel: (0931) 862 8998;
fax: (0931) 861 2396
西兰国际酒店 兰州城关区定西路 133 号
Four-star hotel with all the usual amenities.

Jincheng Hotel (Jincheng Binguan)
209 Tianshui Lu. Tel: (0931) 841-6638; fax: 841-8438
金城宾馆　天水路 209 号
Three-star hotel with air-conditioned rooms; popular with the Overseas Chinese;
seven restaurants and a business centre.

FOOD AND DRINK

anzhou is renowned for its fruits; the earliest fruit orchards in the Lanzhou area were planted during the Western Han dynasty. The city is now ringed with orchards and fields, which during the summer months supply street markets with a profusion of produce, including peaches, plums, apples, dates, walnuts, grapes and vegetables. Roadside melon-sellers sit beside huge piles of watermelons and sweet Gansu melons (a small honeydew melon, peeled and then eaten). The seeds are said to have been introduced to China by American Vice-President Henry Wallace in the early 1940s.

Locals eat the fruit on the spot, spitting out the seeds, which the seller promptly collects, dries and resells. Red dates that have been sun-dried on roofs or in courtyards, then sprayed with white wine and preserved in wine pots, are a local winter treat. Popular throughout northwest China, Lanzhou's most well-known local speciality is *niurou mian*, a spicy noodle soup served with beef and scallions. The restaurant scene seems to be concentrated in the city centre, near the Shengli Hotel on Jiuquan Lu. There are several market areas that are worthwhile: the biggest and most vibrant is located on He Zhong Lu, spread out on either side of Tianshui Lu just south of the Lanzhou Hotel—in the morning you can have a traditional Han Chinese breakfast of *doujiang* (soybean milk) and *youtiao* (fried dough-stick), during the day the market is overrun with stalls selling shoes, clothing and household items, and then around dusk the market is transformed once again, this time into pure food: grilled lamb, spicy hot pot, dumplings, *chunjuan* (deep-fried spring rolls) and *jianbing* (large egg pancake stuffed with cold vegetables and chillies), fried noodles and rice, and sweet bean soups. There are a variety of small restaurants and a fruit/vegetable market just west of the main train station.

EARLY CHINESE TRAVELLERS OF THE SILK ROAD

Zhang Qian: The unrivalled hero of the Silk Road is Zhang Qian, the second-century BC Chinese ambassador-extraordinaire, whose two amazing journeys into Central Asia opened the historic Silk Road and established the first cross-cultural exchanges between East and West. Appointed an envoy to the Western Regions by the Han Emperor Wudi in 139 BC, he was given the task of persuading the Yuezhi tribes in Ferghana to ally themselves with the Chinese and help wipe out the Xiongnu. In the ten

(above) Bodhisattva painting on silk, Khocho, ninth–tenth century AD

years he was held prisoner, he learnt their customs and strategies. He married a Xiongnu woman and had a son before escaping and continuing his imperial mission along the northern Silk Road to Kashgar and Ferghana. Though he failed to achieve a military alliance with the Yuezhi, he was well received and assisted in his further travels through neighbouring kingdoms, including Bactria and Sogdiana.

Hoping to avoid the Xiongnu, Zhang Qian returned via the southern Silk Road—only to fall into the hands of allied tribes. He was held captive for another year, before confusion caused by the death of the Xiongnu leader created conditions for escape. After 13 years, Zhang Qian and an attaché—the only remaining member of his embassy—returned to Chang'an (Xi'an) in 126 BC. He reported in detail on the geography, cultures and economies of the 36 kingdoms of the Western Regions—a new world to the Chinese. Emperor Wudi, keen to expand his influence in Central Asia, was delighted and again sent Zhang Qian to pursue the contacts already established. With 300 men, 10,000 sheep, extra mounts, and quantities of gold and silk, Zhang Qian set off in 119 BC. His representatives went to the courts of Ferghana, Sogdiana, Bactria, Parthia and northern India, and the embassy returned four years later, bringing with it many foreign envoys. Two years later, in 113 BC, Zhang Qian died. His tomb, in Shaanxi Province, has recently been restored.

Ban Chao: In the first century AD, China's power over the oases of the Tarim Basin had been lost to the Xiongnu. Ban Chao, the cavalry commander whose campaigns re-established military control, became known as one of the greatest of China's generals.

Having distinguished himself in battle against the Xiongnu in the region of Hami and Barkol, in northeast Xinjiang, he was given the unenviable task of subjugating the kingdoms of the Silk Road, which had rebelled against China and allied themselves with the Xiongnu. A resourceful soldier and diplomat, he took the kingdoms of Loulan, Khotan and Kashgar either by brute force or cunning strategy, installing pro-Chinese rulers and re-opening the southern Silk Road to trade. He remained in Central Asia for 31 years, crushing rebellions and establishing diplomatic relations with more than 50 states in the Western Regions. Accompanied by horsemen arrayed in bright red leather, he himself went as far as Merv (in Turkestan) and made contacts with Parthia, Babylonia and Syria.

This last contact was made by Ban Chao's envoy, Gan Ying, who in AD 97 was ordered to proceed to Ta Ts'in (in the Roman Empire). He reached the Persian Gulf but was told by the Persians that the way by sea to Ta Ts'in was far and dangerous and that he would have to take three years' supply of grain with him. Gan Ying was deterred by this misinformation (presumably designed to protect the interest of middlemen in the East-West trade) and he turned back. Nevertheless, his travels increased China's knowledge of the Roman Empire. Ban Chao returned to China at the end of his life to receive high honours. He died in 101.

Fa Xian: The monk, Fa Xian, was one of the first of many Chinese Buddhists to make a pilgrimage to India. His account of his overland journey, *A Record of Buddhist Kingdoms*, immortalized him both in China and—following translation—in the West.

Fa Xian's self-imposed mission was to bring back to China Buddhist canons and images to expand the knowledge of this religion in his own country. Accompanied by a number of devout fellow monks, he set forth in 399 on a journey across the southern Silk Road and over the Hindu Kush to India, losing at least one travelling companion to frostbite. Fa Xian stayed for two years in Sri Lanka and eventually took stormy passage by sea back to China in 414.

This great adventure took 15 years, and for the rest of his long life—he died at the age of 88—Fa Xian worked on translations of the Sanskrit sutras he had brought back with him. His record of the journey was an important contribution to the history of the Central-Asian kingdoms in the fifth century.

Xuan Zang: The Buddhist monk, Xuan Zang, is the best loved of all Chinese travellers on the Silk Road. Two accounts of his journey have become Chinese classics—his own historical and geographical *Records of the Western Regions* and a humourous 16th-century novel, *Journey to the West* (or *Monkey*) by Wu Cheng'en, which tells how an odd assortment of companions accompany the monk, vanquishing monsters and overcoming all obstacles.

Foreign travel from China was forbidden when, in 629, Xuan Zang undertook his lone journey on foot and horseback to India. He travelled at night to avoid the sentries in the beacon towers beyond Dunhuang, almost died of thirst while lost in the desert near Hami, and was so lavishly fêted by the King of Turpan that he finally resorted to a hunger strike for permission to continue his journey. Taking the northern Silk Road as far as Kucha, he travelled to Tashkent and Samarkand and then, more or less in the steps of Alexander the Great, southwards to the Peshawar area of modern Pakistan, where in the famous Buddhist university of Nalanda he studied for several years. He spent 14 years in India, Nepal and Sri Lanka before returning to China via the southern Silk Road, through Kashgar, Yarkand and Khotan. By the time he had reached Khotan, news of his return had reached the emperor, who had the monk triumphantly escorted all the way to the capital at Chang'an.

Xuan Zang returned in 645 with 22 horses bearing more than 700 Buddhist works, as well as relics from the Buddha's chair and statues of gold, silver and sandalwood. The Big Goose Pagoda in Xi'an was built to house the sutras, and this is where he worked for the rest of his life, translating them. He died in 664, and the Tang Emperor Gaozong built the Xingjiao Temple outside Xi'an in memory of this great man.

THE EARLIEST DISCOVERIES OF BUDDHIST RELICS

uring his 1935 mission to the region, Sir Eric Teichman wrote in *Journey to Turkistan* that the Chinese 'boil with indignation to read in the books of foreign travellers descriptions of how they carried off whole libraries of ancient manuscripts, frescoes and relics of early Buddhist culture in Turkestan'. Although the Chinese have put a stop to the days of freelance excavations in and around the Taklamakan, many of the ancient Buddhist treasures that survived the sands and swell of Islam for centuries were removed by foreign explorers in a relatively short period of time just after the turn of the century and are now housed in over 30 foreign institutions in England, France, Germany, Japan, Korea, Taiwan, Soviet Union, United States, India, Sweden and Finland.

It is important to note that even before the arrival of Western archaeologists and geographers, many of the buried cities and grottoes along the Silk Road had already been discovered, pillaged or destroyed by the oasis dwellers and tribesmen of the region. In 1863, the first survey team to cross over the Karakoram range into Chinese Turkestan consisted of one Mohamed-i-Hameed, an experienced Indian clerk and surveyor sent by the British to explore the oases of the Taklamakan clandestinely. Only his survey instruments along with some intelligence notes and topographical information collected during his six months in Yarkand were to make the return journey to India. Mohamed-i-Hameed's notebook contained the first reliable confirmation of buried cities in the desert, no longer a legend but an excavatable reality. William Johnson, in 1865, and Sir Douglas Forsyth, a few years later, were the first Western explorers to visit the ancient capital of Khotan and other buried cities in the vicinity of Keriya. Russian explorers were the first to discover some minor buried sites in the Lop Nor in 1877 and the walled city of Kharakhoja, the ancient Uygur capital, in 1879, the same year a Hungarian geological team came upon the Buddhist grottoes at Dunhuang.

The earliest excavations by local treasure hunters and Western archaeologists yielded an amazing collection of Buddhist sutras—some with ancient Indian characters inscribed on birch bark, some written in Sanskrit using the Brahmi alphabet, and others in previously unknown languages (the Bower manuscripts). Those first recovered from the Kucha region in 1889 represented the most remarkable find to date—manuscripts on medicine and necromancy written by monks around the fifth century, the oldest written works known to exist anywhere. Unfortunately, the British, French and

Russians in their haste became sloppy in their quest for manuscripts; forgeries became big business for some ingenious locals who went as far as to create their own characters and languages, puzzling scholars for a number of years (see 'Islam Akhun' on page 313). In spite of this, the genuine manuscripts were testimony to the excellent state of preservation in which many of these Buddhist relics were found and thus began the influx of archaeological expeditions into the Tarim Basin. The discovery of wall paintings and manuscripts in the Turpan region by Russian scholar, Dmitri Klementz, in 1898 signalled the beginning of the great race for the lost treasures of the Taklamakan.

SIR AUREL STEIN

 ir Aurel Stein (1862–1943), considered by the Chinese to be the most heinous of the 'foreign devils' and by Western scholars to be 'the most prodigious combination of scholar, explorer, archaeologist and geographer of his generation', embarked on his first archaeological expedition to Chinese Turkestan in 1900. His amazing discoveries led to honorary degrees from Oxford and Cambridge, knighthood from the British government, the gold medal from the Royal Geographical Society, and numerous other awards. His findings were divided: the murals are to be seen in the National Museum of New Delhi, but the rest lies largely unmarked and poorly displayed at the British Museum, possibly in deference to China's outrage at his successful 'theft'.

Stein was born in Budapest, studied Sanskrit and Persian in Germany, Britain and Austria and joined the administration of the British Raj in 1887. In 1900, well aware of the extraordinary discoveries of Sven Hedin and the potential gold mine that Chinese Turkestan offered archaeologists and historians, he organized his first journey to Khotan to search for evidence of Indian influences on Buddhist art and to undertake 'a systematic exploration of the Silk Road sites'. Stein believed that since native treasure seekers were finding manuscripts and antiquities with careless, unprofessional searches, a thorough investigation would certainly yield more of the same.

At Dandan Oilik where Hedin first travelled, northeast of present-day Khotan, Stein found Sanskrit texts of the Buddhist canon, some dating from the fifth and sixth centuries, in what had once been a library in a monastery. Among the ruins were painted wooden panels depicting a two-humped Bactrian camel, revealing a mix of Indian, Persian and Chinese influences—the term 'Serindian art' was coined by Stein. He continued on to the town of Niya, which was once an important oasis along the southern route of the Silk Road, where he found more wooden tablets, letters inscribed in Kharoshthi, a script of northwest India that dates from the time of Christ. These tablets are concurrent with the arrival of paper from China around the second century AD, for paper was initially rare and expensive. Nearby, he found wooden tablets with clay seals bearing the figure of Athena, with aegis and thunderbolt, as well as other Greek figures, including Eros and Heracles.

Stein's second mission in 1907 (accompanied by his faithful terrier, Dash) took him to Charkhlik, across the haunted Great Desert of Lop, so named by Marco Polo, to Loulan, his only guide being the recently available map of the region by Hedin. At Loulan, Stein found military records and official documents in an old rubbish dump dating from the third century. Little is known about this period of Chinese history, a fact which has only made the Chinese even more enraged about the removal of these documents. Kharoshthi documents on wooden tablets show Loulan had once been an outpost of an ancient Indian empire. Stein next left for Dunhuang, where he made his most remarkable discoveries at the Mogao Caves, the largest rock-temple complex in Central Asia.

The Mogao Caves are unique, partly for the scale of the work, but also for the high degree of artistic achievement in much of the wall paintings and sculpture. They were constructed as shrines to Buddhist gods and as temples where devout pilgrims and other travellers could pray for the success of their journeys. One inscription from August 2, 947 invokes the goddess Guanyin's protection 'so that the district will prosper and the routes to the east and to the west will be open and free, and in the north the Tartars and in the south the Tibetans will cease their depredations and revolts'.

Stein first heard from an Urumqi trader that a Taoist priest called Wang Yuan-lu, or Abbot Wang, had

M. Aurel Stein

stumbled upon a hidden library when workmen were restoring what is now known as Cave 17. Little by little, by playing on Wang's reverence for the monk Xuan Zang (whom Stein also greatly respected), Stein was able to persude the abbot to let him see some of the manuscripts, selected by Wang, with the promise of future donations to his pet project: the complete restoration of the temples. Stein never alluded to the historical importance of these manuscripts and was extremely careful not to breathe a word of his discovery, happily fulfilling Wang's request to remain silent. After a few of the documents had been read, it became evident that Xuan Zang had transported much of the library from India himself and translated many of the Buddhist sutras from Sanskrit. Considering it an omen or a 'quasi-divine hint' as Stein called it, Wang led him to the library itself, 500 cubic feet of manuscripts, piled in disarray. Wang removed the manuscripts a few at a time while Stein and his translator tried to discern which were valuable and worth transporting back to England. Of the 7,000 complete Dunhuang manuscripts, all have been catalogued and moved to the British Library.

The 'library cave' also contained extremely rare temple banners and votive hangings from the Tang dynasty, which survived the Islamic purges of the ninth and tenth centuries partly because, from 781, the Tibetans controlled Dunhuang. In all, Stein hauled off 24 crates of manuscripts and five crates of paintings, for which he paid the incredible price of £130. Stein's reputation was secured when news of the Dunhuang treasures reached Europe. Archaeologists worldwide wanted to come to Chinese Turkestan and search for the lost art and literature of this previously unknown Buddhist civilization.

Stein's third and last successful expedition to China was in 1914, when all his rivals were gone and he saw for himself the destruction wreaked upon the grottoes and sites by careless and rushed archaeologists. He returned to Dunhuang and bought five more crates of manuscripts from Abbot Wang and continued on to Karakhoto, Bezeklik and Astana. By 1930 the Chinese had imposed regulations and restrictions for excavating on their soil and Stein's last expedition, which lasted seven months and was undertaken at the age of 67 with the Harvard Fogg Art Museum, was his only real failure. Stein died in Kabul in 1943 at the age of 82, while seeking permission, as he had for the previous 40 years, to explore Afghanistan, the missing link in his Silk Road explorations.

192. ANCIENT MANUSCRIPTS IN SANSKRIT, CENTRAL-ASIAN BRAHMI, SOGDIAN, MANICHAEAN-TURKISH, RUNIC TURKI, UIGUR, TIBETAN. FROM WALLED-UP TEMPLE LIBRARY, 'THOUSAND BUDDHAS,' TUN-HUANG.

Scale, one-seventh.

1. Sanskrit Prajna-paramita text on palm leaves. 2. Roll with Manichaean 'Confession of Sins' in early Turkish. 3. Book in Runic Turki. 4, 6. Uigur texts in book form. 5. Pothi in Central-Asian Brahmi script. 7. Text in cursive Central-Asian Brahmi written on reverse of Chinese MS. roll. 8. Roll with Sogdian text. 9. Leaf of Tibetan Buddhist Pothi.

193. GIGANTIC ROLL OF PAPER, WITH SANSKRIT AND 'UNKNOWN LANGUAGE' TEXTS IN BRAHMI SCRIPT, FROM WALLED-UP TEMPLE LIBRARY, 'THOUSAND BUDDHAS,' TUN-HUANG.

Scale, one-fifth.

A shows the roll, which is over seventy feet long, partially opened.
B shows the silk painting on top of outer side.

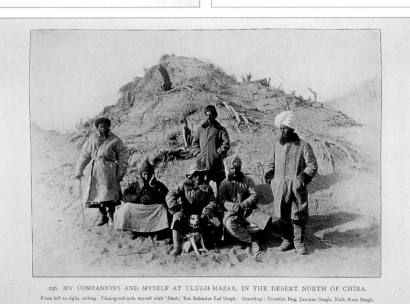

296. MY COMPANIONS AND MYSELF AT ULUGH-MAZAR, IN THE DESERT NORTH OF CHIRA.

From left to right, sitting : Chiang-ssŭ-yeh, myself with 'Dash,' Rai Bahadur Lal Singh. Standing : Ibrahim Beg, Jasvant Singh, Naik Ram Singh.

Aurel Stein (centre) with his faithful terrier 'Dash,' pictured with field companions during March 1908 in the southern Taklamakan east of Hetian. On Stein's right is Chiang who helped negotiate the Dunhuang manuscript deal with Taoist priest Wang Yuanlu

161. STUCCO IMAGE GROUP, REPRESENTING BUDDHA BETWEEN DISCIPLES, BODHISATTVAS, AND DVARAPALAS, IN CAVE-TEMPLE CH. III., 'THOUSAND BUDDHAS' SITE.

194. BUNDLES OF OLD MANUSCRIPT ROLLS, MAINLY CHINESE, IN ORIGINAL WRAPPERS, FROM WALLED-UP TEMPLE LIBRARY, 'THOUSAND BUDDHAS,' TUN-HUANG.

Scale, one-fifth.

DELICATE NEGOTIATIONS

 o at last with many a sigh and plaintive remonstrance, and behind the outer temple gates carefully locked, he set to this great toil, helped now by a sort of priestly famulus whose discretion could be relied on. Previously I had sometimes feared that the little Tao-shih might get smothered under a tumbling wall of manuscript. Now I wondered whether the toil of pulling them out would not cause his slender physique to collapse. But it held out all the same, and by the evening of May 28th all the regular bundles of Chinese rolls, more than 1050 in all, and those containing Tibetan texts had been transferred to neat rows in the spacious main cella of the temple.

The bundles were almost all sewn up tightly in coarse covers of linen (see picture on page 102). But the ends were generally left open, and as Wang (Tao-shih) handed out bundle after bundle through the chapel door, Chiang and myself were just able to see hastily whether, amidst the usual rolls with Chinese texts, there were embedded any Pothi leaves from Brahmi manuscripts, folded-up pictures, or other relics of special attraction. Such we picked out and put aside rapidly. But there was no time to even glance at individual rolls and to see whether they bore anywhere within or without Indian or Central Asian writing.

P erfunctory as the operation had to be in view of the Tao-shih's visibly growing reluctance, I had a gratifying reward for my insistence on this clearing in the discovery of several miscellaneous bundles at the very bottom. They had been used there by the Tao-shih to turn a low clay platform into a level foundation for the manuscript wall above. In spite of the crushing these bundles had undergone, I recovered them from a large number of exquisite silk paintings of all sizes, and some beautiful embroidered pieces. One of the latter was a magnificent embroidered picture, remarkable for design, colours and a fineness of material, and showing a Buddha between Bodhisattvas in life size, which I shall have occasion to discuss hereafter (see picture on page 172).

Perhaps it was a lively sensation of the toil he had undergone and now longed to see ended, or the fear that we were now touching those precious Chinese Sutra texts to which he alone seemed to attach any real value. At any rate the Tao-shih at this stage came to business, so to speak, by asking for a substantial 'subscription' (pu-shih) to his temple. At the same time he protested that any cession of sacred texts or 'Chings' was impossible. I myself was glad to take up the theme; for I had recognized long before that it was my duty towards research to try my utmost to rescue, if possible, the whole of the collection from the risk of slow dispersion and loss with which it was threatened in such keeping.

But at the same time I could not close my eyes to the serious difficulties and objections. I was quite unable to form any definite estimate of the philological value of those masses of Chinese canonical texts which made up the bulk of the hidden library. Their contents were, no doubt, to be found in the complete editions of the Buddhist 'Tripitaka,' printed for centuries past in China, Korea, Japan. Still less was I able to select those texts which for one reason or another were possessed of antiquarian or literary interest. The removal of so many cart-loads of manuscripts would inevitably give publicity to the whole transaction, and the religious resentment this was likely to arouse in Tun-huang, even if it did not lead to more serious consequences, would certainly compromise my chance of further work in Kan-su.

Nevertheless, I was prepared to face these risks rather than forego the endeavour to rescue the whole hoard. Chang-ssu-yeh, in spite of misgivings justified by his knowledge of the local conditions, loyally did his best to persuade the Tao-shih that removal of the collection to a 'temple of learning in Ta-Ying-kuo,' or England, would in truth be an act which Buddha, and his Arhats might approve as pious. He also urged that the big sum I was prepared to pay (I hinted at 40 horse shoes, about Rs.5000 and was resolved to give twice as much, if need be, whatever the excess over my sanctioned grant) would enable Wang to return to a life of peace in his native province, distant Shan-hsi, if Tun-huang should became too hot for him. Or else he could allay any scruples by using the whole sum for the benefit of the temple, which by his restoration he could claim to have annexed as his own with all its contents known and unknown.

But all in vain. The prospect of losing his precious 'Chings' as a whole or in part profoundly frightened the good priest, who had before resignedly closed his eyes to my gathering whatever I thought of special artistic or antiquarian value. For the first time our relations became somewhat strained, and it required very careful handling and our suavest manners to obviate anything like a breach. What the Tao-shih urged with all signs of sincere anxiety was that any deficiency in those piles of sacred texts would certainly be noticed by his patrons, who had helped him with their publicly recorded subscriptions to clear and restore the temple; that in consequence the position he had built up for himself in the district by his pious labours of eight years would be lost for good, and his life-task destroyed. He even vaguely reproached himself for having given up sacred things over which his life patrons ought to have as much right of control as he himself, and doggedly asserted the need of consulting them before moving a step further. And in the depth of my heart I could bear him no grudge for these scruples and recriminations, or even gainsay them.

F or two long days these discussions had to be carried on intermittently with a view to gain time while my examination of the miscellaneous bundles was proceeding. I managed to complete this by the second evening. But on returning to the temple the next day in order to start the close search of the regular Chinese bundles for Central-Asian and other foreign text materials, I found to my dismay that the Tao-shih in a sudden fit of perturbation had shifted back overnight almost the whole of them to their gloomy prison of centuries. His sullen temper gave us further cause for anxiety. But the advantage we possessed by already holding loads of valuable manuscripts and antiques, and the Tao-shih's unmistakable wish to secure a substantial sum of money, led at last to what I had reason to claim as a substantial success in this diplomatic struggle.

He agreed to let me have fifty well-preserved bundles of Chinese text rolls and five of Tibetan ones, besides all my previous selections from the miscellaneous bundles. For all these acquisitions four horse shoes of silver, equal to about RS.500, passed into the priest's hands; and when I surveyed the archaeological value of all I could carry away for this sum, I had good reason to claim it a bargain. Of course, after so severe a struggle I lost no time in removing the heavy loads of Chinese and Tibetan rolls. Until now my devoted Ssu-yeh had struggled to my tent night by

197. WANG TAO-SHIH, TAOIST PRIEST AT "THOUSAND BUDDHAS" SITE, TUN-HUANG.

Wang Yuanlu, the Taoist priest who in 1899 discovered the cache of manuscripts hidden behind a wall. Eight years later the priest succumbed to pressure from Stein and parted with most of the manuscripts for the equivalent of £130

night with the loads of daily 'selections'; but to this task his physical strength would not have been equal. So help had to be sought on this occasion from Ibrahim Beg and Tila, my trusted followers; and after two midnight trips to the temple, under the screening shadow of the steep river bank, the huge sackfuls were safely transferred to my store room without any one, even of my own men, having received an inkling.

The Tao-shih's nervousness had increased by prolonged absence from his clients in the oasis; and now he hastened to resume his seasonal begging tour in the Tun-huang district. But a week later he returned, reassured that the secret had not been discovered and that his spiritual influence, such as it was, had suffered no diminution. So we succeeded in making him stretch a point further, and allow me to add some twenty more bundles of manuscripts to my previous selections, against an appropriate donation to the temple. When later on it came to the packing, the manuscript acquisitions needed seven cases, while the paintings, embroideries, and other miscellaneous relics filled five more. The packing of these was a very delicate task and kept me busy on the days when photographic work was impossible in the caves. There was some little trouble about getting enough boxes without exciting suspicion at Tun-huang. Luckily I had foreseen the chance and provided some 'empties' beforehand. The rest were secured in disguise and by discreet instalments, so everything passed off without a hitch.

The good Tao-shih now seemed to breathe freely again, and almost ready to recognize that I was performing a pious act in rescuing for Western scholarship those relics of ancient Buddhist literature and art which local ignorance would allow to lie here neglected or to be lost in the end. When I finally said good-bye to the 'Thousand Buddhas,' his jovial sharp face had resumed once more its look of shy but self-contented serenity. We parted in fullest amenity. I may anticipate here that I received gratifying proof of the peaceful state of his mind when, on my return to An-hsi four months later, he agreed to let depart for the 'temple of learning' in the distant West another share of the Chinese and Tibetan manuscripts in the shape of over two hundred compact bundles. But my time for feeling true relief came when all the twenty-four cases, heavy with manuscript treasures rescued from that strange place of hiding, and the five more filled with paintings and other art relics from the same cave, had been deposited safely in the British Museum.

Sir Mark Aurel Stein, Ruins of Desert Cathay, 1912

ALBERT VON LE COQ

ir Aural Stein's arch-rival, considered the second most heinous of the 'foreign devils' by the Chinese, was the German Albert von Le Coq (1860–1930). His findings from Chinese Turkestan and those from two other German expeditions, easily filled the 13 rooms that were added on to the Berlin Ethnological Museum for his Turpan Collection.

After working in his father's wine business until the age of 40, von Le Coq decided to study oriental languages including Arabic, Turkish, Persian and Sanskrit, and in 1902 joined the Indian section of the Ethnological Museum in Berlin. In 1904, he left on his first expedition accompanied by Theodor Bartus, the museum handyman, to explore Kharakhoja, Bezeklik, Karashahr, Maralbashi and Shui-pang (north of Turpan), where they found Christian manuscripts, fragments of St. Matthew's Gospel, the Nicene Creed in Greek, and texts on the visit of the Three Kings to the infant Christ. In Hami, Bartus and von Le Coq were wined and dined at the sumptuous palace of the khan, which was furnished with Hetian carpets, silk embroideries, jade carvings and French clocks.

While in Hami, von Le Coq heard of the discovery of ancient manuscripts near the oasis town of Dunhuang. A Turkoman merchant knew of a Chinese priest who had discovered the hidden Buddhist library some five years earlier. At the same time von Le Coq's boss, the noted art historian Albert Grunwedel, also from the Berlin Museum, telegrammed von Le Coq to meet him in Kashgar. Since von Le Coq did not have time to go to both places, he spun a coin, a Chinese silver dollar that came up heads. He left for Kashgar the next day and unwittingly left the wealth of Dunhuang to his rivals, Aurel Stein and Paul Pelliot.

Von Le Coq returned with Grunwedel to the Kucha region. A Japanese team had recently been in the area, and a Russian team hoped to dig there as well. When the Beresovsky brothers arrived, there was some disagreement as to who had the 'right' to dig where. The Russian and German governments had casually laid out 'spheres of interest' and made certain arrangements that were supposed to be respected by the excavators.

Von Le Coq moved on to work at the Kizil Caves, which overlook the Muzart River, and consisted of 'hundreds of temples in the steep cliffs of a mountain range'. Kucha had been a relatively cosmopolitan city and wealthy caravan stop during the days of the Silk Road and was rich in Buddhist culture and art—the Kizil frescoes are considered to be the apex of Central Asian art. Von Le Coq said of one temple: 'the paintings were the finest we found anywhere in Turkestan, consisting of scenes from the Buddha legends, almost purely Hellenistic in character'. The Germans initially found the walls of the caves covered with an inch-thick layer of mould, which was easily washed away with Chinese brandy. One picture done in bright blue pigments showed King Ajatashatru taking a ritual bath in melted butter while a courtier paints the death of the Buddha for his master, since he is afraid to speak the bad news. The other caves contained paintings of the Buddha's temptation by Mara, his sermons and his cremation.

V on Le Coq removed whole murals and the contents of entire temples, but Grunwedel condemned this practice of grabbing art for its value as treasure. Von Le Coq finally left on his own for Berlin after being away two and a half years. Because of the wealth of Buddhist relics that the Germans (including Grunwedel) brought back to be catalogued and studied, von Le Coq did not leave on his second expedition for another six years. However, this expedition was plagued from the start and interrupted by the outbreak of World War I in Germany. It was von Le Coq's last visit to Central Asia and not nearly as lucrative as his first. An extensive account of his excavations is recorded in his book *Buried Treasures of Chinese Turkestan*. Von Le Coq spent his remaining years as the director of the Berlin Museum, arranging exhibits for his treasures.

Although it is commonly thought that all of the German findings from Central Asia were destroyed by Allied bombing in World War II, this is luckily not true. Some of the wall paintings that had been cemented into the walls, and another 28 of the largest ones (almost all from Bezeklik), were totally destroyed in the bombings, after having survived for centuries hidden in the desert sands. All movable objects in the museum were taken to the bunker at the Berlin Zoo, or to the bottom of West German coal mines for safe-keeping; most of the manuscripts had been kept at the Prussian Academy for study. Only 40 per cent of the artwork was in fact destroyed; the remainder is elaborately and extensively displayed in the Museum of Indian Art in Berlin.

F urthermore, not all of the art was lost due to the Allied air raids. Some of the artefacts that had been moved from the museum to the Berlin Zoo bunker were taken by the Soviets when they took control of that part of Berlin in 1945. It is said that they hauled at least eight or nine crates of clay sculpture back to Russia with them and the whereabouts of these treasures is still unknown. The Russians also looted many Indian and Turkestan sculptures from the Berlin Ethnographical Museum. While much of the European painting removed after the war has been returned, nothing has been mentioned of the Silk Road art, despite repeated requests on the part of the German authorities.

Albert von Le Coq, 1860–1930

SVEN HEDIN

edin, an intrepid Swede and the first foreigner to explore the ancient cities and ruins of the Taklamakan, was a geographer and explorer whose discoveries won him two of the Royal Geographic Society's coveted gold medals, a knighthood from the British government, and honorary doctorates from Oxford and Cambridge. He was small in stature, an extremely determined man who published nearly 50 volumes of his travels and adventures, and was well known and admired by the kings of Central Asia and the world. Sadly, when he died in 1952 at age 87, he was forgotten by some and repudiated by others. During both World Wars, he had taken a strong and well-publicized pro-German stance that earned him the enmity of many former friends and colleagues.

Hedin studied physical geography in Berlin under Baron von Richthofen, a renowned Asian explorer. In 1890, at age 25, he made his first scouting trip to Central Asia, and four years later returned for the second of several expeditions that would last a total of 40 years. Hedin was a scientific explorer, and not an archaeologist like Stein or von Le Coq. His interest in the Taklamakan and Tibet was in surveying and drawing maps of uncharted regions. His first near-disastrous journey into the Taklamakan in 1895 was a landmark: it proved that, although it was hard going to travel into the Taklamakan, it was possible, thereby inspiring Aurel Stein and other archaeologists and explorers to follow his example. Hedin's subsequent two expeditions into the Taklamakan, in 1896 and 1899/1900, led him to the cities of the southern Silk Road, where he made remarkable archaeological discoveries of an early Chinese garrison town, and charted the wandering Lop Nor Lake (before heading off to Lhasa disguised as a Buddhist pilgrim). Hedin's discoveries and maps proved invaluable to Stein, who followed in his tracks to Hetian and Loulan. Hedin's findings are displayed in Stockholm at the Ethnographical Museum.

In 1926, Hedin was invited by the Chinese government and German Lufthansa Airlines to map a Berlin-Urumqi-Beijing air route. At this time the Chinese were extremely hostile to foreigners and Hedin's expedition faced numerous bureaucratic hassles, encouraged by rumours in the newspapers that he had come to air-lift art treasures out of China. The artefacts that were unearthed during this trip were all turned over to the Chinese authorities under new stringent policies regarding foreign excavations in the Taklamakan.

Southern Gansu

Dongxiang Autonomous County

From Lanzhou to Linxia is 160 kilometres (100 miles), a five- or six-hour journey by road. The route leads from Lanzhou via Liujiaxia, across the Yellow River and southwest through the scenic, steeply-rutted canyons of Dongxiang Autonomous County.

Most of the 190,000-strong **Dongxiang** minority live in this county. Recognized as a distinct minority only in 1949, the Dongxiang are Muslims of Mongol origin. Their language is basically Altaic Mongolian mixed with Chinese and Turkic, and written with both Arabic and Chinese script. They are probably descendants of Genghis Khan's troops stationed at nearby Hezhou (the old name for Linxia) in the early 13th century, when he attacked the then-powerful Xixia Kingdom. Granted amnesty in the Ming dynasty, they remained in the area, turning from war-making to agriculture and carpet-weaving. They intermarried and converted to Islam.

As Muslims, they became deeply involved in the anti-Qing dynasty rebellions led by the Hui that broke out periodically from the late 18th century onward. Many served in the armies of the Ma family warlords during the first half of this century. Today the more subdued Dongxiang eke out a living growing potatoes, wheat, barley, maize and broad beans on small terraced fields ascending the perpendicular canyons of the region, supplementing their income by herding goats, fat-tailed sheep and donkeys, and with stints on road-construction gangs.

hough their dress is now indistinguishable from the modern dress of other Huis, the Dongxiang women once wore beautifully embroidered jackets and trousers, and on festive occasions, colourful skirts, high-heeled flowery shoes and ornate silver jewellery; green or blue tasselled and decorated pillbox hats indicated their marital status. Sadly, this costume seems to have disappeared some 70 years ago. As strict, conservative Muslims, they still marry off their young daughters at 14 years of age, despite Chinese laws forbidding the practice. At New Year celebrations their wilder Mongol origins surface with such activities as wrestling and 'waging war'—the artful game of throwing clods of earth at each other.

From the county seat of Dongxiang, the road winds through the hills, affording from time to time glimpses of the **Tao (Peach) River** far below. A sudden descent into the strikingly rich and fertile **Daxia River** valley leads to the outskirts of Linxia, the prefectural capital. Along the Tao and Daxia river valleys are rich archaeological sites that have yielded large quantities of Late-Neolithic black- and red-painted pottery of the Majiayao (5000–4000 BC), Qijia (4000–3000 BC) and Banshan (2000 BC) cultures, now exhibited in the Gansu Provincial Museum in Lanzhou.

LINXIA

The **Linxia Hui Autonomous Prefecture**, established in 1945, comprises seven counties with various minority peoples—**Hui, Dongxiang, Baoan, Salar** and **Tibetan**. Apart from the Tibetans, all are Muslim, and the prefecture presents surprising and colourful contrasts.

inxia was probably on two of the three routes that the Silk Road took through Gansu. The ruins of an ancient fort stand in Jishishan County, 84 kilometres (52 miles) from Linxia. Certainly, the city played an important role in the spread of Islam from Central Asia, for it became known as 'Little Mecca', a place of pilgrimage for Muslims from other Chinese provinces and a centre for religious scholarship. Above Dongxiang county seat is the 1,300-year-old **Tomb of Han Zeling (Hamuzeling)**, the first Arab missionary to come to Linxia via the Silk Road.

In the 18th century, the New Teaching (Xinjiao) or Vocal Recollection Sect was introduced to Gansu by a Chinese Muslim, Ma Mingxin, who had travelled to Bukhara and beyond. This rapidly came into conflict with the Old Teaching (or Silent Recollection Sect). The resulting tension, combined with Chinese anti-Muslim repression, culminated in uprisings against the Qing authorities in several provinces. Hochou (Linxia) became one of the main Muslim centres of religious and military activity at this time. A Qing army advanced upon the city in 1871, but was roundly defeated by Muslim forces, allowing the Muslim leader to negotiate with the Qing general, Zuo Zongtang, from a position of strength and to secure permission for the Muslims in the area to remain, while the Han Chinese were forced to move elsewhere. This agreement was bought at the cost of 4,000 horses and 10,000 firearms and spears. Following the Qing victories in northwestern Gansu, thousands of Muslims were resettled in this southern region.

In 1928, forces of the Chinese Republic prevented an army of 50,000 Muslims from entering the city for several weeks, until the Christian warlord, Feng Yuxiang, sent reinforcements from Lanzhou. In a second attack, according to one foreign traveller, the Muslim forces numbered 100,000 and 'with Ahungs (imams) now in their ranks to lash them to fanatical frenzy, the Moslems stormed the Hochow walls. Wave after wave of wild-eyed, besworded Hui-Hui were cut down by Chinese machine guns or blasted to bits by a battery of artillery.' The vengeful Chinese slaughtered the Hui women and children, and razed the Muslim quarter.

Linxia was the birthplace of the powerful Muslim warlord, Ma Zhongying, who once controlled the whole of southern Xinjiang and created the short-lived Republic of Eastern Turkestan in 1933. In the first half of the 20th century, his brothers Ma Bufang and Ma Buqing were military governors of Qinghai, Gansu and Ningxia. Ma Bufang's fierce troops fought the survivors of Mao Zedong's Long March in the winter of 1936–37 as they crossed the Gansu–Qinghai border.

Taoist shrine in Muslim-majority Linxia

THE GOLDEN HORDE

ou could smell them coming, it was said, even before you heard the thunder of their hooves. But by then it was too late. Within seconds came the first murderous torrent of arrows, blotting out the sun and turning day into night. Then they were upon you—slaughtering, raping, pillaging and burning. Like molten lava, they destroyed everything in their path. Behind them they left a trail of smoking cities and bleached bones, leading all the way back to their homeland in Central Asia. 'Soldiers of Antichrist come to reap the last dreadful harvest' one 13th-century scholar called the Mongol hordes.

Peter Hopkirk, *Foreign Devils on the Silk Road*

The Mongol Empire comprised the largest land empire in history, stretching from the Sea of Japan to the Caspian Sea. Between 1218 and 1253 these barbarians had conquered all of Central Asia and Russia, up to the borders of eastern Europe. The Mongols, whose empire spanned a relatively short period of time, were led out of the grasslands by Temujin (1162–1227), later known as **Genghis Khan**, an illiterate political and military genius. He unified and organized the scattered nomadic tribes of Mongolia, Manchuria and Siberia into a disciplined and highly effective military force. After first testing his mounted savages with the conquest of the Xixia Kingdom, Genghis Khan moved south across the Gobi Desert one spring; four years later, in 1215, most of the Northern Chinese Empire had been subdued by the Mongol fighting machine, which then turned its energies towards Central Asia and Eastern Europe, completely destroying the cities of Bokhara and Samarkand in 1220. The death of Genghis in 1227 and his son Ogotai in 1241 forced the Mongol generals to break off their European campaign, which was then approaching western Europe.

Kublai Khan (1216–1294), the grandson of Genghis, completed the conquest of China in 1279 and founded the Yuan dynasty, establishing his capital at Khanbalik (present-day Beijing). Less ruthless and more tolerant than his grandfather, Kublai permitted a certain degree of religious freedom, resulting in the conversion of many Mongols to Islam. Since the Mongols controlled much of the territory of the old Silk Road, overland trade was re-established with Europe and a cosmopolitan culture flourished. Marco Polo's father and uncle, visiting the empire in the 13th century, were asked to bring 100 Christian priests to China on their return journey so that the Mongol ruler could learn more about the Western religion; Marco Polo stayed in China for 17 years serving under Kublai Khan. The Yuan dynasty signified the first time in Chinese history that a barbarian people had conquered the whole of the country. The Chinese were oppressed by the foreign invaders and initially not allowed to hold political or military positions.

The Mongols proved to be poor and corrupt administrators, however. A Chinese adviser to the court remarked 'you may conquer a great empire on a horse, but it cannot be ruled from the back of the horse'. The Mongol Empire began to disintegrate in the late 1200s and fell apart completely with the death of Kublai. Chinese rule was restored with the Ming dynasty in 1368.

Tamerlane (1336–1405), a descendant of Kublai Khan, was a Tartar, or Mongol Turk, born to a chief's family near Samarkand. A devout Muslim and vicious leader, he came to the throne in 1369 at Samarkand. He reunited the scattered kingdoms of the Mongol Empire, invading India and ruling over large parts of Central Asia. In 1398, his armies sacked Peshawar, the Punjab, Lahore and Delhi, and in 1401 they captured Baghdad. It was said that when Tamerlane left Delhi he had so completely devastated the city that no living thing was seen among the ruins for more than two months. Tamerlane died whilst preparing an invasion of Chinese Turkestan.

Babur, a fifth-generation descendant of Tamerlane, in 1526 established the Mughal Empire in India. Lasting until 1748, it was considered one of the most advanced empires in the world, and extended from the Himalayas to southern India, from Kabul to Bombay.

(following pages) Hui gentlemen in Linxia

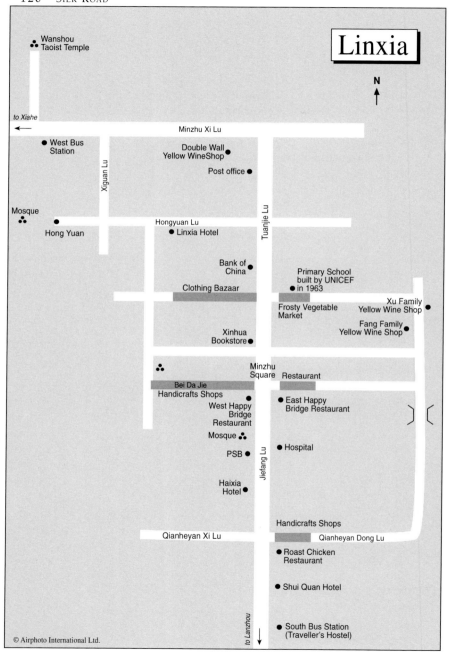

SIGHTS

The fine villa and headquarters of Ma Buqing, now the Children's Palace of Huancheng Dong Lu, has some outstanding examples of the brick carving for which the city was once famous. Another residence, Hudie Lou (Butterfly Villa), is occupied by the military and closed to visitors.

Many of Linxia's streets are lined with high mud walls, broken by grey brick archways and wooden doors painted black-and-red, which lead into small garden courtyards surrounded by single-storey residences. Other streets are oppressed by the usual nondescript governmental blocks of grey concrete.

BEI DAJIE

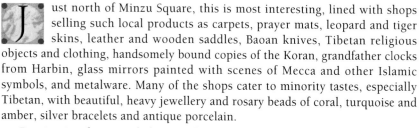 ust north of Minzu Square, this is most interesting, lined with shops selling such local products as carpets, prayer mats, leopard and tiger skins, leather and wooden saddles, Baoan knives, Tibetan religious objects and clothing, handsomely bound copies of the Koran, grandfather clocks from Harbin, glass mirrors painted with scenes of Mecca and other Islamic symbols, and metalware. Many of the shops cater to minority tastes, especially Tibetan, with beautiful, heavy jewellery and rosary beads of coral, turquoise and amber, silver bracelets and antique porcelain.

Dominating the city's skyline are the green minarets and cupolas of its 20-odd mosques. They are decorated with intricately carved granite, limestone and wood. During the Cultural Revolution all but 12 mosques in this Muslim city were destroyed; today, all money for restoration and the construction of new mosques is given privately by the Muslim community. Children study Arabic independently at the mosques after regular school hours until the age of 12, when the language is offered in public schools. Many mosques house young seminarians clad in flowing black or white robes; the lucky ones study Arabic in Beijing at the Foreign Languages Institute but only a select few have been to Mecca. The call of the muezzin can be heard five times a day throughout the city, beckoning worshippers to the mosques.

Many Muslim men and women wear a plain white square cap and are easily confused with restaurant workers. Hui women dress modestly with a cowl-shaped lace headdress—green for unmarried women, black for married women, and white for the elderly. Enormous round crystal-lensed glasses with brass fittings are extremely popular among the older Hui gentlemen in Linxia—a status symbol at up to Rmb500 a pair. A traveller in the early 1930s noted the difference between Linxia and other Han cities:

> In its teeming streets and crowded bazaars one can almost believe himself in the native quarter of some Levantine city. Tall, light-skinned, heavy-bearded men

swagger with the haughtiness of an aggressive, consciously superior race. Women, clad in coloured pantaloons and veiled like their Moslem sisters in the Middle East, call to their boisterous children in whose play groups no Chinese child is welcome.

HONG YUAN

The city's extensive main park has paths winding through its many small gardens, a greenhouse, a small pond with paddle-boats, bridges and a children's amusement park next to a small zoo. There are pagodas in the park, and a tea garden which serves *sanxiangcha* (three-flavour tea) and sunflower seeds underneath carved wood and vine awnings. The Han presence is virtually absent; most visitors are Muslims in veils and skullcaps.

WAN SHOU (LONG LIFE) TAOIST TEMPLE

This lies on the hills north of the city, just up the road perpendicular to the West Bus Station. A funicular tram hauls passengers from the city to the villages above, or you can follow the steps leading up past the many levels carved into the mountain to the main temple at the top. There are panoramic views of the city, its mosques and the surrounding valley and mountains. Originally built during the Ming dynasty, the temple was destroyed during the Cultural Revolution and restoration began in 1983, with all monies donated by the Taoist community. There are now about 15 monks working and studying in the many temples scattered along the bluff. At the summit there is a series of gardens and courtyards with a teahouse and Muslim restaurant, while wooded paths lead to temples on adjacent peaks. It is a relaxing place to spend an afternoon and many locals come for picnics on their day off.

LIANHUA MOUNTAIN

In **Kangle County** near Linxia, this is the site of an annual six-day *hua'er*, or folksong festival, during the sixth lunar month (July). Han, Tibetan, Hui, Dongxiang and Baoan men and women all take part, forming teams of ten, each team trying to outlast the others in singing spontaneous responses to the songs of other groups. Love songs and historical ballads are the most popular.

LINXIA PRACTICAL INFORMATION

TRANSPORTATION

Buses several times a day to/from Lanzhou (East Bus Station, above which is a Travellers' Hostel) and to/from Xiahe and Hezuo (West Bus Station); unreliable service to Xining, the capital of Qinghai.

Young Hui woman of Gansu

ACCOMMODATION

Linxia Hotel (Linxia Fandian)

9 Hong Yuan Lu. Tel (0930) 621-2805; fax 621-4412

临夏饭店　红园路 9 号

Most comfortable accommodation in Linxia; Muslim and Chinese restaurants.

Shui Quan Hotel (Shui Quan Binguan)

Jie Fang Nan Lu. Tel (0930) 621-4967/8

水泉宾馆　解放南路

Next to East Bus Station; clean and comfortable; Muslim restaurant.

Haixia Hotel (Haixia Fandian)

Jie Fang Bei Lu. Tel (0930) 621-2590, 621-3209

海峡饭店　解放北路

Centrally located; basic Chinese accommodation; communal toilets and no showers.

FOOD AND DRINK

S mall Muslim restaurants and noodle stalls serve bowls of flat noodles with five fragrant sauces, mutton noodle soup with raw garlic and turmeric-/cumin-flavoured *bing* (flatbread); some specialize in roast chicken and mutton. Street vendors offer sticky rice cooked in bamboo leaves served with honey or the sweet *mozhou*—a mould of glutinous rice, egg, milk, sugar and raisins. Tea shops serve the local Hui speciality tea—*sanxiangcha*—in bowls with a lid and saucer, green tea leaves, rock sugar, dried *longyan* (dragon eyes) and apricot pits. A constant stream of hot water is added, so that one bowl lasts an age. Both of the two-storey teahouse-cum-restaurants (the East and West Happy Bridge Muslim Restaurants, overlooking Minzu Square and the night market) serve good noodles and tea, and are excellent vantage points from which to oversee the action in the square. There are also several good small restaurants just south of the square. Yellow wine shops are advertised by large white-fringed blue banners with the characters for *huang jiu* (yellow wine). A warm welcome is guaranteed at the Fang and Xu Family Yellow Wine Shops where the jovial proprietors pour the hot, pale yellow wine into large bowls. It is made from a small grain of rice fermented for one year, and is subtle but very strong. Traditionally, the wine is drunk for breakfast, accompanied by a bowl of scalded mutton soup spiced with spring onion and yellow wine. The shops, which open at 5 am, are crowded with Muslims on their way to work.

THE BAOAN AND SALAR OF JISHISHAN COUNTY

T his county lies to the west of Linxia, near the Gansu–Qinghai border. The three-hour bus journey from Linxia to Xiahe, where the Labrang Monastery is located, passes through the villages along the narrow Daxia River valley. They present an interesting cultural contrast between Islam and Buddhism. One village clusters around a small Muslim mosque, while another is adorned with tall Tibetan prayer flags. Around the threshing-floors stand huge haystacks strewn over high wooden frames, which from a distance make the villages 'look as if they were all poles', according to one foreign traveller. During the harvest, groups of Tibetan farmers take frequent breaks in the fields, drinking yak-butter tea and eating *tsampa* under the shade of colourful umbrellas.

The local Baoan people are amongst the smallest of China's minorities, barely numbering 8,000. Like their Dongxiang neighbours, they are of Mongolian origin and probably migrated from homelands in northern Xinjiang during the Yuan dynasty. Written in Chinese, their language is comprised of a high percentage of Mongolian words. During the late Yuan and early Ming dynasties, the Baoan converted to Islam and settled in the Tongren region of eastern Qinghai Province. Although they intermarried with the local people—Tibetans, Tu, Han and Hui—the Baoan have maintained their unique language and customs, and like the Dongxiang, were recognized by the Chinese as a distinct minority in 1949.

B y 1860, this small Muslim community, located amidst a predominantly Tibetan Buddhist population, found itself subjected to increasing religious persecution and friction over water rights. The Baoan headmen decided to migrate eastwards into the Jishishan Mountains, and the community settled into compact villages amongst other Muslims, growing wheat, maize and fruit, and tending small flocks of sheep. The Baoan, swept along with the Muslim uprisings of the late 19th century and the 1920s and 1930s, were heavily taxed and forced into labour by the Ma warlords.

From their long association with the Tibetans, the Baoan learnt the art of making knives, which is their best-known handicraft. Baoan knives are adorned with elaborate inlaid brass, copper, horn and bone handles, and used by the minority peoples in Gansu and Qinghai. Baoan dress once resembled that of Mongols and Tibetans, but today their attire is more like the Hui. Only on festive holidays is their nomadic ancestry apparent in sports such as wrestling, shooting and horse racing.

Marriages are lively occasions and usually arranged by the families or sometimes a go-between. The imam is invited to officiate at the ceremony in the bride's home and after reading the scriptures he throws handfuls of red dates and walnuts upon the wedding party. Before the bride leaves for her new home, she scatters the threshold of her parents' home with handfuls of grain mixed with tea leaves to express her attachment to her family and her desire for its continued prosperity. She traditionally rides away on a horse, since a mule, being sterile, is considered inauspicious.

Most of the 60,000 members of the Turkic-speaking Salar nationality live across the Qinghai border in Xunhua Salar Autonomous County, but some can be found in Jishishan County. The Salar are thought to have come from Samarkand in the 14th century. According to popular legend, they were considered bandits and troublemakers by fellow Turkic tribes, were encouraged to choose exile and were sent off with a white camel, a bag of earth and a gourd of water. The camel was to lead them to a new land where the earth and water matched their samples. After leading them across Xinjiang to the Qinghai–Gansu border, the camel turned to stone, whereupon the Salars found the water and earth of this new land to be identical to that of their homeland, and they settled down.

Salar marriages usually are arranged by parents or go-betweens, as is typical among Muslims. The weeping teenage bride is escorted out of the house by her parents; she mounts a horse and rides around the courtyard three times, scattering the five grains of prosperity upon the gathered family. On the birth of a child, a fire is set in front of the doorway at home to keep visitors away.

The Salars have a rich oral tradition of stories, myths and songs and they always participate in the *hua'er* song festivals at Lianhua Mountain. Baoan dancing is heavily influenced by the strong and lively movements of traditional Tibetan dance.

Tibetan lamas dance at Labrang

GANNAN TIBETAN AUTONOMOUS PREFECTURE

XIAHE

his small hill-encompassed dusty town, lying along the banks of the Daxia River at an altitude of 3,000 metres (9,700 feet), is a county seat within the Gannan Tibetan Autonomous Prefecture. Its historic role has been the servicing of the great Tibetan monastery of Labrang.

Today, shops along the main street supply the simple requirements of the Tibetan farmers and semi-nomadic herdsmen from the grasslands as well as those of the local monks. The two-storey wooden shops, mostly run by the Hui, stock Tibetan religious objects such as hand-printed sutras, moulds, prayer wheels, musical instruments, bells and *vajras* (thunderbolts), as well as hand-tinted photographs of the late Panchen Lama and pictures of the current youthful one. Silversmiths skilfully work jewellery orders for Tibetan ladies, and cobblers handcraft high-quality sturdy leather boots, saddles and bridles. The town is thronged with colourful pilgrims between harvests. Local watermills grind roasted barley into flour (*tsampa*), the staple of the Tibetan diet.

Living conditions for many Tibetans are very poor: high mud walls surround large, communal compounds of dilapidated two-storey wooden shacks, the lower floor usually housing the kitchen, storage rooms and livestock. A simple stepladder leads to the upper-storey balcony and living quarters. Each balcony has a white pot-bellied stove for the daily burning of fragrant cypress leaves. The roofs provide storage for branches and straw, which are used for fuel. Cow and yak-dung pats are left to dry on the walls; the stench is intense all year round. More prosperous families live in single compounds, in houses supported by carved and brightly decorated wooden pillars.

The surrounding valley is serene, with yaks pulling ploughs in the nearby fields. The grasslands, excellent pasturage for herds of yaks and horses, begin about 30 kilometres beyond Xiahe. In the summer, they are carpeted with wild flowers, and Chinese beekeepers spend the short summer here, moving their hives every 20 days.

The 260-kilometre (160-mile) journey from Lanzhou to Xiahe takes a bus seven or eight hours. The road, via Linxia, climbs through the yellow, barren loess hills of the Yellow River basin, cutting hair-raising bends. It traverses Guanghe County, where garlic is a local speciality. Buses stop along the way to allow passengers to stretch their legs and buy ripe melons from the roadside stalls during the summer season. Bad weather can slow the journey considerably and make it even more nerve-racking. Long-distance buses leave from Lanzhou's West Bus Station daily.

It is possible to climb to the top of the Gongtangcang Stupa, which stands on the bank of the river, from where one can enjoy a bird's eye view of the Labrang Monastery.

SIGHTS

LABRANG MONASTERY (LABULENG SI)

This majestic lamasery is one of China's six great monasteries of the Gelugpa (Yellow Hat) Sect. The others are Ganden, Sera and Drepung, Tashilunpo in Tibet and Taersi in Qinghai. Labrang was founded in 1709 by the first Jiamuyang, or Living Buddha, called E'angzongzhe, a scholar-abbot who came from nearby Ganjia. Within the Tibetan religious hierarchy, his current incarnation as the Sixth Jiamuyang ranks next in importance only to that of the Dalai Lama and the Panchen Lama. Once the home of 4,000 scholarly monks, Labrang had jurisdiction over more than 100 smaller monasteries and gained its wealth through taxes and donations.

During the 1920s, when much of Gansu and eastern Qinghai languished in the grip of Muslim warlords, the flourishing commercial activity and power of the monastery became a source of envy to the Ma family warlords, who attempted to impose heavy fines to be paid in rifles and silver. In protest, the young Living Buddha and his entourage left the monastery, which caused an immediate cessation of trade and exacerbated age-old religious tensions. The warlord troops occupied the area and were attacked by Tibetan soldiers, who took pleasure in disembowelling their prisoners. The Muslims attacked again, using machine guns to mow down the Tibetans, and reoccupied Labrang, offering a reward of three silver dollars for each Tibetan head.

 uring the Cultural Revolution many temples were destroyed, and monks were forced to return to their home villages to work. The monastery reopened in 1980, and many of the older monks returned to Labrang. The government has restricted enrolment, but nevertheless there are now some 1,300 monks. Young entrants, who receive a monthly salary from the state, must be 18 years of age and have completed middle school. However, many little boys wearing magenta robes are present in the monastery, apparently receiving a traditional religious education. The handsome compound in Tibetan style now has only a dozen or so temples, compared to more than 80 in its heyday. The lamasery contains 60,000 mostly bronze Buddhist statues and a rich collection of Tibetan Buddhist manuscripts, including scriptures and discourses on philosophy, history, medicine and the arts.

Extensive restoration and rebuilding has taken place, and most of the wall paintings are new. In 1985, a fire caused by faulty wiring swept through the Great Chanting Hall, gutting the building, which has now been restored. The state has allocated some Rmb100,000 annually since 1981 for restoration. An exhibit of sacred objects saved from the fire in the Hall is housed in the museum, including bronze saddles, clothing, elephant tusks, musical instruments, muskets and suits of chain mail. Intricate and colourful examples of yak-butter sculpture, from the festival held annually on the 15th day of the first lunar month, are on display. The insides of the temples are dark, mystical and exotic, permeated with the smell of burning yak butter. Photography is prohibited.

Traditionally, there are six colleges at Labrang that confer Tibetan degrees equivalent to those of Western universities. These are the colleges of Tibetan Medicine, Esoteric Teaching, Astronomy, Higher and Lower Theology, and the Wheel of Time. Monk students must pass examinations in order to proceed to the next level of study. Music, dancing and painting also are taught, with some courses involving up to 15 years of intensive study.

The College of Tibetan Medicine was established in 1784 by the Second Jiamuyang. Presently about 35 monks study here. The courtyard walls are brightly painted with medicinal plants and flowers. The temple houses a large statue of the White Tara goddess, a companion of the bodhisattva Avalokitesvara (known as Guanyin in Chinese, an important bodhisattva in Mahayana Buddhism, embodying compassion and wisdom) and a coral- and turquoise-studded funeral stupa of the revered teacher of the current Dalai Lama and the late Panchen Lama.

The mystifying and complex Tibetan study of medicine is based on the Indian humours of bile, wind, and phlegm, which correspond to the human frailties of greed, anger and sloth. Tibetans believe physical sickness is also spiritual sickness; the diagnosis is in determining which humour is imbalanced, and correcting it with a variety of herbal remedies, prayers, amulets, exorcisms and bloodletting. Tantric texts enumerate 84,000 possible illnesses. Traditionally, 11 years of training were required to become a Tibetan doctor.

 In the **Temple of the Eleventh Buddha**, dating from 1809, shelves of sutra boxes line the walls, with an upper balcony giving access to the higher ledges. Victory banners of yellow and red are draped grandly between the pillars, gently brushing the face of the main statue. The yak-butter lamps burn for 24 hours a day with butter donated by pilgrims.

The School of Lama Dancing was established by the Fourth Jiamuyang in 1879, destroyed in 1958 and rebuilt a year later. At present 40-odd monks study dance, and twice a year they perform their slow, dramatic turning movements while wearing fearsome masks depicting various gods. Yama, the most terrifying, was originally the ancient Hindu god of death, and is the Tibetan Lord of the Dead and King of Religion; he is usually depicted with the head of a buffalo, adorned with rings of severed heads and skulls, riding naked on a blue bull.

The **Temple of Maitreya** was founded in 1788. Maitreya is the future, or coming Buddha and tradition assures that if the pilgrim catches a glimpse of Maitreya's crown, he will not suffer in the Buddhist realms of hell after death. Statues of bodhisattvas line the inner temple, four on either side. Giant prayer wheels flank the entrance. As the prayer wheels are spun (always clockwise, symbolizing how man revolves around Buddha as the planets revolve around the sun), the scrolls contained within release prayers and invocations to the heavens, earning merit for the pilgrim. Beside the Temple of Maitreya is the Debating Square, where monks hold formalized scriptural debates during the sixth and seventh lunar months.

he most sacred building is the golden-roofed **Jokhang Temple**, built in 1907. Two golden deer stand beside the Wheel of Law, recalling the Buddha's first sermon at Sarnath Deer Park. The upper forecourt is lined with bronze prayer wheels. The statue of Sakyamuni Buddha at the top of the inner altar was made in India 2,500 years ago by Buddhist disciples.

The College of Lower Theology is being used as the main prayer hall until the Great Chanting Hall has been built. The college itself is temporarily relocated in the **Temple of Tsong Khapa** (1940). Tsong Khapa (1357–1419) was the founder of the Ganden monastery near Lhasa whose reforms led to the founding of the Yellow Hat sect. The temple walls are lined with 1,000 statues of Manjusri (the Embodiment of Divine Wisdom) donated by the tutor of the present Dalai Lama and Panchen Lama.

Other buildings at Labrang include the **Temple of the White Umbrellas** (1907)— umbrellas are a token of royalty and symbolize the protection of the Dharma, or faith. There is also the **Temple of White Tara** (1940) and the **Temple of Manjusri** (1928). A new library houses some 60,000 volumes of sutras and religious literature. The printing workshop offers a fascinating glimpse of monks hand-printing rice-paper strips of scriptures using carved wooden blocks. In the kitchens, giant copper kettles and huge cauldrons once were used to prepare meals for thousands of monks on special occasions. One cauldron more than three metres (ten feet) in diameter could cook 2,250 kilograms (5,000 pounds) of rice, oil and meat at one time—but it took a day and a half.

There are many important religious ceremonies and festivals that take place at Labrang in which monks, locals and nomads from the grasslands take part. Tibetans use a lunar calendar, meaning that dates for the festivals change from year to year. One of the most important is the Monlam Festival (Great Prayer) celebrating Buddha's victory over his six opponents, which takes place three days after the Tibetan New Year (late February or early March). The celebrations last about three weeks in Lhasa, but are shortened to four days at Labrang. On the first morning, an enormous *thanka*, a sacred painting of the Buddha on cloth, measuring 20 by 30 metres, is unfurled on the hillside facing the monastery on the opposite side of the Daxia River (known as 'Sunning the Buddha'). The elaborate ceremonies that follow include processions, bathing rituals and many prayers. On the second day, masked Cham dances are performed by students from the College of Dancing led by the god Yama. The third day has a night ceremony with a display of yak-butter lanterns and sculptures, holy food presented to the gods, and on the last day the Maitreya statue is paraded throughout the monastery.

XIAHE PRACTICAL INFORMATION

Xiahe consists of one dusty main street; the monastery is accessible by foot.

TRANSPORTATION

By road: daily buses to/from Hezuo, Linxia and Lanzhou; bus station is at the northern end of the main street.

ACCOMMODATION

 vailable at the **Minzu Fandian**, tel (0941) 712-1593, basic Chinese accommodation; **Daxia Binguan**, tel (0941) 712-1546, cleaner and more comfortable with English-speaking guides to Labrang. The charming **Labrang Hotel**, a twenty-minute walk past the monastery overlooking the river, offers the most comfortable accommodation with traditional Tibetan architecture, a good restaurant, and central heating in the winter. A modern three-star wing has now been added to this hotel. The **Baihailuo Binguan**, which is about five minutes' walk up the main street from the bus station, is a new hotel with clean double rooms. The **Jinlun** (Goldenwheel) **Hotel**, tel (0941) 712-2305; fax 712-3125, is the newest hotel in town and has a good restaurant located on the main street. Both hotel and restaurant are closed in the low season.

FOOD AND DRINK

Xiahe has a few restaurants along the main street but the standard of hygiene is low. Local fare consists primarily of fried noodles or noodle pieces in soup with beef, and turmeric/cumin *bing*; vegetables are relatively scarce. Several teahouses serve *sanxiangcha*; they are pleasant places to relax and play cards with the locals.

HEZUO AND GANLHO DZONG

About 70 kilometres (43 miles) southeast of Xiahe is **Hezuo**, the governmental seat of the Gannan Tibetan Autonomous Prefecture. This small town, opened to foreign visitors in 1990, is an important trading post for the Tibetan nomads who roam the grasslands of southern Gansu. The numerous shops sell goods essential to nomadic life, including saddles, stirrups, colourful warm blankets and clothing, leather goods, hand-crafted knives and numerous canned goods and household necessities. Dried goods stores sell apricots and other dried fruit, walnuts, almonds, peanuts, spices, rock and brown sugar.

SIGHTS

In the circle in front of the bus station, there is a large bronze statue of a deer, representing the Buddha's first Sarnath sermon. The market is situated on the unpaved roads extending from the circle. Monks from Labrang and the local monastery, Hui farmers and real Tibetan cowboys mill about here, sporting stylish leather boots, belts and wide-brim black hats. Just west of the bus station is the mosque, a three-tiered rounded pagoda-like structure for the predominant Hui community. On the outskirts of town are Tibetan houses made of mud bricks with hand-carved wooden doors. Tibetans from all over Gansu come to study at the Minority Teachers Institute in Hezuo, where the Tibetan language is taught. There is a youthful, vibrant feeling to this large trading post, providing an excellent stopover for those travellers heading north from or south to other Tibetan communities in the grasslands of Gansu and Sichuan.

The former Gelugpa monastery of Ganlho Dzong lies on the outskirts of the town. It once rivalled Labrang in size and beauty, but was destroyed in 1967 during the Cultural Revolution. Two halls and a 13-storey temple have now been reconstructed; the beautiful murals and figures inside the temple are among the best examples of contemporary workmanship.

uring the summer months horse- and yak-races are held by the semi-nomadic Tibetan tribes of the area, who live in tents during the summer and move down to sheltered valleys to spend the winter in stone dwellings well-stocked with blocks of *mar* (yak butter) and bags of *qingke* (mountain barley). Several nature reserves have been established in the southwestern corner of Gansu Province in recent years. The most important are the giant panda reserve of **Baishuijiang** and a bird sanctuary for swans, bar-headed geese and other migratory birds in the grassland county of **Luqu**.

Hezuo Practical Information

Like Xiahe, this is a one-street town and everything is accessible by foot.

Transportation

By road: daily buses to/from Xiahe, Linxia and Lanzhou as well as Luqu and points south and west in the grasslands.

Accommodation

Available at the **Hezuo People's Government Guesthouse**, a ten-minute walk south of the bus station past the movie theatre.

Food and Drink

Within the market area is your best bet: small Hui restaurants offer better than average Muslim cuisine, and many noodle variations served with beef, mutton or vegetables. Small wooden shacks, constructed around a clay oven, serve large flatbreads (sesame, salty or sweet) and the ever-popular turmeric/cumin *bing*.

HEXI CORRIDOR

ince ancient times the Hexi or Gansu Corridor has been the principal communications link between China, Central Asia and the West. It is bound to the south by the **Qilian Mountains**, whose melting snows sustained the settlements, and to the north by the vast Tenggeli and **Badain Jaran** deserts and the Mazong, Heli and Longshou mountain ranges.

The earliest known inhabitants of the corridor were the Wusun, ancestors of the **Kazakhs** and the first victims in a series of enforced migrations westward into Central Asia. The Wusun were driven out by the Yuezhi, an Indo-European tribe who, in turn, were pushed west by the Xiongnu in the second century BC. The Yuezhi king's head was used as a drinking cup by the victors. Emperor Qin Shihuangdi (reigned 221–210 BC) built part of the Great Wall around this strategic area in an effort to contain the Xiongnu armies. Zhang Qian, the brave and devoted envoy of Emperor Han Wudi, was held captive in this 'panhandle' for ten years by the Xiongnu, before escaping to continue his explorations westwards. The Han dynasty (206 BC–AD 220) subdued the marauding Xiongnu and created four prefectures within the corridor, not only to establish a strong presence but also to declare its ambition to advance into Central Asia. The westward movement of the defeated Xiongnu eventually led in the fifth century to the rape and plunder of Europe by their descendants under Attila the Hun.

The decline of the Han dynasty led to the rise in power of a Mongol horde or the Xianpi (Hsien-pi), who in the late fourth and early fifth centuries set up a series of states, known as the Later, Southern, Northern and Western Liang dynasties. The northward expansion of the Tibetans forced neighbouring tribes, such as the Tuyuhun, ancestors of the **Tu** people from the Kokonor Lake area in Qinghai, to take refuge here in the seventh century. The Ganzhou Uygurs gained dominance in the tenth century and, with capitals at Dunhuang (formerly Shazhou) and Zhangye (formerly Ganzhou), took firm control of the trade route. These various kingdoms frequently sent tribute to the reigning Chinese dynasty.

he Hexi Corridor formed part of the Xixia Kingdom, which was ruled from the 11th to the early 13th centuries by the Tanguts. Xixia figured in a three-way balance of power with the Song and at first the Liao, then their successors, the Jin. The Tanguts were later overthrown by the Mongols. The 72 tombs of the Xixia emperors lie outside Yinchuan, the capital of Ningxia Autonomous Region.

The towns along the Hexi Corridor were well equipped with caravanserais to accommodate the traffic heading east and west. Through these centres, the interchange of ideas and new merchandise eventually filtered into the heartland of China.

The 1,892-kilometre (1,175-mile) rail journey from Lanzhou to Urumqi follows the path of the Silk Road through the Hexi Corridor. The corridor itself is more than 1,200 kilometres (750 miles) long, at its broadest about 200 kilometres (125 miles) wide and at its narrowest only 15 kilometres (nine miles). The view from the train window is mesmerizing: gravel pits etched out between craters of mud and telephone poles stand in dried-up rivers; bridges and irrigation ditches lie useless in the cracked earth; oases of trees and green fields come into view sporadically; a train station consists of clusters of tracks next to a mud shack with a diligent outback train-company employee waving green and red flags; passengers appear from nowhere; and to the south lie the distant snow-covered mountains of Qinghai.

The railway route follows the Zhuanglang River, which rises in the mountainous **Tianzhu Tibetan Autonomous County**, established in 1952. More than 44,000 Tibetans live in this region, breeding cattle, sheep and special herds of white yaks in the rich pastureland. The county seat is at Anyuanyi, a stop on the line. Tianzhu Tibetan women are distinguished by the long strips of coloured cloth, embroidered and embellished with coral, shells or silver, which they attach to their braids. The women also wear ornate heavy earrings and necklaces. During the winter the herdsmen and their families make pilgrimages to **Kumbum Monastery** in Qinghai, and in the late summer they hold horse races.

WUWEI

fter driving out the pastoral Xiongnu in 121 BC, the Han dynasty established one of four commanderies at Liangzhou, as Wuwei was then known, making it the political and commercial centre of the Hexi Corridor. With the chaos that followed the fall of the Han dynasty in 220 AD, many scholars sought safety in Wuwei, far from the intrigues of the capital at Chang'an. The Later Liang (Hou Liang) dynasty capital was located here between 386 and 403, and the town became a centre for Buddhist studies.

Wuwei reached its zenith during the Tang dynasty, when it saw an endless stream of foreign trade caravans. By the eighth century the city had a diverse population of more than 100,000 Chinese, Central Asians, Tibetans and Indians. The rich pasturelands in the vicinity facilitated horse breeding, which yielded hides used to make coracle boats and armour. Grapes, introduced along the Silk Road, thrived in Wuwei, and its wines were, according to the monk Xuan Zang, 'fine and rare'. Itinerant magicians, fire-eaters and acrobats entertained locals at the temples and a distinctive style of music developed in Wuwei called 'Xiliang'. It combined traditional Chinese melodies with those of the oasis kingdom of Kucha in Western Xinjiang, and it remained popular for five centuries.

Wuwei became part of the Xixia Kingdom (11th to 13th centuries) before the Mongols swept through and destroyed it so completely that only in the mid-1980s did scholars recover the lost Xixia language. Marco Polo, passing through some decades after the fall, nevertheless was impressed, finding 'traders and artisans and . . . an abundance of corn'. The wandering Venetian added that 'in Wuwei is found the best musk in the world, the yaks are as big as elephants and the pheasants as big as peacocks'. In the 19th century, Wuwei was a stop on the opium route running across Ningxia to Taiyuan, the capital of Shanxi Province.

Wuwei leapt to fame with the discovery in 1969 of the 'Flying Horse of Gansu', the 245-millimetre-high (9.7-inch) bronze statue of a 'celestial horse' depicted in full gallop, with one leg on the back of a swallow, the bird's head turned in astonishment. This work is now a centre-piece in foreign exhibitions of Chinese archeological treasures. The caves, tombs and ancient monuments in the Wuwei district have yielded other rich finds of pottery, bronze, jade, lacquerware, silk remnants and stone tablets.

SIGHTS

uwei is surrounded by fertile fields of grain and vegetables, which in late summer form wide carpets of pink and yellow. The markets overflow with fruit, melons and vegetables (chillies, tomatoes, aubergines and cabbages) as well as tobacco, grain, horse bridles, rope, grain baskets and huge woven mats used to line horse-drawn or hand-pulled carts. Workshops trim and cut sheepskins and other hides. The streets of the residential quarters of the city are lined with high straw and mud plaster walls pierced by old carved wood entrances to small courtyards. A small section of the gate of the old city wall stands in ruins southeast of the city; an outsized bronze copy of the Flying Horse graces the city park on Shengli Jie.

KUMARAJIVA PAGODA (LUOSHI SI TA)

This pagoda on Bei Guanbei Jie was built in the seventh century to commemorate the Buddhist monk, Kumarajiva, one of early China's four great translators of Indian Buddhist texts. Born of an Indian father and a Kuchean princess in Kucha, he became a monk at the age of seven and, later, a renowned teacher throughout the Western Regions. He lived in Wuwei from 386 to 403, preaching and translating some 300 volumes of Mahayana (the 'Greater Vehicle') scriptures from Sanskrit to Chinese.

HAIZANG TEMPLE (HAIZANG SI)

This temple lies about three-quarters-of-an-hour's walk northwest of the city, in the grounds of a park with a boating lake. Several humped bridges lead to its beautifully arched gate. The temple's exact date of construction is unknown, but records place its restoration in 1482. It is a complex of pavilions, terraces and halls, but little statuary remains.

LEITAI HAN TOMB (LEITAI HAN MU)

t the northern end of Baiguan Zhong Jie (about one kilometre from the centre of town) are the Taoist temple and underground Han-dynasty tomb in which the Flying Horse and other treasures were discovered in 1969. The terrace on which the temple stands dates from the Jin dynasty, the halls from the Ming. The entrance to the tomb of an unidentified general of the Eastern Han dynasty is below the terrace. The cave was used by peasants for storage before the discovery in 1969 that it contained a tomb. A well dug by monks during the Ming was converted into a ventilation shaft. The tomb consists of seven rooms with an arched entrance embellished with a tree pattern. The walls and ceilings are of small oblong bricks; the lozenge pattern of black and grey bricks forms a dado. Traces of flower paintings can be seen in the centre of the ceilings, and lotus-shaped oil lamps were found in niches in the walls. Photography is prohibited inside the empty tomb.

WUWEI MUSEUM (WEN MIAO)

The Wen Miao or Confucius Temple (just south of the Tianma Binguan), first built in 1437, is a graceful complex of temple halls, pavilions, corridors, bridges and ponds set in two large courtyards. The museum houses a collection of stone inscriptions, pottery, stone and wooden artefacts, calligraphy and paintings. Of particular interest is the Xixia Tablet, which was discovered at the Dayun Temple in 1806 and declared a national treasure in 1961. The inscription, in the extinct Xixia script on one side and translated into Chinese on the other, has provided the key to deciphering this script and a literature lost for more than 700 years. A Xixia dictionary was published in 1129 but disappeared after the Mongol invasion in the 13th century. Russian explorers discovered a copy when excavating in Xinjiang in 1907–1908, and another copy later surfaced in Japan. Subsequent research in China and Japan has depended on the Xixia Tablet as the main source for comparative linguistic studies. In 1986, a leading Chinese linguist published decodings of more than 5,000 Xixia characters, which are structured rather like Chinese characters. The inscription praises the ancestors of the Xixia state and gives details of its history and economy.

DAYUN TEMPLE AND BELL TOWER (DAYUN SI)

On Heping Jie, down a dusty street lined with mud houses, the bright walls of Dayun Temple stand hidden behind a huge red-wood gate. Built on the site of a former Liang-dynasty palace, the temple was famous in the Hexi Corridor during the Tang dynasty. Only two halls remain, but they contain some impressive bronze statues. This is where the Xixia Tablet was discovered in the 19th century. The two-storey Bell Tower supports a handsome bell decorated with flying apsaras, heavenly kings and dragons. It was cast in the Tang dynasty, and its ring, audible for three miles, was said to resemble thunder. There is a good view of the city from the second storey.

WUWEI PRACTICAL INFORMATION

oday, Wuwei is essentially a Han city, with a population of over a million employed in agriculture, spinning, sugar refining and carpet manufacturing. Strangely enough for a population this size, Wuwei is not very large and there are no public buses.

TRANSPORTATION
Either by road or rail: daily buses to/from Lanzhou, Zhangye and Jiayuguan (bus station is on Nanguan Xilu); several trains daily either way on the Lanzhou-Urumqi line (train station is two kilometres from town—frequent mini-bus service from the bus station and centre of town).

ACCOMMODATION
Available at either the **Liangzhou Binguan**, 68 Dong Dajie, tel (0935) 221-2450, which offers basic but clean lodging or the **Tianma Binguan**, 2 Jianguo Jie, (0935) 221-5170, a more luxurious hotel favoured by Overseas Chinese with the Heavenly Horse Travel Service across the street.

FOOD AND DRINK
Focus of the night market on Xi Da Jie in front of the city park: fried noodles and dumplings in a spicy soy sauce, grilled mutton skewers and a wide variety of flatbreads, liver *gyros*, cold meats (pork and lamb), quail egg soup served in small iron pots, and excellent deep-fried sweets. Soft-serve ice cream and beer are also available.

YONGCHANG

After leaving Wuwei the railway veers northwest, cutting across the eroded remains of the Great Wall near the town of Yongchang, lying to the south. A fascinating theory connects the empire of ancient Rome with the Yongchang area.

n 54 BC, the Roman general Crassus invaded the Central Asian kingdom of Parthia with an army of 42,000 legionaries. At the ensuing Battle of Carrhae the Romans were routed; 20,000 were slain and 10,000 captured. The Roman historian Pliny recorded that his countrymen were marched to the eastern borders of Parthia in the region of the Oxus River of Central Asia, where they served in the armies of Parthia and intermarried with the local population.

At about the same time, a branch of the Xiongnu murdered several Chinese envoys sent to negotiate with their *shanyu* (chieftain), then residing near the borders of the Kingdom of Sogdiana close to the Talas River in Kazakhstan. In 36 BC, a Chinese punitive expedition was sent out under the Protector-General of Central Asia, Kan Yanshou. A detailed description of the successful siege on the Xiongnu town appears in the *Chinese History of the Former Han Dynasty*, recording that 'more than a hundred foot-soldiers lined up on either side of the gate (and drilled) in a fish-scale formation'—probably referring to the testudo, a battle formation used by Roman legions, in which interlocking shields protected the heads and legs of soldiers.

The theory that these soldiers might have been the same Romans captured by the Parthians at the battle of Carrhae was presented by Homer H Dubbs in his book *A Roman City in Ancient China*. Dubbs held that the 145 foreign soldiers (Romans) captured by the Chinese eventually married local women and settled near present-day Yongchang, where in AD 5 a town named Liqian (Lijien) was established—a name once used by the Chinese for Syria and the Eastern Roman Empire. This name was later changed to Jielu, meaning 'prisoners captured in the storming of a city'.

Shandan

he grasslands just south of Shandan were pastures reserved for imperial use. During the Sui dynasty more than 100,000 horses earmarked for post, war or state service grazed here. During the Tang dynasty horses were tended in herds of 120, with as many as 40 herds under a single 'inspectorate'. The horses were branded in many places to show age, ownership, stamina and origin. All carried the character *guan* (official) on their right shoulders. Thirty strokes of the bamboo rod was the stipulated punishment for any official who was short of a single horse.

In 1948, an important Neolithic site was discovered in Shandan County. The Shandan Siwa Culture, characterized by coarse double-handled painted pottery and by phallic stone models, apparently replaced the Yangshao Culture in Gansu in the 11th century BC and survived until 770 BC. Shandan is also the home of the Bailie School, founded in 1937 by a New Zealander, Rewi Alley (1897–1987), who had arrived in China in the 1920s. The school, part of the Chinese Industrial Co-operative Movement, trained rural orphans to organize and operate small factories manufacturing such items as paper, glass, rugs and bricks.

Zhangye

The prefecture of Zhangye is in the forefront of Gansu's efforts to wrest land from the desert; reafforestation and irrigation systems have dramatically changed the face of the area over the last 20 to 30 years. Some 68 million trees have been planted as windbreaks around tilled fields, thus easing the threat of the encroaching sands of the Badain Jaran Desert.

One of the military commands established along the Hexi Corridor after the Xiongnu expulsion by the Han dynasty was in Zhangye (formerly Ganzhou). In 609, the Sui-dynasty emperor attended a grand trade fair for merchants and envoys from 27 foreign states, and the town flourished as a centre of East–West trade until the Tibetans wrested control from the weakened Chinese Empire in the next century.

 riven from their Yenisei River homelands by Kirghiz warlords during the ninth century, the Uygur tribes scattered, and established several states. Ganzhou became one of the principal states, controlling the trade route and enjoying friendly relations with the Chinese. The kingdom was more powerful than its sister state at Dunhuang and prospered until 1028, when the Tanguts swept in and established the strong Xixia Kingdom (11th to 13th century).

After Zhangye had become part of the Mongol Empire, the peripatetic Polo family (Marco, his father and uncle) sojourned here for a year, awaiting orders from Kublai Khan. Marco commented on the city's many Buddhist monasteries, temples and statues and on the presence of 'three fine large (Nestorian) churches' in the city. The Franciscan missionary, Odorico da Pordenone, a papal emissary journeying through China in the early 14th century, noted that 'the towns and villages were so closely strung along the great caravan route that on leaving one the traveller could spy the walls of the next'.

During the Ming dynasty Zhangye and Jiuquan were major garrison towns for the million men who guarded the Great Wall. Zhangye's stature seems to have diminished by the late Qing period, however, for one 19th-century traveller commented (and could well do so today), 'as all Chinese towns are practically a copy of one another, it is unnecessary to weary the reader with a description of it'. Nevertheless, a magisterial appointment here was considered a veritable goldmine, being far enough away from Beijing to be free of official interference.

 hangye's renowned temples survived the Muslim rebellions that devastated other cities in the region late in the 19th century. The indefatigable missionaries, Mildred Cable and Francesca French, wrote in the 1920s in *Through Jade Gate and Central Asia*: 'Looking down into the city from the wall, one's first impression is the beauty of the reed-filled lakes, and the number of splendid trees. From the midst of these the gay, glazed-tiled roofs of numerous temples appear, and a high pagoda built in Indian style catches the eye . . .'

Sights

Giant Buddha Temple (dafo si)

The pagoda mentioned in Mildred Cable's diary dates from 582 and is Zhangye's oldest building. But the main attraction in this ancient city is the Giant Buddha Temple which houses China's largest reclining Buddha, a 34.5-metre giant (see picture on page 148). The temple makes a stop off in Zhangye almost obligatory, and is highly recommended to even the most temple-weary travellers. **Dafo Si** was constructed during the Western Xia dynasty (1038–1227). According to legend a monk named Cui Mie, following beautiful music to its source, found no musician but, instead, a tiny reclining jade Buddha. This auspicious omen prompted him to collect donations to build a temple including a giant Buddha, which was completed in 1098. It was named Kasyapa Tathagata Temple, and then in 1411 the Ming Yongle emperor granted the temple the name *Baojuesi*, meaning Precious Revelation. The temple is also said to be Kublai Khan's birthplace, and the place where the corpse of his mother, the Nestorian princess Sorqoqtani, was brought to lie in state. Behind the clay Buddha covered in gold leaf stand ten disciples, while around the hall 18 *luohan* (saints) stand. In 1995, an enormous cache of Buddhist scriptures, some more than 500 years old, were found in 12 cabinets hidden in a double wall. The rolls, totaling 6,647, were printed during the Ming Yongle period (1403–1424), and while consisting primarily of scriptures on paper also included some on satins, Buddhist music and paintings. A further 200 scriptures date from the Qing dynasty (1644–1911). Researchers regard the find as the most significant since the discovery in 1900 of the Dunhuang manuscripts.

HORSE'S HOOF MONASTERY (MATI SI) AND GOLDEN PAGODA (JINTA)

 ixty kilometres (37 miles) south of Zhangye, in the **Qilian Mountains**, are numerous groups of Buddhist temple caves carved into the sandstone, the most important being Mati Si (Horse's Hoof Monastery) and Jinta (Golden Pagoda). While the murals and statues of Mati Si caves have been destroyed, those of Jinta—dating from the fifth to the 14th centuries AD—are exceptionally well kept. Access, however, is difficult and requires climbing at certain spots. Take a local guide and a powerful torch to make the most of them. The caves of Mati Si were an important religious centre, and the monastery has been restored numerous times in the last 400 years. The caves are north of Mati Si and contain several statues and frescoes; there is a bronze statue of Guanyin, and at the foot of the cliff are the Halls of Sutras and the Hall of the Three Buddhas, restored in 1858. Protective roofs were built around some of the caves. Tibetan lamas raise yaks here.

ZHANGYE PRACTICAL INFORMATION

TRANSPORTATION
By rail or road: daily buses to/from Shandan, Wuwei, Lanzhou, Jiuquan and Jiayuguan and several through Qilian Shan to Xining in Qinghai. Several trains daily either way on the Lanzhou–Urumqi line.

ACCOMMODATION
Available at either the **Zhangye Binguan**, tel (0936) 821-4018, next to the Giant Buddha Temple, or at the **Ganzhou Binguan**, tel (0936) 841-1001, on Nan Jie near the Bell Tower.

PLAYING THE GUEST

he Taoyin, as I have said, was always merciful to his European friends, and the dinner was much shorter than the average Chinese repast. There were only some twenty-five courses, and these were eaten with the full complement of knives, forks and spoons; not a chop-stick to be seen, though I, for one, as soon as I had learnt the knack of using them, always used chop-sticks on the exotic Chinese food rather than banal Western cutlery. It may be of interest to record the menu, so far as I was able to identify the courses. Hors d' œuvres including, in addition to the usual items, slices of hard-boiled egg which had been buried for some years and had turned quite green, were eaten during as well as before the meal.

MENU

Tea and Dessert
Hors d' œuvres
Syrup dumplings

Shark's fin with shredded chicken

Pigeon's eggs
Pork fritters

Traveller-fish soup
Bamboo-root stewed in syrup

Roast chicken
Mince dumplings

Dried Chuguchak sturgeon

Sea-slug soup
Tinned oranges
Stewed chestnuts
Cold roast pork
Veal fritters
Fish tripe
Cabbage soup

Stewed pears stuffed with rice

Pastry dumplings
Baked mutton
Roast pigeon
Mutton fat fritters
Seaweed soup
Lotus seeds in syrup
Boiled rice
Tea and dessert

W hat was almost always a trial at Yamen banquets was the drink. Except on great occasions when one or two bottles of a sticky brand of French champagne were produced and administered in small quantities, there was nothing to drink but a peculiarly evil-smelling kind of brandy. One was seldom pressed to eat, for which one was thankful enough, but it was impossible to avoid at least sipping the brandy between every course. A Chinese host talks much more about his cellar than about his cook; to refuse to drink with him means that you do not like his wine, an imputation which causes him much loss of face. Apart from the conventional politenesses, which one soon learns to give and take as a matter of course, there is nothing stilted or ceremonious about Chinese conviviality, even on official occasions. The etiquette seems to be for a guest to behave as if he were in his own home, lolling about on his chair, getting up from table in the middle of dinner and walking about for a few minutes, and so on. When conversation flagged at our own parties it was generally safe to start the Chinese off on a kind of "fingers-out" game which was very popular. In this, two players put out their right hands at the same time, either closed or with one or more fingers outstretched, at the same time shouting a number which they guess will be the total number of fingers out for both hands. Whenever one of the players shouts the correct number, he makes the other drink his health. The fingers go out and the numbers are shouted with amazing rapidity, and when three or four such contests are going on at the same time the effect on the gaiety, or at any rate noisiness, of the party and on the circulation of the liquor is remarkable.

C P Skrine, Chinese Central Asia, 1926

JIUQUAN

tone tools—axes, knives and grinders—found in the Jiuquan area are evidence of a Stone Age culture existing here between 4,000 and 5,000 years ago. The powerful Yuezhi tribe displaced the Wusun and occupied the land between Jiuquan and Dunhuang from the fourth to the second centuries BC. By the Former Han dynasty (206 BC–AD 8), the Yuezhi had been driven out by the Xiongnu, and it was during this period that Jiuquan (then known as Suzhou) entered the historical records. A Han army under General Huo Qubing defeated the Xiongnu, and the Jiuquan protectorate was established in 107 BC.

Jiuquan (meaning 'Wine Spring') was the first town encountered 'within the wall' by eastbound travellers and is located 20 kilometres (12 miles) from the Jiayuguan Pass of the Great Wall. The city was rebuilt in the middle of the fourth century AD, following an earthquake, and traces of the city's southern gate still remain. During much of the fourth and fifth centuries northern China was torn by fighting, which resulted in a great exodus of refugees into the Hexi Corridor and areas south of the Yangzi River. This migration coincided with the spread of Buddhism arriving from the west, creating a diverse and flourishing township filled with foreign merchants. Between the seventh and eighth centuries, Tuyuhuns, Tibetans, Turks and the Tanguts of the Xixia Kingdom successively occupied the area.

When Genghis Khan's troops attacked the city in 1226, the Xixia soldiers held out for several days. The Yuan (Mongol) dynasty emulated the Han practice of establishing self-sufficient military colonies, in Jiuquan and throughout Inner Asia. Prosperity returned and post stations were established throughout the corridor—there were 99 of them between here and Beijing. Marco Polo spent a year in Jiuquan (referred to as 'Succiu' in his book) and remarked on the presence of Nestorian Christians, as he usually did, and the lucrative trade in rhubarb, which grew wild in the mountains.

he amazing three-year Silk Road journey of the Portuguese Jesuit, Benedict de Goes, ended tragically in Jiuquan in 1606, where he died starving and penniless, after demoralizing delays in his attempts to reach fellow Catholics in Beijing. De Goes noted that the foreign quarter was guarded and locked each night, much like the Jewish ghettoes in European cities. Foreign traders who resided in Jiuquan for more than nine years were forbidden to leave China.

During the uprisings that swept through Gansu, Ningxia and Xinjiang in the late 19th century, Jiuquan was occupied for three years by Muslim rebels and most of the ancient buildings and temples were destroyed. In 1873, the Chinese General, Zuo Zongtang, took command of 15,000 troops and bombarded the city walls with German Krupp guns. The fall of the town, described by Zuo as 'the most perfect feat of my military career', resulted in the slaughter of nearly 7,000 Muslims and the end

Wen Miao, a Confucian temple, and now a museum, in Wuwei

of the rebellion in Gansu. The Muslims of the Hexi Corridor were resettled in southern Gansu and Zuo swore that 'their seed will no longer remain in these three prefectures, and one need not worry about collusion between Muslims inside and outside the Jiayu Pass'.

 he archaeologist, Sir Aurel Stein, visited in 1907, and again in 1914, while exploring the Southern Mountain (Nan Shan) range. Stein was grandly escorted into town by mounted soldiers wearing straw hats and carrying huge banners, and was wined and dined by local dignitaries.

The modern population of 100,000 is mostly Han Chinese, though a small mosque tucked away amidst bare and crowded courtyards off Dong Dajie confirms a Muslim presence. Hunting in the nearby mountains is a popular pastime for many locals. The economy revolves around quarrying, mining and manufacturing; and Jiuquan is one of China's most important satellite-launching centres.

The local speciality product, 'night-glowing cups', are produced in a third-floor factory at the corner of Dong Dajie and Minyi Jie, one block east of the Drum Tower. Made of locally-mined black and green Qilian jade, these cups are designed stemmed, thimble-shaped or three-legged, in the ancient style. According to a 2,000-year-old legend, King Zhoumu was presented with one of these cups, which glowed when filled with wine and placed in the moonlight. The Tang poet, Wang Han, wrote:

Grape wine from a night-glowing cup is good,
I want to drink, but the pipa urges me to mount my horse.
Lying drunken on the battlefield would be no laughing matter,
Tell, how many soldiers ever did return?

Sadly, the mysterious cups do not seem to glow in modern moonlight!

SIGHTS

 t Jiuquan's central intersection stands the Drum Tower, which occupies the site of a fourth-century watchtower from which the two-hour night watches were sounded. When the city greatly expanded late in the 14th century the watchtower was converted into the Drum Tower. The existing simple structure is a 1905 reconstruction; inscriptions above each of its four gateways announce 'East is Hua Shan' (near Xi'an), 'West is Yiwu' (Hami), 'South is Qilian Shan' and 'North is the Great Desert' (Gobi).

JIUQUAN MUSEUM (JIUQUAN BOWUGUAN)

Situated on Gongyuan Lu (a continuation of Dong Dajie), this has a small collection of locally excavated items, including Eastern Han pottery, small Han bronzes, mirrors and lamps, and painted bricks from the Wei and Jin periods. Also on view are a model of the Ding Jia Zha 5 Tomb excavated in 1977, and an exhibition of its lively wall paintings depicting daily life during the Eastern Jin. The tomb is off the Jiuquan–Jiayuguan road.

JIUQUAN YUAN (WINE SPRING GARDEN)

The town's derives its name from this famous site. The garden is reached by continuing east from the museum. Tradition tells how Han Wudi, wishing to congratulate General Huo Qubing upon his victory over the Xiongnu, sent an envoy to Jiuquan with a present of excellent wine. But there was not enough for all his officers and men, so the fair-minded General Huo poured the wine into the spring so that all could share equally. The spring still flows, and the park has several pavilions, handsome archways and a small lake.

THE WENSHUSHAN CAVES

ifteen kilometres southwest of Jiuquan, the earliest of these date from the fifth century. Wenshushan was the most important religious centre in the area during the Wei, Sui and Tang dynasties. Unlike other cave temples, these are not carved out of the cliffs but out of the hillside, and are relatively small. There are a great variety of small temples, halls of the Buddha and pavilions carved in an ornate style at the entrance to the caves. The Wenshushan Monastery was referred to as the 'three hundred Buddhist cells' during the Qing dynasty, but after 1865 these cells were destroyed by Hui rebels; the existing buildings are restorations. During the Qing dynasty the monastery buildings were maintained by local families and no monks lived here. There are Lama Halls of the Sutras and some Buddhist temples at the front of the mountain and more Taoist temples in the back. Most of the statues and frescoes reflect a Tibetan style; the oldest cave is the Qian Fo Dong (Thousand Buddha Cave), which is in a style similar to that of the Mogao Caves (at Dunhuang) of the Northern Wei dynasty.

In the 1920s, Mildred Cable and Francesca French visited the temples here, remarking that 'hundreds of shrines stand on the mountainside and numerous guesthouses have been built to accommodate the thousands of pilgrims [many of them Tibetan] who gather each year' during the fourth lunar month. At other times the caves were unattended. 'The shrines are connected by a labyrinth of small, steep paths, which wind in and out around and over the hillside, at each turn of the road revealing a temple.' **Tibetan** herders live in plains around the caves and the area has been part of the Uygur Minority Autonomous County since 1953.

JIUQUAN PRACTICAL INFORMATION

TRANSPORTATION
By road or rail: hourly buses to/from Jiayuguan, daily buses to/from Dunhuang and Zhangye. Several trains daily either way on the Lanzhou–Urumqi line.

ACCOMMODATION
Available at either the **Jinquan Binguan**, 2 Cangmen Jie, tel (0937) 261-2641, or the **Jiuquan Binguan** on Nanguan Jie, tel (0937) 261-4211.

China's largest reclining Buddha, 34.5 metres long, at the Giant Buddha Temple in Zhangye. The temple is also said to be the birthplace of Kublai Khan

(right) The Hongsha River cuts a gorge through the Qilian Mountains near Jiuquan. The camel caravan passing along the valley floor gives an idea of scale

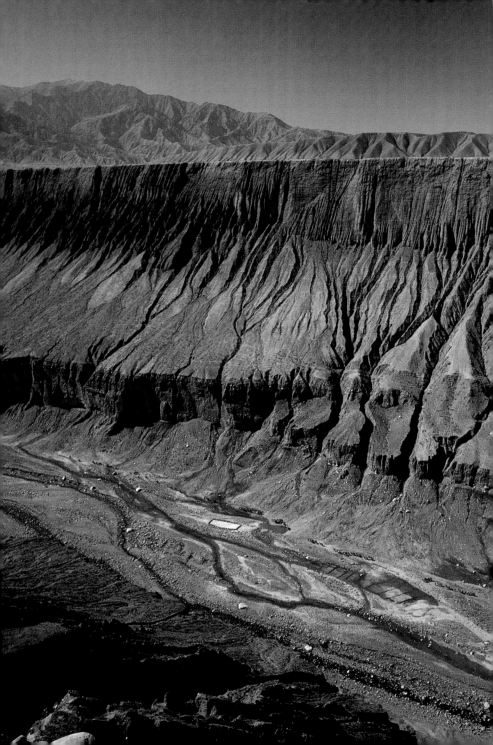

JIAYUGUAN

 oday, Jiayuguan (population 115,000) is an industrial centre producing chemical fertilizer, cement, coke and iron from raw materials mined in the nearby mountains. But in the vicinity are many deserted forts and wind-eroded beacon towers. Jiayuguan was originally a Han outpost and in 1372, during the Ming dynasty, a fortress was built to protect the last frontier of the Chinese empire. Historically, Jiayuguan was a small township engaged in local trading, catering to the needs of the military garrisons stationed at the fort.

More than 1,000 tombs of the Wei (220–265) and Western Jin (265–316) were located between Jiayuguan and Jiuquan. Many of them can be distinguished by small mounds on the desert scrub surface. However, only one tomb, designated number six, is open to the public. This three-chamber tomb includes almost 700 painted bricks depicting all facets of daily life—farming, mulberry picking, herding, hunting, military encampments, butchering and entertainments. No mortar was used in the tomb's construction, and its occupant was probably an aristocrat. The paintings are executed with bold, simple lines using mainly black, ochre and terracotta pigments. Taxis can be hired to the tombs, or alternatively hire a bike, buy some provisions including a couple of litres of water, and ride there. Distance is 28 kilometres round trip on flat roads.

Jiayuguan has an excellent Great Wall Museum located on the southern edge of town, close to the bus stop for Jiuquan, on Lanxin Lu. Exhibits include a wealth of Wall relics, interpretive materials on the ramparts' construction and maps of the different routes of Great Walls during various dynasties. The museum is open Monday–Saturday, 8.30am–12.00 noon and 2.30pm–6.00pm; Sunday, 10am–4pm.

JIAYUGUAN PASS

 his is the most impressive site in the Hexi Corridor, and the pervading sense of history is overwhelming. The pass stands between the snow-capped Qilian Mountains to the south and the black-hued swells of the Mazong (Horse's Mane) Mountains to the north. To the east of the pass is China, and to the west the boundless sweep of desert that was the beginning of the barbarian Western Regions of ancient times. The demarcation line has always been the Great Wall of China and in particular Jiayuguan, meaning 'Barrier of the Pleasant Valley'. As early as the Han dynasty, records speak of a pass (fort) in this region, and during the Song period 'there was a pass, but not a city, which served as a checkpoint' against smuggling. During the 14th century a Ming-dynasty army under the command of General Feng Sheng drove the last of the Yuan armies northwest out of the Hexi Corridor. Realizing the necessity of keeping the Mongols out beyond the Great Wall and the strategic significance of this position, General Feng set about building and reinforcing the wall in 1372, and adding this fort, which became known as 'The Greatest Pass under Heaven' and formed the westernmost extreme of the Great Wall during the Ming dynasty.

The walls of the fort are an imposing 10.7 metres (35 feet) high and 733.3 metres (3,406 feet) in perimeter. The complex consists of inner and outer ramparts, with bowmen's turrets and pavilioned watchtowers. The outer ramparts once enclosed barracks, storehouses, a temple to the God of War, a theatre for entertaining the troops, and a freshwater spring. The whole was surrounded by a defensive ditch. A local story tells how the fortification was so carefully planned that, on completion, only one brick was left over.

ittle now stands between the outer and inner walls except the theatre and, opposite, the museum, which was once a temple. At the eastern end, the three-storeyed Guanghua Men (Gate of Enlightenment) rises over the inner wall, overlooking an outer courtyard and guarding an arched 20-metre (65-foot) tunnel through the wall. The gate was built in 1506 and is reached by a steep ramp up the inner face of the wall. The corresponding western gate, the Rouyuan Men (Gate of Conciliation), leading to the desert, was said to have been shunned by the soldiers garrisoned here, for it was used only by those travellers facing the unknown dangers beyond, not the least of which were the reputed demons of the Gobi Desert. Over both gates are 17-metre-high towers adorned with flying eaves. At all four corners are the blockhouses, bowmen's turrets and watchtowers. The view from the gates of the surrounding grey and yellow desert increases the centuries' old feeling of independence and isolation.

The earliest known traveller to make the journey through the pass into the formidable desert was Laozi (Lao Tzu) in the fifth century BC. Laozi, the supposed author of the great Chinese classic of Taoist thought, the *Dao De Qing* (*Tao Teh Ching*), was reputed to have been between 160 and 200 years old when, disillusioned that many ignored his teachings, he rode his black buffalo out of the Hexi Corridor into the oblivion of the Western Regions.

It was not until 400 years later that Emperor Han Wudi's envoy, Zhang Qian, came through the Jiayuguan Pass on his way to and from the Western Regions, opening up the route to traders, pilgrims and later envoys from the West. Foreign merchants, their camel caravans laden with tribute gifts and goods, waited here for permission to proceed eastwards into China, sometimes for months at a time.

In the early 20th century, Cable and French wrote: 'The scene was desolate beyond words, and if ever human sorrow has left an impress on the atmosphere of a place, it is surely at Jiayuguan, through whose portals for centuries past a never-ending stream of despairing humanity. . . disgraced officials, condemned criminals,

Jiayuguan fortress at the western end of the Ming-dynasty Great Wall

homeless prodigals, terrified outlaws, the steps of all those have converged to that one sombre portal, and through it have for ever left the land of their birth. The arched walls are covered with poems wrung from broken hearts.' One example goes:

> Looking westwards we see the long long road leading to the New Dominions,
> Only the brave cross the Martial Barrier.
> Who is not afraid of the vast desert?
> Should the scorching heat of Heaven make him frightened?

It was the custom of every westbound traveller to throw a stone at the western wall. If the stone rebounded it meant he would return home; if not, he knew he would die among strangers. If the stone echoed against the wall, the venture would be prosperous.

The Great Wall descends at first steeply southwards from Jiayuguan and then stretches on across the corridor towards the Qilian Mountains, broken in many places

and almost buried by sand in others. This stretch of the wall dates from the Ming dynasty and is punctuated every three kilometres or so by eroded watchtowers.

Public buses (summer only) and taxis (get a group and bargain) go to the fort, or rent a bicycle at the Jiayuguan Binguan for the five-kilometre journey.

JIAYUGUAN PRACTICAL INFORMATION

The city is small and easy to find your way around; taxis are available in front of the Jiayuguan Binguan.

TRANSPORTATION

By road, rail or air: flights to/from Dunhuang and Lanzhou several times a week (the airport is ten kilometres from town; Gansu Jiayuguan International Travel Service for bookings); hourly buses to/from Jiuquan, daily buses to/from Dunhuang, Zhangye, Wuwei and Lanzhou; several trains daily either way on the Lanzhou–Urumqi line (the train station is five kilometres from town, bus number 1 from the city centre).

continued on page 158

THE GREAT WALL

by William Lindesay

n the minds of most, the Great Wall is a stone dragon dipping and thrusting its way through the mountains north of Beijing towards its seaside terminus at Old Dragon's Head, Shanhaiguan on the Bohai coast. But for most of its length — the defence passes through eight northern provinces — it is more like a serpent of mud. Tail ends of this monster of man's creation, the most extensive and labour intensive building project in human history, can be found directly on the Silk Road in Gansu Province.

Though nearly all of the Great Wall marked on contemporary maps dates from the Ming dynasty (1368–1644), the complex structure had its origin some 20 centuries earlier, during the Warring States period. Rulers of northern and central kingdoms built defensive walls to protect their lands from invasion by neighbouring states. Once these kingdoms were conquered and unified in 221 BC by Qin Shihuangdi, China's first emperor built what can be regarded as the first Great Wall. One of his generals, Meng Tian, linked up the former kingdom walls of the Zhao, Yan and Qin states with new ramparts to form the Qin-dynasty Great Wall. Its low earthen mound remains can be seen near its starting point at Lintao, south of Lanzhou, and around Guyuan, southern Ningxia, which lies directly on a northern branch of the Silk Road out of Xi'an.

With the fall of the Qin and the rise of the Western Han dynasty, the empire expanded, especially westwards. The development of the Silk Road, and the construction of the Great Wall which shadowed it, were an integral part of the expansion. But the new territory came under constant threat from invasion by the Xiongnu, a nomadic tribe. Defence of newly conquered land in the west became a major problem for Han emperors. At first, the Han courts tried to appease the nomads with tribute, but this only achieved short-lived peace. Chao Cuo, a minister under Emperor Han Wendi, offered stronger advice on defending the western regions: 'The Xiongnu eat meat and cheese, wear skins and furs, and possess no farmsteads nor fields. They lurk along the border, ready to invade once garrison troops are withdrawn. It will profit the emperor to dispatch generals, officials and troops to colonize the frontier. Families should be resettled there to farm the land, and high walls fronted by deep ditches should be built to stop the Xiongnu's southerly advance.'

T he minister's advice was implemented, with the Han Great Wall being built through the whole length of the Hexi Corridor as far as the eastern shores of Lop Nor in eastern Xinjiang — this westernmost extent being first proved by the explorations of Sir Aurel Stein. During this time the four prefectures of Wuwei, Zhangye, Jiuquan and Dunhuang were established. The best-preserved sections of the Han Great Wall can be found in the vicinity of the two main gates of Yumenguan and Yangguan, west of Dunhuang, which once functioned as check points on the Northern and Southern Silk Roads respectively. Those passing through the gates were questioned, and permission was required to proceed. Merchants carrying goods were taxed.

A special characteristic of the Han Wall at its western end are the layers of tamarisk twigs which were alternated with rammed earth to provide more stability during the rampart's construction.

For centuries after the Han dynasty, Wall-building in the west lost its importance since capitals of ruling dynasties were located far to the east and the main threats to them originated from the north, particularly from the Mongols. During the Ming dynasty however, a Great Wall was once again built through the Hexi Corridor. The line of the Han Wall was largely retraced by the new defence, but its most westerly extent was Jiayuguan, not Lop Nor. The first beacon tower on the Ming Great Wall hangs precariously on a cliff above the Taolai River, which has cut down into desert the gravel at the foot of the Qilian Shan, the snow-capped mountain range which forms the spectacular backdrop to the walls and gate towers of the Jiayuguan fortress (see pictures on pages 156 and 152–3). Remains of the Ming Great Wall, a rammed earthen rampart

Crumbling rammed earth Great Wall of the Ming dynasty, east of Zhangye in Gansu Province

The Taolai River at the very western end of the Ming Great Wall. Rammed-earth remains of a watchtower and ramparts can be seen at the top right

like a giant, desiccated worm-cast, can be seen throughout the length of the Hexi Corridor, but most spectacularly in Shandan County where the form of the structure is well preserved and runs virtually unbroken for more than 80 kilometres. The use of locally available materials for building were essential, and in the desert that meant clay. This was dug from the ground in front of the actual line of the intended Wall, thus accentuating the height of the Wall itself. Groundwater was tapped and moistened clay was compacted between wooden frames. Once the frame was removed, the hot desert sun baked the structure to rock hardness.

The Ming Great Wall, stretching from Jiayuguan to Shanhaiguan was extended during the late Wanli period (1572–1620) with the building of the 'Liaodong Sidewall' from Shanhaiguan to the Yalu River on the present-day border between China and North Korea. In the west the Wall came under little threat, but in the east it did to a certain extent thwart re-invasions from the Mongols, while ultimately it stood proudly unchallenged on steep mountain ridges as a statement of the might of the great Ming empire. However, it never faced the test it was built to withstand: Manchu armies from the northeast were allowed to pass through the Wall at Shanhaiguan by a renegade fortress general who had heard that rebels were in control of Beijing and that Emperor Chongzhen had hung himself. That spelt the end of Wall building.

During the Qing dynasty, invaders came not from the grasslands and desert regions north of China, but over the sea from Europe, Japan and North America. Interestingly, Jiayuguan at the very west end of the Wall continued to be manned and function as a check point, while observation towers were built in the region bordering Chinese Turkestan. The Kangxi emperor commissioned Jesuits in 1708 to make a survey of the Ming Wall which was completed a decade later and presented as a 12-metre-long map, now in the Nanjing Museum.

ACCOMMODATION

Available at the **Jiayuguan Binguan**, tel (0937) 622-6983, on the main circle across from the post office, with its own restaurant and bar or the international-style **Changcheng Binguan**, tel (0937) 622-5266, between the train station and city centre, which caters almost exclusively to Western and Japanese tour groups.

FOOD AND DRINK

Primarily Muslim with some Sichuan and Mongolian flavours; there are numerous small restaurants on the streets emanating from the main circle. For breakfast, street stalls serve a spicy porridge of doufu and pork.

The only Travel Agency in Jiayuguan is the Gansu Jiayuguan International Travel Service, located behind the Jiayuguan Binguan, which has a fleet of mini-buses for tours to the sites.

JIAYUGUAN TO DUNHUANG

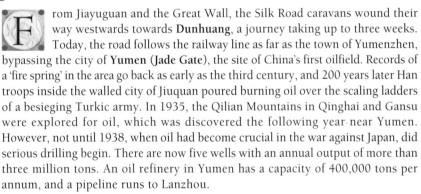

rom Jiayuguan and the Great Wall, the Silk Road caravans wound their way westwards towards **Dunhuang**, a journey taking up to three weeks. Today, the road follows the railway line as far as the town of Yumenzhen, bypassing the city of **Yumen (Jade Gate)**, the site of China's first oilfield. Records of a 'fire spring' in the area go back as early as the third century, and 200 years later Han troops inside the walled city of Jiuquan poured burning oil over the scaling ladders of a besieging Turkic army. In 1935, the Qilian Mountains in Qinghai and Gansu were explored for oil, which was discovered the following year near Yumen. However, not until 1938, when oil had become crucial in the war against Japan, did serious drilling begin. There are now five wells with an annual output of more than three million tons. An oil refinery in Yumen has a capacity of 400,000 tons per annum, and a pipeline runs to Lanzhou.

Some 61 kilometres (38 miles) southeast of Yumen are the **Changma Buddhist Caves**, three small groups of caves dating from the Five (907–960) and Song (960–1279) dynasties. The site is located in a wide valley surrounded by the Da Ban Mountains. There are many interesting frescoes depicting Buddhas, bodhisattvas, terraces, pavilions, lotus designs and statues, all probably influenced by the Mogao Caves and developed by local families who had also supported the work at Dunhuang and were eager to earn merit.

Along the road small patches of fields give way to sand bluffs and occasionally herds of grazing camels, sheep or goats. A handful of houses make up a settlement surrounded by the rare glimpse of green trees. To the south the lower foothills of the Qilian Mountains remain in view, but soon the dark Mazong range to the north slides over the horizon. The desert changes constantly: sometimes dunes, sometimes flat with small mounds of sand around grey-green camel thorn bushes. Farmers' carts are harnessed to donkeys or donkeys and camels together. Further on, tufts of green, yellow and brown scrub are interspersed with fertile strips along the tree-lined road. The oasis of Yumenzhen has orchards and fields of sunflowers and corn. The road briefly veers north of the railway line, passing the ruins of the city of **Qiaowan**, built by the Qing emperor Kangxi (reigned 1662–1723).

Anxi

nxi straddles the junction of the two Silk Road trade routes and was once of considerable importance; some geographers called it the very heart of Asia. Caravans of precious jade dug from the **Karakash River**, near Khotan on the southern route, made regular stops at Anxi during the second and first centuries BC. During the Tang dynasty the headquarters of the 'Protectorate of the Western Lands' was stationed here, which made Anxi the principal base for Chinese military expeditions into Central Asia.

The old town was completely destroyed during the 19th-century Muslim rebellions, and thousands of the inhabitants slaughtered. The rebuilt town presented a dismal appearance to early 20th-century travellers. In 1907, Sir Aurel Stein found nothing indicating Anxi's former importance; he stored his Dunhuang treasures at the local *yamen* (magistracy) before exploring an ancient line of beacon towers along the Shule River to the west. During the 1920s Mildred Cable and Francesca French made several visits and were rewarded with official permission to explore the city walls at will—local custom forbade women to do so except on special holidays—and they were able to discern the main cart tracks leading toward Urumqi to the northwest, Lanzhou to the southeast and the Lop Nor to the southwest. By this time the camel caravans from Mongolia were trading domestic utensils, paraffin, cloth and sugar for the wool, cotton, carpets and jade of Central Asia. Biting winds blew daily, a problem much alleviated in recent years by a tree-planting programme. 'In the winter shops were closed and everything was at a standstill,' the missionaries wrote, 'every household lived, ate and slept on its dung-warmed *kang* . . . (and) many whiled away the weary hours with the fumes of the opium pipe.'

Anxi remains a small township best known for the Buddhist caves at **Elm Forest Temple (Yulin Si)**, also called **Wanfo Xia**, in the mountains some 70 kilometres (43 miles) to the south, whose history spans some 1,400 years. The caves were hewn out of the cliffs in the sides of mountain gorges. There are about 41 existing caves from the Tang, Five Dynasties, Song, Xixia, Yuan and Qing periods. These caves were probably first constructed at the same time as those of Dunhuang. Most of the

Tri-colour pottery camel and musicians (Tang dynasty, 618–907 AD), unearthed at Zhongbao Village, Xi'an City

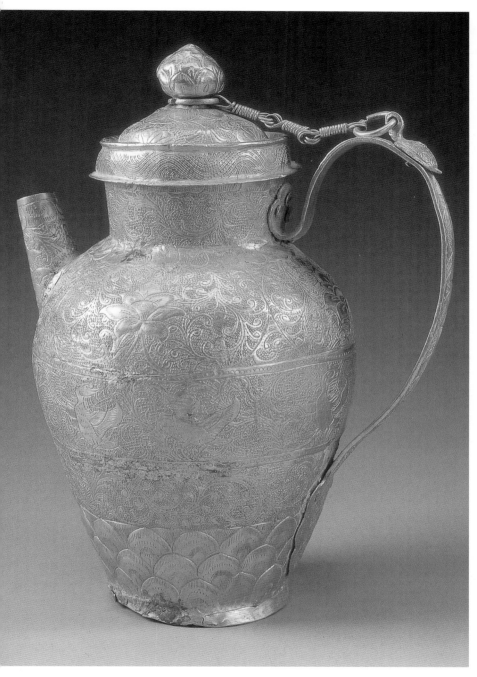

Gold pot decorated with mandarin ducks and climbing plants, height 21cm, diameter at centre 11cm, (Tang dynasty, 618–907 AD), excavated from Xianyang Northwest Medical Apparatus and Instruments factory site, Shaanxi in 1969

caves have coffered ceilings (inlaid panels) but there is an extremely rare one that has a wide cone-shaped ceiling. Many of the frescoes are in poor condition, although there are a few excellent examples of Tang art. The surrounding scenery is stunning.

DUNHUANG

Tourists and scholars alike are attracted to this desert town of 14,000 inhabitants to see for themselves China's richest treasure-house of ancient Buddhist murals and sculpture, the **Mogao Caves**.

n the early days of the Silk Road, Dunhuang (meaning 'Blazing Beacon') was an important trading centre and during the first century BC, the westernmost outpost of China. In 121 BC, following General Huo Qubing's military victory over the Xiongnu, Dunhuang was fortified and settled by the Chinese. The Great Wall was extended to Dunhuang and a line of fortified beacon towers stretched westwards into the desert. By the second century AD Dunhuang had a population of more than 76,000 and was a key supply base for the caravans that passed through the city: those setting out for the arduous trek across the desert loaded up with water and food supplies, and others arriving from the west gratefully looked upon the mirage-like sight of Dunhuang's walls, which signified safety and comfort. Dunhuang prospered on the heavy flow of traffic. The first Buddhist caves in the Dunhuang area were hewn in 353. Merchants, pilgrims and other travellers constructed cave shrines to ensure the donor success in his journey through the demon-filled perils of the open desert, and in gratitude for dangers overcome.

The Tibetans took over Dunhuang in the latter half of the seventh century. Weakened by internal dissension, they were driven from the Hexi Corridor by the private army of the Chinese warlord, Zhang Yichao, in 851. Zhang received rewards and titles from the Tang court, and became the effective ruler of Dunhuang, succeeded by various family members until 911, when the Uygur kingdom of Shazhou was established. Throughout the period of Uygur domination the leaders of Dunhuang were still Chinese, and political marriages took place between the Dunhuang ruling house of Cao and the daughters of the King of Khotan. The Cao family contributed to many of the caves at Mogao.

Dunhuang fell to the Xixia Kingdom in 1036 and later to the Mongols in 1227. In the early 16th century, the city came under the sway of the Muslim Chaghatai Khanate, which then ruled most of Uyguristan, and seems to have been partly abandoned. The Qing dynasty re-established control, and in 1760 Dunhuang was resettled.

As news spread of the survival of the caves and of Abbot Wang's discovery in 1900 of the Dunhuang manuscripts, foreign archaeologists began turning up in Dunhuang, buying valuable manuscripts and scroll paintings, and removing statues. The richness of the material created a whole field of study known as 'Dunhuangology' (see Special Topics and Literary Excerpt on pages 97–112).

In *The Gobi Desert*, the missionaries Cable and French describe the town during the 1930s:

> he people of Tunhwang viewed themselves as the élite of the Gobi land, and were abnormally proud of their oasis. They had plenty of money to spend and opened their markets freely to goods from other places, but prided themselves on being a self-supporting community, not only in respect of food, but also in regard to brides and bridegrooms, and they did not approve of marriages arranged between their own children and those of other towns. The market-place was always busy with merchants coming and going, the professional story-teller took his stand each day to amuse the moving crowd, and gaily dressed women came in carts from the farms for a day's shopping and to see their friends. The granaries overflowed with wheat, and the town reckoned itself to be the safest and most prosperous place imaginable, priding itself on its trade-route nickname of 'little Peking'.

SIGHTS

A bustling market operates daily in the southwest part of town. Department stores stock the simplest of goods—ropes, rolls of plastic, nuts and bolts, basic household goods and endless rows of canned foods, including donkey meat (can-openers, however, are not available).

MOGAO CAVES (MOGAO KU)

he Mogao Caves, which honeycomb the cliff-face of the Mingsha Hills, 25 kilometres (16 miles) southeast of Dunhuang, are the world's richest treasure-trove of Buddhist manuscripts, wall paintings and statuary. Hewn over a millennium spanning nine dynasties, from the fourth to the 14th centuries, they mark the height of Buddhist art. In a tiny oasis huddled against the western side of a steep valley, the caves are hidden from view, invisible until you are directly in front of them. Surrounding the green valley are sand dunes and desert, which make a striking contrast. The geographical position has contributed to the degradation of the caves; southwestern winds and sands blow directly in, eroding the walls and paintings.

History relates that in 336, a monk called Lie Zun came upon the cliff and had a vision of a thousand golden rays of light shining upon him like as many Buddhas. The

monk asked a pilgrim to have one of the smaller caves painted and consecrated as a shrine to ensure his own safe journey. Other pilgrims and travellers followed, and for the next thousand years temples and shrines were hewn out of the cliff, painted and decorated by the pious or fearful to guarantee the success and safety of their journeys (see picture on page 107). Lie Zun ended up founding what Mildred Cable would call, 15 centuries later, 'a great art gallery in the desert'.

he first foreigners to visit the Mogao cave temples were the Russian explorer, Colonel Nikolai Przewalski, and a Hungarian geological expedition, both in 1879. But it was the discovery in 1900 of a cache of manuscripts in Cave 17 by the self-styled abbot, a Taoist priest name Wang Yuanlu, that brought orientalists rushing to Dunhuang. There were more than 50,000 manuscripts from the temple library, including religious texts and documents on history, customs, literature, art, mathematics, medicine and economics. These treasures were sealed up in a small hidden cave by Buddhist monks in the 11th century, presumably to save them from the ravages of war with the Xixia. The Viceroy of Gansu was anxious that the finds be protected, but could not afford their transhipment to Lanzhou; he simply ordered the caves resealed. In order to pay for his restoration plans, Abbot Wang took it upon himself to sell some of the manuscripts to excited foreigners.

In 1905, while visiting Hami, the German archaeologist, Albert von Le Coq (see pages 109 to 111), heard from a Turkoman merchant of the discovery of the hidden library. As the temples were still active, it would have been impossible for foreign excavators to remove the wall paintings. The library, however, was a different matter. Greatly tempted but pressed for time, he tossed a coin to decide if he should go. 'Heads win, tails lose!' he wrote. 'Tails . . . came uppermost, and I had my horse saddled and began our journey to Kashgar'; thus he missed out on this 'mine of fabulous treasure'. Sir Aurel Stein arrived at Dunhuang two years later and persuaded the abbot to re-open the cave containing the manuscripts (see pages 99 to 108). Night after night, Stein and his translator secretly perused bundles of documents. Manuscripts in Chinese, Uygur, Sogdian, Tibetan, Sanskrit, Runic-Turkic and unknown languages were revealed, including a printed version of the *Diamond Sutra* dating from 868 AD. One of the world's oldest printed books, this important Mahayana Buddhist text states that phenomena are all illusion; it is so called because it is 'sharp like a diamond that cuts away all unnecessary conceptualization and brings one to the further shore of enlightenment'. Stein left Dunhuang with a collection of almost 10,000 documents and wall paintings, which is now divided between the British Museum in London and the National Museum in New Delhi.

Cave housing the Great Buddha at Mogao, near Dunhuang

The celebrated French sinologist, Paul Pelliot, unaware that Stein had preceded him, also gained access to the 'library cave' in 1908 and was 'stupefied'. By the light of a candle he studied about a thousand documents per day, selecting the rarest and most valuable (including a Nestorian version of the Gospel of St John) and finally negotiating a fee of £90 for them. The Musée Guimet in Paris now houses Pelliot's collection. Upon showing some of the manuscripts to scholars in Beijing, the authorities ordered an embargo on the remaining texts. In 1911, Zuicho Tachibana on a mission for the Japanese noble, Count Otani, spent eight weeks gathering material in Dunhuang, followed by the Russian, Sergei Oldenburg, in 1914.

 n 1923, Langdon Warner, an American from the Fogg Art Museum at Harvard University, arrived to see what was left of the wall paintings, and to determine what pigments had been used. Enraged by the graffiti and desecration wrought by the uncaring White Russian soldiers and by the unconscious damage caused by pilgrims, he wrote to his wife: 'My job is to break my neck to rescue and preserve anything and everything I can from this quick ruin. It has been stable enough for centuries, but the end is in sight now.' Warner removed the wall paintings (using his own, not particularly successful technique) from Caves 324 and 328, the last of which contains the best group of sculptures at Mogao.

Still in good condition are nearly 500 caves with over 45,000 murals and 2,000 pigmented stucco figures (the sandstone of the ledge being too loose to carve). Because of the aridity of the surrounding desert the wall paintings and statuary have been preserved for over 15 centuries. Most of the art dates from the Northern and Western Wei, Northern Zhou, Sui and Tang dynasties. The Five, Northern Song, Western Xia and Yuan dynasties are also represented. (Of the remaining caves, 23 are from the Wei, 95 from the Sui, 213 from the Tang, 33 from the Five Dynasties, 98 from the Song, three from the Xixia, nine from the Yuan, and six are undated.)

The paintings are divided into several religious categories, including the Jataka stories, which relate the adventures of Sakyamuni in his previous incarnations, and aspects from the Buddhist sutras depicting universal suffering, transmigration and karmic causality. Sir Aurel Stein commented:

> T hroughout these legendary scenes with their freely drawn landscape backgrounds, their Chinese architecture, the bold movement and realism of their figures, a distinctly Chinese style prevailed. It was the same with the graceful and often fantastic freedom of the cloud scrolls, floral tracery and other decorative motifs. But all the principal divine figures . . . bore the unmistakable impress of Indian models transmitted through Central Asian Buddhism. Hieratic tradition had preserved for these Buddhas, Bodhisattvas and saintly attendants, the type of face, pose and drapery originally developed by Graeco-Buddhist art, whatever modifications Chinese taste had introduced in technique of treatment and colouring.

Most of the caves are rectangular and connected by a series of balconies, walkways and ladders. The paintings cover an area of 45,000 square metres, and the colours (predominantly green, blue, white, black and pink) are still strong and bright, though in some areas the pigments have changed; oxidization is particularly apparent in the vermilion reds, which have turned dark chocolate. For several months in 1920 some 400 White Russian soldiers from Siberia found refuge in these caves, and the soot from their campfires compounded earlier damage caused by incense burned during the annual celebrations of the Buddha's birth; this blackened the murals over the ages. The soot was removed by restorers in the 1960s and 1970s.

The Wei dynasty (386–581) caves are almost all on the third tier. Graeco-Indian influence in clothing, hair and facial features is strongly apparent in all the pre-Tang caves. The quiet emotional expressiveness of the Buddhas, bodhisattvas and disciples contrasts sharply with the lively aggression of the heavenly kings and guardians in the post-seventh-century statues. The sculptures in the Wei caves show wide faces, large noses, thin lips, high cheekbones and curly hair; the female statues are fuller breasted.

he Wei dynasty was founded by the Turkic-speaking Toba people. The preceding years of turmoil had produced a reflowering of Buddhism and the art from this period reflects the high value placed on the ideals of enlightenment and the transcendence of the painful material world. The Chinese liken the serene smile of the Buddha in cave 259 to that of the Mona Lisa; other Wei caves, including 272 (Northern Wei) and 249 (Western Wei), show an elegant style and narrower faces. The black, green and white colour scheme in 432 is striking. Jataka stories, illustrated in caves 275, 428 and 257, depict the adventures of Mohesaduo, Shipi, and Prince Xudana among others. Cave 254 shows the Buddha's defeat of Mara (illusion), who tempts him with desire, taunts him with reason and attacks him with storms and flaming rocks, but the Buddha does not succumb and finally achieves enlightenment. Cave 249 is painted with scenes from Chinese mythology. The Wei paintings often depict the donors who paid for the excavation of the caves as servants or supplicants, usually small in size.

All of the Dunhuang murals, with the exception of the Yuan-dynasty caves, are not frescoes but tempera, or water emulsions. The technique was quite complex: on top of a layer of clay another layer of a cement-like substance was spread on the wall and then polished. This was followed with the background colour, lightly applied in a pale red or dark grey, and finally the painting itself. The colour paints were made from mineral powder and metal oxides. The paintings have lasted for so many centuries because of the type of pigment used, and many of the colours (some of which were imported) are still surprisingly bright.

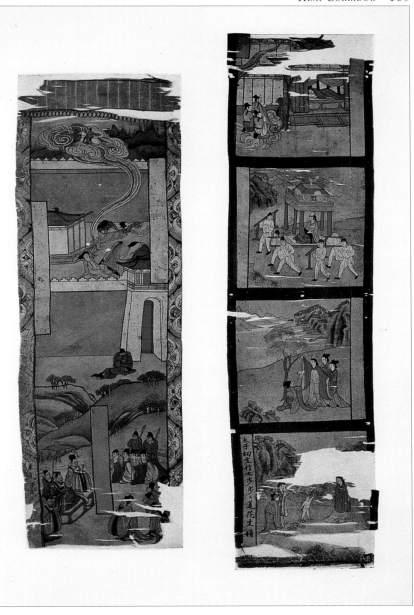

Buddhist banners painted on silk gauze more than one metre in length, depicting the life story of Buddha. Acquired by Stein and lodged in the British Museum in London

(left) *Terracotta bodhisattva at Mogao, near Dunhuang*

orth of the Wei caves are those from the brief Sui dynasty (581–618); several are transformed Wei caves. Some square caves have a niche in the far wall, coffered ceilings, and scenes from Chinese mythology. Many caves had an antechamber that has since collapsed. The sculpture is in good condition and more formal in style than the Wei; the figures of the Buddha, which have lost much of the Gandharan influences, are clearly defined and wear Chinese garments. The faces of the statues are fuller, with long ear-lobes and loosely draped clothing, the upper body is disproportionately bigger—the rules of the time decreed that a larger upper body indicated power and divinity.

Other Sui caves include 244 and 427. The Pure Land doctrine and the teachings of Amitabha were developed during this time and figure in several murals. The Pure Land, or Western Paradise, is a Buddhist afterworld of luxurious palaces, pavilions, courtyards and gate-towers; these murals show architectural structures of great complexity and splendour. The paintings also contain scenes from the Jataka stories and contain a more varied subject matter than in the Wei paintings. The ceilings are frequently decorated with lotus flowers and show a rich use of symmetrical patterns. Above all, the Sui caves mark the end of foreign influence and the transition to the more indigenous styles of the Tang dynasty.

By the Tang dynasty (618–907) the donors were depicted in much larger forms and richly attired. Celestial musicians appeared in the early murals, to be replaced in later caves by the flying apsaras (angels) for which Dunhuang is so famous. The numerous Tang caves reflect the highest artistic achievements at Dunhuang. Most are square, with three levels to accommodate taller statues; others, with reclining Buddhas, have been carved wider. Sculpture during this time was largely neglected in favour of painting; most murals are signed by the artist. The existing sculpture, however, is highly accomplished, extremely realistic and gentle; there is less of a distinction between men and gods. Some beautiful examples are in Caves 57, 332 and 444 (early Tang) and 320 (mid-Tang). There are many figures of bodhisattvas, humans who delayed their achievement of nirvana to assist others in their quest. They wear ornaments and jewels, resembling Tang nobles.

he ornamental Tang paintings depict a wide variety of stories from the Buddhist canon (especially in Caves 152, 320 and 172 of Guanyin and Amitabha), which replace the Jataka story themes. The figures are dressed in rich, aristocratic costumes with flowing robes and turbans. Bodhisattvas figure prominently in the Tang caves. The paintings and designs cover entire walls with designs influenced by Persian and Indian styles, and arabesques of flowers and plants instead of geometric patterns.

By the time of the Five (907–960), Song (960–1279) and Xixia (1115–1234) dynasties there was no more space left on the cliff to make new caves. Some caves were restored, others redone or enlarged. Old paintings have thus been discovered lying under new ones. The Five-dynasties caves are on the lower half of the cliff; the little sculpture that remains resembles that of the Tang, as do the paintings from this period. The murals are larger but seem to lack the skill and dedication of earlier art. The Song and Xixia art is indistinguishable and consists mostly of restoration work. The sculpture from these dynasties is lifeless and a poor imitation of the Tang style. Likewise, the wall paintings seem to be colder. Although the art of the seventh century was innovative (particularly that of the Northern Song dynasty), with the human form drawn clearly and the scenery more abstract, there is only one example of it; Cave 61 shows a landscape of Wutai Shan, Shanxi.

uring the Mongol Yuan dynasty (1279–1368) many caves were restored. The wall paintings from this period are frescoes, a European technique that was introduced probably through Nepal. The murals depict various mandalas (Tibetan geometric representations of the cosmos) and bodhisattvas. A group of caves decorated in Tibetan style, dating from the Yuan dynasty, is rarely opened. After the Yuan dynasty no outstanding developments in art or architecture took place in Dunhuang. Following centuries of renown, the Mogao Caves faded until their rediscovery at the turn of this century. On the site there is a small museum and the Dunhuang Research Academy, where almost 200 Chinese and international scholars carry out research.

The Mogao Caves are located 25 kilometres southeast of Dunhuang. Buses leave for Mogao (small ticket office on Dingzi Lu, across from the Dunhuang Guesthouse) twice a day: at 8 am returning at 11 am, and at 1 pm returning at 4 pm. Alternatively, you can hire a taxi. Tickets to enter the caves start at 86 yuan for a half-day admission. Those wanting to see more can buy the 120 yuan ticket, or even make a special requests to enter an individual cave for between 60–200 yuan each. In an attempt to save the caves from damage by humidity introduced by visitors, the mural and statuary of eight caves have been replicated in a museum in front of the honeycombed cliffside. Entrance to this museum is only 10 yuan.

MINGSHA SAND DUNES AND CRESCENT LAKE

The high yellow sand dunes of Mingsha offer the best picture-book desert scenery that travellers are likely to see along the entire length of the Silk Road. They lie just three kilometres (two miles) south of the city and offer a stunning view of the surrounding desert in one direction and of the Dunhuang oasis in the other. Visitors can ride bicycles, hire a taxi or take a bus out to the edge and then climb the 250-metre (820-foot) Mingsha dune, which overlooks the small and mysterious Crescent Lake. The steep climb is hard going and best undertaken barefoot. The descent is no problem—simply slide down. There are also camel rides into the dunes.

continued on page 176

Embroidered silk hanging more than 1.25 metres square showing Buddha between disciples and bodhisattvas, with donors in adoration below

Painted Buddhist banners on silk gauze, more than one metre in length, depicting bodhisattvas. Both these relics were acquired by Aurel Stein

TABULA RASA

 Sandy now opened one of the scrolls that he had brought. It was snowy white; there was not a trace of so much as half a letter upon it. 'Master,' he said, handing it to Tripitaka, 'This scroll has got no writing in it.' Monkey then opened a scroll; it too was blank. Pigsy did the same; only to make the same discovery. 'We had better look at them all,' said Tripitaka. They did so, and found that all were blank. 'I must say it's hard luck on the people of China,' sobbed Tripitaka. 'What is the use of taking them these blank books? How shall I dare face the Emperor of T'ang? He will say I am playing a joke on him and have me executed on the spot.'

Monkey had by now guessed what had happened. 'Master,' he said, 'I know what's at the bottom of this. It is all because we refused to give Ananda and Kasyapa their commission. This is how they have revenged themselves on us. The only thing to do is to go straight to Buddha and charge them with fraudulent withholding of delivery.' They all agreed, and were soon back at the temple gates. 'They've come back to change their scriptures,' said the bands of the blessed, laughing. This time they were allowed to go straight in. 'Listen to this!' shouted Monkey. 'After all the trouble we had getting here from China, and after you specially ordered that we were to be given the scriptures, Ananda and Kaspaya made a fraudulent delivery of goods. They gave us blank copies to take away; I ask you, what is the good of that to us?' 'You needn't shout,' said Buddha, smiling. 'I quite expected that those two would ask for their commission. As a matter of fact, scriptures ought not to be given on too easy terms or received gratis. On one occasion some of my monks went down the mountain to Sravasti with some scriptures and let Chao, the Man of Substance, read them out loud. The result was that all the live members of his household were protected from all calamity and the dead were saved from perdition. For this they only charged gold to the weight of three pecks and three pints of rice. I told them they had sold far too cheap. No wonder they gave you blank copies when they saw you did not intend to make any payment at all. As a matter of fact, it is such blank scrolls as these that are the true scriptures. But I quite see that the people of China are too foolish and ignorant to believe this, so there is nothing for it but to give them copies with some writing on.' Then he called for Ananda and Kasyapa, and told them to choose a few scrolls with writing, out of each of the thirty-five divisions of the scriptures, hand them over to the pilgrims, and then inform him of the exact titles and numbers.

T he two disciples accordingly took the pilgrims once more to the Treasury, where they again asked Tripitaka for a little present. He could think of nothing to give them except his golden begging bowl. He told Sandy to find it, and holding it up before him with both hands, he said to the two disciples, 'I am a poor man and have been travelling for a long time. I fear I have nothing with me that is suitable as a present; but perhaps you would accept this bowl which the Emperor of China gave me with his own hand, that I might use it to beg with on the road. If you will put up with so small a trifle, I am sure that when I return to China and report upon my mission, you may count upon being suitably rewarded. I hope on these terms you will this time give me scriptures with writing on them, or I fear his Majesty will be disappointed and think that all my efforts have been wasted.' Ananda took the bowl with a faint smile. But all the divinities in attendance–down to the last kitchen-boy god–clapped one another on the back and roared with laughter, saying, 'Well, of all the shameless...! they've made the scripture seekers pay them a commission!' The two disciples looked somewhat embarrassed; but Ananda continued to clutch tightly at the bowl.

Wu Ch'en-En, Monkey, translated by Arthur Waley

arco Polo referred to them as the 'rumbling sands', and indeed the dunes do make a sound like thunder or a drum-roll as the wind sweeps across them. Local legend tells how in ancient times a Chinese general and his army, bound for the Western Regions, camped in the dunes beside the sweet blue waters of Crescent Lake. Noise from the encampment attracted the enemy, who attacked in the dead of night. The Han army beat their war drums to call the troops to arms. Suddenly, in the middle of the battle, a fierce wind blew up, filling the sky with sand and burying both armies. This is why, to this day, the wind blows across the sand's surface to the roll of war drums.

'The skill of man made the Caves of the Thousand Buddhas, but the Hand of God fashioned the Lake of the Crescent Moon,' goes a popular saying at Dunhuang. A solitary sand-jujube (*Eloeagnus latifolia*) grows beside this miniature lake, half-enclosed by reeds.

Dunhuang County Museum (Dunhuang Bowuguan)

This small museum is on Dong Dajie, just east of the main circle. Exhibits include utensils and clothing from the Western Han period, stone carvings and silk fragments, and, from the Mogao Caves, a few of the remaining Northern- and Western- Wei-dynasty scrolls that were left behind by the foreign explorers, revealing the astrological, medical and economics' knowledge of the period.

White Horse Dagoba (Bai Ma Ta)

Among fields of corn and the remains of the ancient city walls southwest of the city (about 40 minutes on foot) lies the nine-tiered dagoba dedicated to the gallant white steed that carried the Kuchean monk, Kumarajiva, east along the Silk Road. Upon his arrival at Dunhuang in AD 384, the horse became ill. One night, Kumarajiva dreamt that the horse spoke to him: 'Teacher, I am in fact the White Dragon of the Western Sea, and because of the task set you to spread the Buddhist teachings I came especially with you on the journey. Now you have already entered the pass and the road ahead holds no danger, I shall accompany you no further, so let us part here.' Kumarajiva clung to the horse's tail, weeping in despair. The horse told him that nearby were heavenly horses from which he could choose a reliable mount, but Kumarajiva was inconsolable. Suddenly there was a loud neigh, and the monk woke from his dream. Just then a servant came in to announce the death of the great white horse. Sick at heart, Kumarajiva buried the horse and built the elegant White Horse Dagoba on its grave.

Yumenguan and Yangguan Passes

The remains of these two important Han-dynasty gates are about 68 kilometres (42 miles) apart, at either end of the Dunhuang extension of the Great Wall. Until the Tang dynasty, when the gates fell into disuse, all caravans travelling through Dunhuang were required to pass through one of these gates, then the westernmost passes of China.

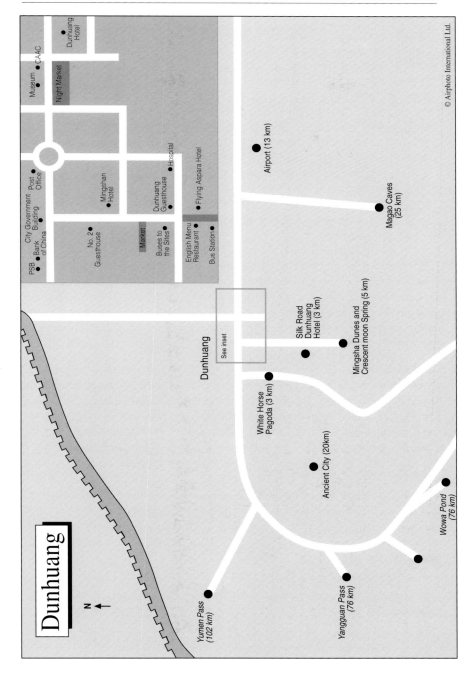

Dunhuang

N ←

© Airphoto International Ltd.

Museum
CAAC
Dunhuang Hotel
Night Market
PSB
City Government
Bank of China
Post Office
Mingshan Hotel
No. 2 Guesthouse
Market
Dunhuang Guesthouse
Hospital
Buses to the Sites
English Menu Restaurant
Flying Aspara Hotel
Bus Station

See inset

Dunhuang

Airport (13 km)

Magao Caves (25 km)

Silk Road Dunhuang Hotel (3 km)

Mingsha Dunes and Crescent moon Spring (5 km)

White Horse Pagoda (3 km)

Ancient City (20km)

Wowa Pond (76 km)

Yumen Pass (102 km)

Yangguan Pass (76 km)

umenguan lies about 80 kilometres (50 miles) northwest of Dunhuang. It was originally called the 'Square City', but because the great jade caravans from Khotan entered through its portals, it became known as the Jade Gate Pass. In the third and fourth centuries turmoil swept through Central Asia, disrupting overland trade, and the sea route via India began to supplant it. By the sixth century, as caravans favoured the northern route via Hami, the pass was abandoned In 1907, Sir Aurel Stein found bamboo slips naming the site as Yumenguan, and in 1944, Chinese archeologists discovered relics confirming this. With its 10-metre-high (32-foot) mud walls pierced by four gateways, the square enclosure covered an area of more than 600 square metres (718 square yards) in the midst of unbounded desolation.

Yangguan lies 75 kilometres (47 miles) southwest of Dunhuang but consists of only the ruins of a high beacon tower. In order to visit either site, you must hire a taxi or rent a car from CITS.

DUNHUANG PRACTICAL INFORMATION

A bustling fruit and vegetable market operates daily in the southwest part of town. Department stores stock a wide variety of goods, including basic household necessities, canned meats, local wines and fruit juices. Dong Dajie is lined with arts and craft stores selling copies of the Mogao paintings, murals and statues in every size, shape and form.

TRANSPORTATION

Daily flights to/from Lanzhou, four times a week (daily during peak season) to/from Urumqi (airport is 13 kilometres east of the city, bus from CAAC booking office on Dong Dajie); several buses per day to/from Liuyuan per day, the closest railhead on the Lanzhou–Urumqi line; daily buses to/from Jiayuguan or Jiuquan; buses to/from Hami depart every other day; irregular service to/from Golmud in Qinghai.

ACCOMMODATION

Silk Road Dunhuang Hotel (Dunhuang Shanzhuang)
Dunyuet Lu. Tel: (0937) 882-2088; fax: (0937) 882-2086;
(Hong Kong booking, tel: (852) 2525 3661; fax: (852) 2537 3790);
email: webmaster@the-silk-road.com; www.the-silk-road.com
敦煌山庄　敦月路
A four-star Han dynasty architectural gem set in gardens. Ethnic Chinese courtyard villas with antique or replica Ming dynasty furniture. Business centre, Western and Chinese restaurants.

Grand Su Hotel (Grand Su Binguan)
5 Shazhou Bei Road. Tel: (0937) 882 9998; fax: (0937) 882 2019
敦煌太阳大酒店　沙州北路 5 号
Four-star hotel situated some distance out of town. A quiet and comfortable place to relax after exploring Dunhuang's treasures.

Dunhuang Hotel (Dunhuang Binguan)
14 East Yangguan Road, eastern end of Dong Dajie. Tel: (0937) 882 2415; fax: (0937) 882 2195
敦煌宾馆　东大街
Four-star hotel with comfortable accommodation primarily for tour groups; Chinese and Western restaurants, bar in the lobby.

Dunhuang International Hotel (Dunhuang Guoji Dajiudian)
28 Ming Shashan Lu. Tel: (0937) 882 8638; fax: (0937) 882 8318
敦煌国际大酒店　鸣沙山路 28 号
Three-star facility located south of the city centre, about 6 km drive away from the Singing Sand Mountains.

FOOD AND DRINK

ike most Han cities, there are many small restaurants throughout the city including a few that serve excellent Sichuan cuisine. Those with English menus are concentrated around the bus station on Dingzi Jie and tend to serve Muslim food. During the afternoon heat, it is best to take refuge in one of the cold drink cafes and have a beer, fruit juice or yoghurt. The night market is the most lively place for dinner: spicy hot pot and mutton skewers are by far the most popular foods as well as noodle soup, flatbreads and cold meats. Around the circle, vendors set up round tables with lounge chairs from where you can drink, eat and watch the action (*sanxiangcha* is served).

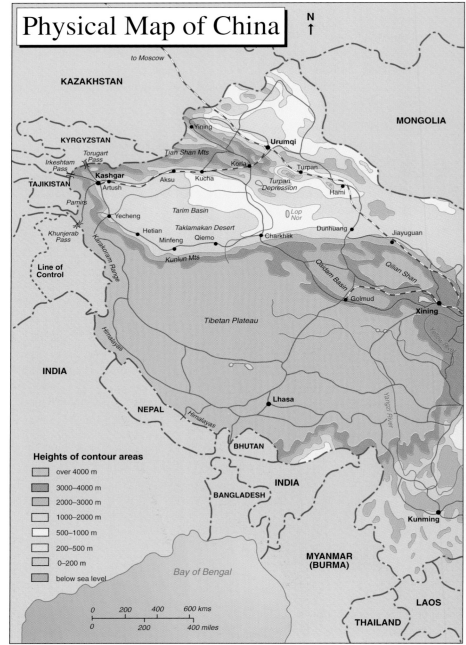

Physical Map of China

N

KAZAKHSTAN

to Moscow

MONGOLIA

KYRGYZSTAN

Yining

Urumqi

Torugart
Pass

Tian Shan Mts

Irkeshtam
Pass

Korla

Turpan

TAJIKISTAN

Kashgar

Artush

Aksu

Kucha

Turpan
Depression

Hami

Pamirs

Yecheng

Tarim Basin

Lop
Nor

Khunjerab
Pass

Hetian

Minfeng

Taklamakan Desert

Qiemo

Charklhik

Dunhuang

Jiayuguan

Line of
Control

Karakoram Range

Kunlun Mts

Qaidam Basin

Qilian Shan

Golmud

Xining

Tibetan Plateau

Himalayas

INDIA

Lhasa

NEPAL

Himalayas

Yangzi River

BHUTAN

Heights of contour areas

- over 4000 m
- 3000–4000 m
- 2000–3000 m
- 1000–2000 m
- 500–1000 m
- 200–500 m
- 0–200 m
- below sea level

INDIA

BANGLADESH

Kunming

MYANMAR
(BURMA)

Bay of Bengal

LAOS

| 0 | 200 | 400 | 600 kms |

| 0 | 200 | 400 miles |

THAILAND

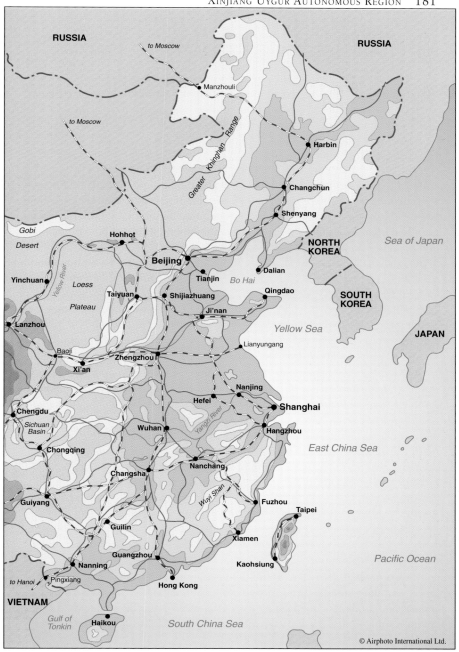

© Airphoto International Ltd.

Xinjiang Uygur Autonomous Region

T he northwest region of Xinjiang ('New Dominion') occupies over 1.6 million square kilometres (over 600,000 square miles), one-sixth of China's territory, making it about the size of Alaska, or three times the size of France. It borders Tibet, Qinghai, Gansu, Inner Mongolia, Mongolia, Kazakhstan, Kyrgyzstan, Uzbekistan, Tajikistan, Afghanistan, Pakistan and India. A region of stunning contrasts—ranging from the Turpan Depression, the lowest point in China, to some of the highest, in the Heavenly Mountains—Xinjiang's many natural sights offer pine-studded mountain pastures, wind-rippled sand dunes, icy jagged peaks, pocked limestone pinnacles, and clear blue fresh- and saltwater lakes. The province has two distinct geographical regions divided into north and south by the **Heavenly Mountains** (**Tian Shan**), which extend the width of the province. North of the Heavenly Mountains is the **Junggar Basin**, a semi-arid expanse of grasslands and marshes irrigated by the **Manas** and **Ulungur** rivers. Pastoral nomadism is the dominant way of life in this region. To the south lies the **Tarim Basin**, where prosperous agricultural oases surround the fearsome **Taklamakan Desert**, which means in Uygur 'enter and never return'. The Taklamakan swallows all rivers except the 1,262-kilometre (789-mile) Hetian-Karakash and the Tarim, which flows around the northern rim.

Divided in ancient times into 36 separate kingdoms, Xinjiang became an area of major strategic importance after the opening of the Silk Road, inducing China to assert its suzerainty whenever it could, the first time under the Han in the first century AD and then, briefly, under the Tang dynasty. The reassertion of Chinese domination and repression during the Qing dynasty eventually led to the Muslim rebellions of 1862–1873, fronted by Yakub Beg. These revolts, which swept through the northwest, were savagely suppressed by the Chinese, and Xinjiang became a province under the Qing rulers in 1884. With the fall of the Qing dynasty in 1911, Xinjiang was left to self-rule; a succession of warlords ruled over Xinjiang until 1949. An attempt to establish an independent state culminated in the founding of the short-lived Eastern Turkestan Republic in 1945. After 'liberation', many of the Muslims welcomed the change in government and the area was declared the Xinjiang Uygur Autonomous Region in 1955.

With a population of over 20 million, Xinjiang is home to 13 nationalities—**Uygur, Kazakh, Han, Hui, Xibo, Mongol, Kirghiz, Uzbek, Manchu, Russian, Tartar, Dahour** and **Tajik**. It is divided into five autonomous prefectures, six autonomous counties, 74 counties, seven prefectures and eight municipalities.

Much of China's mineral wealth lies hidden in the region, including oil, iron, coal, gold, silver, antimony, copper and jade. Oil exploration in co-operation with American, French and Japanese companies is under way deep in the Taklamakan Desert and **Junggar Basin** (see Special Topic on pages 322 and 323). Along the southern rim of the Taklamakan, China tests nuclear weapons and, with the help of French and American teams, has set up nuclear power plants. Agricultural produce includes fruit, vegetables, wheat, rice, sorghum, maize, cotton, tobacco, oil-bearing crops and sugar beets; the Chinese commonly refer to Xinjiang as 'the land of fruits and melons'. On the slopes of the **Altai Mountains** grow spruce, cypress and pine trees.

Xinjiang was subject to a myriad religious and economic influences from the civilizations of India, Greece, Persia and China, and its arid climate provided excellent conditions for the preservation of its buried archeological treasures. Unfortunately, little remains for the modern traveller; much of the wall paintings and statuary have been defaced or are in poor condition. However, this should in no way deter those wishing to visit these magnificent Buddhist grottoes and ancient ruined cities. Over recent decades the region's Cultural Relics Bureau and Archeology Institute have undertaken excavations and explorations in the Taklamakan Desert, the Turpan Depression, the Yili River valley and the Altai district, discovering microlithic tools, nomadic rock carvings, ancient tombs and burial objects, as well as entire cities.

evelopment of the transportation network within Xinjiang continues. The Nanjiang Railway has reached Kashgar. It was completed in 2000, and in the north is the line connecting Urumqi to Almaty via the Turk-Sib route. The region's 24,000 kilometres of roads need constant maintenance and are often blocked by wind blown sands, washed away in flash floods, or rent by earthquake fissures. Despite these challenges, new roads are laid where a few decades ago it would never have been thought possible. Highway 312 for example, opened in 1995, crosses the Taklamakan between Lun Tai in the north and Minfeng in the south (see map on page 184 and Special Topic on pages 322 and 323).

Since the break-up of the USSR, ethnic Russian, Kazakh, Kirghiz and Uzbek traders are flocking into Xinjiang from the newly independent states. They come to sell objects such as Russian overcoats and watches, and return home laden with Chinese goods. In Urumqi and Yining, some hotel discos are filled with Russians. It can take up to seven hours to go through customs at Korgas, the border near Yining, because of the volume of goods and people. Kashgar's famous market now has a special enclosure, the Trading Market for Foreigners, packed with eager buyers and sellers despite the entrance fee. Chinese tourists and traders are increasingly travelling over the borders also, to visit relatives and to make money.

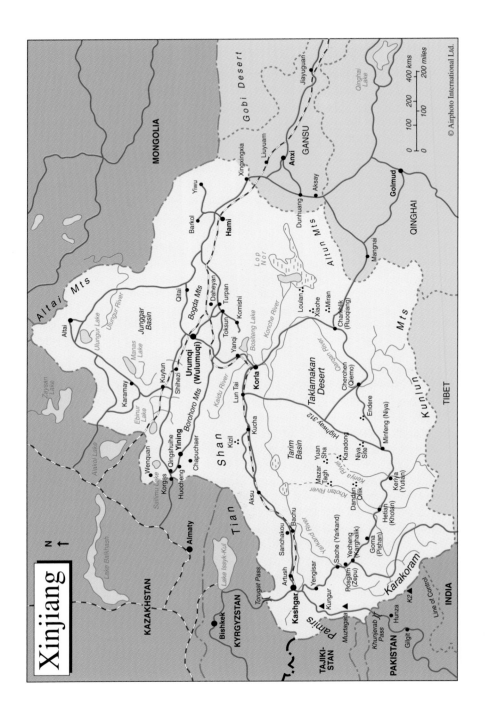

ANXI TO HAMI

he journey by camel or cart along the first leg of the northern Silk Road from Anxi to Hami (the first major town in Xinjiang) usually took two weeks. Cable and French called the desert along this stretch a 'howling wilderness', the monotony broken only by changes in the difficult desert surface. The water at each stop was, by turns, muddy, brackish or sulphurous. Even the indefatigable Xuan Zang, crossing this stretch of desert and finding himself lost and without water, turned back briefly before gathering his determination to continue, half-dead, towards Hami (see Special Topic on page 97).

During the first decades of this century, access to Xinjiang was difficult and time-consuming, requiring passports, permits and frequently the personal approval of the governor hundreds of miles away in Urumqi. Caravans and travellers were required to stop at a very inhospitable rocky ravine known as **Xingxingxia**, where soldiers manning the frontier checkpoint rigorously investigated all-comers. Delays were long and tiresome, and the area was infested with murderous bandits.

HAMI

The city of Hami is the capital of Hami Prefecture, which includes the **Barkol (Balikun) Kazakh Autonomous County** and Yiwu County. The city's population of over 130,000 comprises numerous minority groups, including Uygur, Kazakh, Hui and Mongol, but the majority are Han Chinese.

In 1986, archaeologists excavated more than 80 tombs and discovered 50 well-preserved corpses, complete with fur hats, leather boots and colourful woollen clothing, said to be more than 3,000 years old.

erhaps the earliest reference to Hami (or Yiwu, Yizhou or Kumul, as it was variously known) was in a book made of bamboo slips and bound together with white silk, found in a second-century BC tomb in Henan Province. This record, discovered in the third century, is an account of the quasi-mythical travels of Emperor Mu, the fifth emperor of the Zhou dynasty, who, on returning from his visit to the Queen Mother of the West, stayed in Hami for three days and received gifts of 300 horses and 2,000 sheep and cattle from the local inhabitants.

Hami was considered by the Chinese the key to access to the northwest, but they were not always successful in keeping the city free of nomadic incursions. In AD 73, the Han general, Ban Chao, wrested the area from a Xiongnu army and established a military and agricultural colony. In the sixth and early seventh centuries, Hami was incorporated in turn into the empires of the Eastern and Western Turks, which at their peak stretched from Manchuria westwards to beyond the Aral Sea. But, with the assertive military posture of the Tang emperor Taizong, Hami and many other Central Asian oases had come under the protection of a military protectorate-general by 640. The Buddhist monk, Xuan Zang, spent several weeks in Hami recuperating from his near-fatal desert crossing.

Marco Polo, who traversed the 'province of Kamul' on his way to the court of Kublai Khan in the 13th century, rejoiced at a most hospitable local custom: 'I give you my word,' he wrote, 'that if a stranger comes to a house here to seek hospitality he receives a very warm welcome. The host bids his wife do everything that the guest wishes. Then he leaves the house and goes about his own business and stays away two or three days. Meanwhile the guest stays with his wife in the house and does what he will with her, lying with her in one bed just as if she was his own wife; and they lead a gay life together. The women are beautiful and vivacious and always ready to oblige. ' This adulterous behaviour was frowned upon by one of the Mongol khans, who prohibited its practice. For three years the people of Hami obeyed; then, laden with gifts, they begged the khan to allow them to return to their age-old tradition, 'for their ancestors had declared that by the pleasure they gave to guests with their wives and goods they won the favour of their idols and multiplied the yield of their crops and their tillage.' The perplexed khan replied sternly: 'Since you desire your own shame, you may have it.'

uring the Ming dynasty, Hami sent tribute missions to the emperor and found itself invaded from time to time by its powerful oasis neighbour, Turpan. In 1681, it was annexed by the Oirat Mongols, who had displaced the Chaghatai rulers in their growing Kashgarian Empire.

From 1697 to 1930 a succession of Uygur Hami kings held nominal sway over Hami, first sending tribute to the Qing dynasty, then becoming embroiled in the various Muslim revolts that swept through Xinjiang. In 1880, the brilliant Chinese general, Zuo Zongtang, after defeating the rebel ruler of Kashgar, Yakub Beg, set up his headquarters in Hami in anticipation of a military confrontation with the Russians, who had occupied the Yili Valley region in the west. He contributed to the rebuilding of Hami following a Muslim uprising. In 1887, Sir Francis Younghusband, British explorer, soldier and mystic, noted that the environs of Hami were strewn with ruins and that there were only about 6,000 inhabitants. Younghusband and Colonel M Bell had journeyed overland from Beijing by separate routes, planning to meet up in Hami before travelling on to India together. Younghusband was late and described his eventual meeting with Bell, months afterwards at the end of his journey, as follows:

Colonel Bell told that he really had waited for me a whole day in Hami—this place in the middle of Central Asia, nearly two thousand miles from our starting point—and, astonished at finding I had not turned up to date, had proceeded on his way to India.

ven Hedin and Albert von Le Coq both met the last Hami king before his death in 1930. Von Le Coq was entertained at a banquet accompanied by large quantities of Russian liqueurs and French champagne, which the king, though Muslim, had no qualms about drinking. The rooms of the palace were furnished with jade, porcelain, fine carpets and silk embroideries, and, incongruously, a cuckoo-clock. Hedin described the king as 'a portly little man of 70 years, with a reddish complexion, friendly eyes, aquiline nose, and snow-white beard'. Northeast of the city the king had a summer palace, an amalgam of Chinese and Persian architecture, with a beautiful garden encompassing the ancient ruins of a Buddhist temple.

Upon the king's death, 'princely state' status gave way to Chinese bureaucracy, characterized by overbearing tax 'reforms' and insensitive Han officials, resulting in a rebellion that spread across Xinjiang under the leadership of the young Muslim, Ma Zhongying. Hami at that time consisted of three walled towns—old, new and native Uygur. But a traveller passing through soon after the rebellion wrote: 'Ruins lay everywhere, and most of the native city had been reduced to heaps of rubble.'

Today, Hami, the eastern gateway to Xinjiang, is a rich agricultural oasis fed by more than 100 underground water channels, or *karez*, which bring cold water from the melting snows of the Heavenly Mountains. During the summer months, Hami produces its famous melons, hops and many other kinds of fruit, grains and pulses.

ore than 30 types of Hami *gua* (melon) are grown here as well as watermelons, although the Chinese consider those grown in adjacent Shanshan County the best. The delicious, crisp and fragrant melons were sent by the kings of Hami as a tribute to the Qing court of Emperor Qianlong, who was delighted with their texture and flavour, hence the name Hami melon. The fields around the city are devoted to the cultivation of these melons, of which more than 40,000 tons are produced annually. They ripen from late June, when they begin appearing in the markets, but are sweetest in September.

The district has natural resources of coal, iron, gold, rock salt, titanium and tungsten. Industrial output includes carpets, cement, clothing, plastics, beer and canned fruits. Like Turpan, Hami is in a fault depression about 200 metres below sea level, and temperatures are extreme, from a high of 43°C (109°F) in summer to a low of –32°C (–26°F) in winter.

UYGUR FOOD, DRINK AND A FEW WORDS

A lthough Uygur cuisine is less varied and complex than those of Sichuan, Yunnan and other parts of China, it maintains a spicy edge that blends well with the selection of meat and vegetables available. *Laghman* is found everywhere—a mutton stir-fry with fresh eggplant, string beans, tomatoes, and hot green peppers served over thick noodles. Rice is rarely eaten except on special occasions and on Sundays at the bazaar when small restaurants prepare *poluo*, a tasty fried rice pilaf prepared with squash or mutton, accompanied by *manta*, a thin-skinned dumpling filled with mutton and onion. Despite the intense heat, the most common midday meal is *chushira*, a hearty wonton soup spiced with red peppers and herbs. Night markets and bazaars are never without *kebab* vendors—and a choice of grilled mutton, fat or liver skewers—or clay bread-making ovens that make a wide variety of *nan*, flatbreads that are salty, sweet, filled with meat or plain. Another product of these ovens, popular with tea in the morning, is *samsa*, a small square packet of dough filled with mutton fat and onions, and baked like bread. *Apke* is hard to miss in the bazaar (roughly translated as goat's head soup), it consists of a large cauldron with the goat's head prominiently displayed atop a coil of intestines that have been cleaned, stuffed with meat, flour, eggs and oil, and then reunited in a simmering broth with the remaining entrails.

For drink, the Uygurs prefer a rough, broken black *chai* (tea), sold in bricks that are indistinguishable from pressed sticks and twigs. A popular summer drink (best in Turpan) is made from the juice of rehydrated peaches or apricots, known by its Chinese name *bingshui*, literally 'cold water'. *Durap*—a refreshing mixture of chipped ice, fresh yoghurt and sweet honey—and hand-churned vanilla ice cream, *maroji*, are extremely popular in Kashgar and along the southern Silk Road.

Uygurs speak a Turkic-Altaic language influenced over time by various Central Asian dialects; very few understand Mandarin and they are delighted to hear foreigners make an attempt at their language. The following word list, with no excuses for the transliteration, is only a start:

es salaam aleikum—peace be upon you	*wa aleikum es salaam*—and upon you
yakshee musiss?—how are you?	*yakshee*—good
yakshee emess—no good	*harashor*—great
haah—yes	*emess*—no
kanj pul?—how much?	*kanj kilomitir?*—how many kilometres?
rachmet—thank you	*kechurung*—excuse me/sorry
kosh—goodbye	*posh*—get out of the way
sen ismim nema?—what is your name?	*sen naden kelding?*—where are you from?
tamaka—tobacco	*mohorka*—Xinjiang blend rolled in
bazaar—market	newspaper
ash—food	*autobuz*—bus
ashkana—restaurant	*bir*—one, *shkia*—two, *yuetch*—three,
lamaz—mosque	*tut*—four, *beich*—five, *oute*—six,
mazar—tomb	*yete*—seven, *sekiz*—eight,
bilhet—ticket	*tukus*—nine, *oun*—ten
biket—bus station	

A Uygur family at home in Urumqi

SIGHTS

TOMBS OF THE HAMI KINGS

 ituated in the leafy, mud-walled suburbs two kilometres (just over a mile) south of the city, these are Hami's most important remaining monument. Only two or three of the nine kings appear to be buried here with their families. The tombs are said to have been built by the seventh king (with the Qing government contributing 20,000 taels of silver) and completed around 1840, after more than 20 years' construction. However, the royal tombs may date from the early 18th century: a stone tablet, dated 1706, was erected at the palace (no longer extant), stating that carpenters had been invited from Beijing to construct a number of large-scale buildings for the beautification of the city.

The poorly preserved tomb complex has two mud-brick mausoleums with Islamic domes surmounting multi-tiered, wooden, Chinese-style eaves. The interior of one is painted in a blue-and-white flower design. The third mausoleum is completely Islamic in style, square with a domed roof, its high walls and façade decorated in blue, turquoise and white tiles. A large mosque, whose four walls are inscribed with religious scriptures and colourful designs, completes the complex.

Nearby stand the remains of the old city wall, extending for about 100 metres, which once protected the palace. Further west is an ancient poplar tree called the Nine Dragon Tree and a tiny mosque used by the local villagers.

GAI SI'S TOMB

This lies on the same road, closer to the city—a simple mud-brick hall with a wooden verandah and green-tiled dome. This *mazar*, or holy tomb, is dedicated to the memory of Gai Si, one of the three Muslim missionaries believed to have come from the Middle East during the seventh century. Gai Si died at Xingxingxia, where the Hami kings later erected a simple memorial to him. In 1945, local Hami Muslims collected money to build the present *mazar*, and his remains, scattered during the military occupation of Xingxingxia in 1939, were gathered here. A large number of people participated in the reburial ceremony; the holy man's beard was, it is said, miraculously still intact.

THE HAMI CULTURAL OFFICE MUSEUM

Situated on Jianguo Lu, this houses the corpses and other finds from the 3,000-year-old graves excavated at Wupu, 20 kilometres (12 miles) southwest of Hami. The graves were excavated first in 1978 and again in 1986. Fifty corpses were unearthed from the graves, along with large quantities of brightly coloured striped woollen cloth, a full-length cloak in excellent condition, pottery and wooden utensils. Research on the corpses is being carried out at museums in Urumqi, Shanghai and Beijing.

Of particular interest is a carved 'stone man' gravestone from the fifth or sixth century. A few of these (some several metres high) are scattered about the grasslands of northern Xinjiang, marking graves of the Eastern and Western Turkic period, and are primitively but powerfully carved. No other museum in Xinjiang displays the 'stone man' carvings. There are also samples of Neolithic rock carvings from the northern part of the Hami region, depicting camels, wild goats and scenes of hunting and warfare. These are similar to carvings on rock faces in the northern Altai Mountains and in Hunza, Pakistan.

Lafuqueke

One of a number of ancient city ruins in the Hami area, this lies 60 kilometres (40 miles) southwest of Hami, and is thought to have been a county seat during the Tang dynasty. The extensive ruins, some 600 m (2,000 ft) long and half as wide, include remains of a Buddhist temple (with traces of frescoes), a dagoba, barracks and watchtowers. The site is unexcavated and lies partly under cultivated fields and a graveyard.

Hami Practical Information

The city is spread out and has little character. Most visitors only overnight in Hami before continuing on to either Turpan or Dunhuang. Transport is by road or rail: daily buses to/from Turpan and Urumqi, every other day to/from Dunhuang; several trains daily either way on the Lanzhou-Urumqi line.

Accommodation

ither across the street from the bus station at the **Dong Ying Guesthouse** (Dong Ying Zhao Dai Suo), tel (0902) 223-3296, basic facilities with communal toilets and public showers (double Rmb34), or at the **Hami District Guesthouse** on Jianguo Nan Lu, tel (0902) 223-3140, a 15-minute walk from the bus station, a large complex beyond a shaded park with Chinese and Muslim restaurants, travel services and bike rental (dorm Rmb80 for four beds, double Rmb280).

Food and Drink

Available at the Nong Mao night market, a large outdoor market lined on both sides with small Chinese and Muslim restaurants, just behind the bus station off Bing He Lu: kebabs and nan, cold and fried noodles with mutton and vegetables, Hami *pijiu* as well as local fruit in season.

Yili (Ili) Kazakh Autonomous Prefecture

The Yili (Ili) Kazakh Autonomous Prefecture lies along the border with the CIS. Its capital, Yining, is closer to the Kazakhstan city of **Almaty** than to Urumqi and only 60 kilometres (35 miles) from the border. The prefecture takes its name from the Yili

THE SWORD OF PURITY

slam was first introduced to China by Arab traders and missionaries travelling along the Silk Road during the Tang dynasty. In Xinjiang, Islam pervades almost every facet of society: the *muezzin's* call to prayer from the minarets of the many mosques spread throughout the oasis towns, the ubiquitous skull caps worn by all men, the copies of the Koran and other religious material piled up in front of the mosques, the veiled women in the bazaar—all are constant reminders of the devotion and pervading existence of this belief. After Muhammad's death, holy men, travelling to the Indian subcontinent and east to China along the Silk Road, converted many to Islam; Arab sea traders built mosques and made converts in South China, in Guangzhou and Xiamen.

Islam—Arabic for 'submission to God'—was founded by the Prophet Muhammad, born in the city of Mecca (Saudia Arabia) in AD 570. Muhammad declared that there was but one God; he saw himself as God's messenger and preached a universal brotherhood in which all men were equal. As an able statesman and commander, he unified the Arab nations. The people of the Middle East were ready to accept Muhammad's new religion after centuries of fighting splintered khanate wars. Islam flourished, and within a century it had stretched from Persia to Spain.

Every Muslim has five fundamental religious duties, known as the Pillars of Islam. He must recite the creed, *La illaha illa 'llah Muhammad Rasulu llah* ('There is no God but Allah, and Muhammad is his prophet'), pray five times a day facing Mecca, fast during the month of *Ramadan*, give alms to the poor and make a pilgrimage to Mecca.

he Koran is the holy book of Islam, consisting of written and oral records compiled during Muhammad's lifetime and in the years immediately following his death. It contains the philosophy and moral code of Islam and is considered the true word of God as revealed to Muhammad; it is the supreme authority to which every Muslim looks for guidance. The teachings of Islam were first revealed at Creation but since then man has continually erred and God's prophecy has become obscured with false interpretations. Prophets are periodically

sent to earth by God to reaffirm his word; they are considered divine and include the Hebrew patriarchs, Abraham and Moses, as well as Jesus. Muhammad was sent by God to restore purity. He was the last prophet; the next will be the Messiah. Muslims call the followers of prophets—including Jews and Christians—*ahl-e-kitab*: 'People of the Book'.

Islam suffered a major split immediately after the death of Muhammad in 632. Since he had not clearly named a successor, there were violent power struggles and two main sects emerged: the Sunnis, the larger sect (to which the Uygurs belong), who follow elected leaders called *caliphs*; and

An elderly gentleman of Turpan

the smaller sect, the Shias (or Shiites), led by hereditary leaders called 'imams', direct descendants of Muhammad through his daughter Fatima. The Ismailis, the followers of Aga Kahn (an offshoot of the Shias), include the Tajiks of western Xinjiang.

River, which flows from the Heavenly Mountains into Kazakhstan. In the second century BC, clans of the Yuezhi tribe, driven westwards by the Xiongnu, attempted to settle here but were pushed southwestwards by the Turkic-speaking, nomadic Wusun tribe who, according to Chinese historians, had blue eyes and red beards. They established control over the Yili River valley and founded the Wusun state. In his second mission to the Western Regions, Zhang Qian in 119 BC initiated diplomatic relations between the Wusun and the Han court, which eventually led to the introduction of the 'heavenly' horse to China. The **Kazakhs** are the descendants of the Wusun and today total over 365,000, outnumbered by the Han Chinese and Uygurs in the prefecture's overall population of over 1.6 million. Most Kazakhs live in yurts in the surrounding grasslands and foothills of the Heavenly Mountains.

 ili's rich pasturelands were trampled by almost every Central Asian power from the Xiongnu to the Chinese. In 744, a Tang-dynasty army defeated the ruling Western Turkic Khanate, strengthening the Chinese control of the new northern Silk Road by-passing the Caspian Sea. In 1218, Genghis Khan annexed Yili. Upon his death in 1227, his four sons inherited the great Mongol empire. Chaghatai, the second son, inherited Turkestan, Xinjiang and most of Khorasan, and is thought to have made his capital in **Almalik**, near Yining. The Mongols established strong East–West land communications, and a number of papal envoys from Rome eventually traversed the region, converting locals as they went. In 1340, Richard of Burgundy and five other friars were murdered by Muslims at Almalik, where a Catholic church had been built and a Nestorian community also existed. In the latter part of the 13th century, Kublai Khan garrisoned troops here under the command of his son. Subsequently, the mighty Tamerlane, Kublai Khan's accomplished grandson, inherited control over the area.

During the 16th century Kirghiz and Kazakh hordes made frequent incursions into the Yili River valley, until they were ultimately defeated by the Oirat Mongols. The Qing emperor Qianlong defeated the Oirats in 1758 after an arduous campaign in the Junggar Basin, where tens of thousands of Mongols were massacred. The Qing government established the headquarters of the Yili General in Huiyuan City and founded a military colony at Yining, where large numbers of settlers (Chinese convicts and exiles, Uygurs, Manchus and others) were brought in to farm and develop new land, a policy that successive Chinese governments were to emulate. The nomadic pastoral community also increased in numbers with the arrival of 70, 000 Buddhist Mongol Torguts fleeing tsarist Russia.

When Yakub Beg's rebellion spread to Yili in 1871, the Russians occupied the area and stayed for a decade, until the Treaty of St Petersburg was signed, giving Russia trade, customs and consular rights in Xinjiang (and a nine-million-rouble indemnity) in return for most of the territory it had seized.

In 1944, a Kazakh-Uygur independence movement established the East Turkestan Republic, which soon came under Soviet influence, and by 1949 Yili was, for all intents and purposes, Russian territory. The Chinese Communist government reasserted its control over the area by sending in large numbers of demobilized Chinese soldiers as production-construction corps, and in 1958 it established pastoral people's communes. By the 1960s, and the Sino-Soviet split, there was much dissatisfaction amongst the **Kazakhs** and **Uygurs**, resulting in a mass exodus of more than 60,000 to the Soviet Union before the borders were closed. Cross-border trade between the two countries resumed in 1984 at Korgas.

KARAKHOTO: THE BLACK CITY

The Russian expeditions to the Taklamakan, though numerous and long-lasting, never yielded a wealth of treasures equal to those of Stein or von Le Coq. In 1905, the Beresovsky brothers went to Kucha but found little. In 1908, the Russians made their first and only significant discovery, when Colonel Pyotr Koslov led an exploratory mission to the Sino-Mongolian border. The expedition came across the remains of a fortress in the Gobi Desert, the old city of Karakhoto, probably what Marco Polo had referred to as the city of Etzina. Koslov reported, 'The walls of the city are covered with sand, in some places so deeply that it is possible to walk up the slope and enter the fortress.' At the west gate they '. . . found a quadrangular space whereon were scattered high and low, broad and narrow, ruins of buildings with rubbish of all kinds at their feet'. Karakhoto had been destroyed 600 years earlier, in the 14th century. The last ruler, Kara Tsian Tsiun, had designs on the Chinese throne and attacked the Chinese, who retaliated with a vengeance. Assaulting Karakhoto, the Chinese cut off the town's only water supply, massacring the inhabitants as they tried to flee, and then levelled the city. Before he was killed, Kara Tsian Tsiun filled the well with the state treasury, supposedly casting a spell over the spot so no one would find it. Koslov missed the gold but did manage to find Buddhist manuscripts, coins and books (enough to fill ten crates) from among the sandy ruins, as well as several Buddhist paintings on silk, linen and paper in a royal tomb. These treasures are now on display at the Hermitage in St Petersburg.

YINING (KULJA)

Yining, called Kulja by the Uygurs, has a rangy, almost wild frontier feel about it. It is now a booming city filled with traders; the faces of its people are a mixture of Russian, Chinese, Kazakh, Mongol, Kirghiz, Tajik, Uzbek, Tartar and others. The buildings of the city are spread out and the centre of the old town is dominated by the grassy Qing Nian Gong Yuan (Young People's Park). There are rose and tulip gardens along the many paths in the park. In the evening, Uygur and Kazakh families and intimate couples have picnics while young and old men sit in separate groups, relaxing, playing chess and smoking *mohorka* and *nishee*. Outside the entrance are several pool tables, where fierce betting takes place after the heat of the day has passed. Since Yining has few Western travellers as of yet, you are bound to become an object of endless but amiable curiosity.

ome of the buildings are Russian-style, designed with grand mouldings and columns, often painted blue and white and crowned with red stars, like the old Yili Hotel on the post office square. Single-storey family residences are decorated with carved wooden window frames, painted bright colours, called *nalichniki* in Russian. Many households maintain flower gardens and often have orchards in their courtyards. Shops supply the basic needs of an agricultural and pastoral community. At the Post Office, professional scribes assist locals in addressing envelopes in various languages to all parts of Central Asia and the Middle East. Russians, Kazakhs, Uygurs and other Turkic minorities send letters and cloth-wrapped parcels of Chinese silk flowers and scarves, candies and shoes to relatives abroad, scattered throughout the republics of Central Asia, Turkey and Australia. Since 1984 a growing number of Central Asian citizens have been coming to Yining, either as tourists or for family reunions.

Among the many minority peoples living in the city are a few hundred Russians, or Eluosi, descendants of 18th-century settlers. They have their own Orthodox church, graveyard and primary school, which opened in 1985. A section of the Yili River is reserved for the exclusive use of the Eluosi fishermen.

There are more than 100 mosques in Yining, frequented mostly by Huis and Uygurs. The largest is the **Uygur Mosque** on Jiefang Nan Lu, built during the reign of Qing emperor Qianlong (reigned 1736–1796). A three-tiered gateway leads to a courtyard and a large, simple prayer hall, which is painted blue and surrounded by a Chinese-style wooden verandah with red beams and flying eaves. A more handsome building is the **Shaanxi Mosque** on Shengli Jie, No 1 Alley. Its ornate Chinese-style gateway is similar to that of the Grand Mosque in Xi'an. Its prayer hall dates from the 18th century.

(left) A seasonal settlement of yurts below the snow-clad Pamir Mountains on the border between Xinjiang and Tajikistan

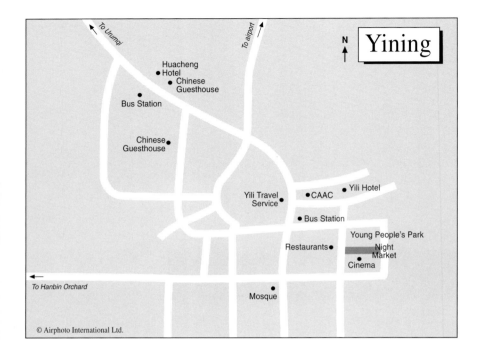

he city's name Yining comes from the Uygur word Kulja meaning 'The Golden Roofed Temple', named after a temple 3.6 kilometres northeast of the city, a famous lamasery built at the end of the Ming dynasty. The temple was destroyed by Amursana of the Junggar tribe and a small fort was built here in 1762 by Emperor Qianlong. Nothing is left but a dirt terrace (the remains of the Qing fort) and to the north, Tibetan statues and tiles with animal designs at the site of the temple.

The Yili Prefecture is the main producer of fruit in northern Xinjiang and its fertile fields yield apples, peaches, pears, apricots, cherries and walnuts. There are several township communes located on the outskirts of Yining where visitors can pick their own fruit. The Hanbin Orchard, located two kilometres west of the city on Xinhua Lu, is an extremely peaceful commune suitable for pleasant walks and shady naps. Large plots of fruit trees are intermixed with small family plots of corn and squash interspersed with wild hemp. Walk, ride a bicycle, or hire a donkey cart; city bus number 3 takes you part of the way.

I n the Yili River valley, the Kazakhs make a goat's cheese called *kurut*—small hard dry cakes with a strong flavour that resembles that of the Greek feta available in Yining. In addition to *kurut*, the Kazakhs enjoy *kumiss*, a strong wine made from fermented mare's milk. The old Russian women of Yining brew an excellent honey and wheat beer known in Kazakh as *piwa*, easily recognized by its rubber cork.

YINING PRACTICAL INFORMATION

Yining is easily accessible by air or road. It is a friendly, easy-going city, definitely worth going out of your way to visit. Tourists should get their Kazhak visas in their home country before visiting Yining.

TRANSPORTATION

Flights to/from Urumqi are scheduled daily (CAAC Booking Office (Tel: 0999/8044328) is in the Yilite Hotel on Jiefang Lu); daily buses to/from Urumqi, Kucha (which continue on to Aksu, Kashgar and Hetian) and other points within the Yili Prefecture depart from the main bus station on Jiefang Lu. The road to Kucha is spectacular, through the lush river valley and grassy foothills of the Heavenly Mountains. It is possible to cross the border to Kazakhstan by road at Korgas, one hour from Yining. However, at present, visas for non-Chinese are only obtainable in Beijing.

ACCOMMODATION

Tao Yuan Hotel (Peach Garden Grand Hotel).
100 Yili River Road. Tel: (0999) 832 5300
桃园大酒店　伊犁河路 100 号
Three-star hotel situated near the Yili River.

Ili Friendship Hotel
7, Third Lane, Stalin Street. Tel: (0999) 802 3901; fax: (0999) 802 4631
伊犁友谊酒店　斯大林街三巷七号
Two-star hotel located in the centre of Yining, 500 metres from the long distance bus station, 5 km from the airport.

Huacheng Hotel (Huacheng Binguan)
Ahemaitijiang Jie, No 7 Alley. Tel: (0999) 812 5050; fax: 812 1640
花城宾馆　阿合买提江街
Close to the main bus station, with a Chinese restaurant and cars for hire.

(following pages) Kazakh herding camels at Sayram Lake, near Yining

Yili Hotel (Yili Binguan)
Jiefang Lu. Tel: (0999) 802 3126; fax: 802 4964
伊犁宾馆   解放路
Clean, comfortable rooms, large shaded gardens and fountains with dance hall and
outdoor pool hall.

FOOD AND DRINK
The Mie Xin Tian Chi Dian on Hong Qi Lu (opposite the Young People's Park) serves
large bowls of tea to accompany sweet breads, pastries, ice cream and tarts in a cool,
spacious Russian-style teahouse. Next door is an even larger Uygur restaurant that
offers the usual *laghman*, *manta*, *samsa*, kebabs and nan. In front of the movie theatre
(on the south side of the park), carts sell dried fruit, nuts and small dry cakes of *kurut*.
On the same street there are many food stalls that specialize in *apke*, cold noodles,
and kebabs—a rowdy night market atmosphere with lots of drinking. Do not forget
to try *piwa*, the local brew with the rubber stopper made by the old Russian women
of Yining. Curbside refrigerators sell fresh or frozen yoghurt, ice cream, cold drinks
and other refreshments.

QAPQAL (CHAPUCHAER) XIBO AUTONOMOUS COUNTY

he Qapqal (Chapuchaer) Xibo Autonomous County lies 20 kilometres (12
miles) southwest of Yining. Among the pilgrims Emperor Qianlong sent to
settle in the Yili region were soldiers of the **Xibo** nationality, whose
homeland is in present-day Liaoning Province, far away in northeast China near
North Korea. In 1764, the soldiers and their families, numbering over 3,000, set off
on a westward trek that took them a year to complete; they travelled in small Mongol-
style carts with tin-rimmed wooden wheels, copies of which can be seen in the
Guandi Temple. Originally these settlers were to stay for three years, but the emperor
extended their sentence to six. Petitions to return to their homeland resulted in a
further extension of 60 years, so the Xibos gave up all hope of returning and gradually
established eight walled towns, opening up the land to agriculture and jealously
guarding their cultural heritage. Their descendants (the eighth and ninth generations)
now number 18,000. They have retained their language and script (similar to
Manchu), unlike their 50,000 or so brethren in the northeast. On the 18th day of the
fourth lunar month, the Xibo commemorate the day their ancestors set off on their
westward journey by holding picnics and archery and wrestling contests. The Xibo
have strong, sturdy physiques, square jaws and flattish faces. Some of the old women
continue to wear traditional dress, a long, dark-blue gown over black trousers and
a white head cloth. They are expert archers and many young athletes from this county
compete in China's Olympic team.

HORSES

China's ability to maintain control over Central Asia and the lucrative Silk Road trade rested, ironically, on trade with the same nomadic barbarian tribes that presented the most serious threat to Chinese rule. One of the most sought-after commodities of this trade was horses.

The growing power of nomadic peoples occupying vast stretches of forest, tundra and desert lay in their horsemanship and manoeuvrability. The introduction of the stirrup, in the third century BC (if not earlier), which freed the riders' hands, gave the nomadic warriors a superiority in the saddle recorded to this day in the English expression 'Parthian shot', initially a reference to the Parthian's ability to turn in the saddle and discharge arrows at pursuers.

The building of the Great Wall was the reaction of China's sedentary, agricultural society against attacks from the mounted, roving Xiongnu armies that threatened Qin dynasty territory in the second century BC.

From far-off Ferghana (in present-day Uzbekistan), 5,000 kilometres northwest of Chang'an, news came of divine 'blood-sweating' horses renowned for their stamina and speed. Anxious to improve the stock of his military mounts, the Han emperor Wudi in 102 BC dispatched an army of 40,000 men to demand a supply of these mounts from the Ferghana court. The Han forces were defeated, and a second army of 60,000 troops had to be dispatched to smooth negotiations before 3,000 of these highly-prized horses could be brought back along the Silk Road to the Chinese capital. The horses did in fact appear to sweat blood, but this seems to have been caused by a mundane skin bacteria rather than any special genetic trait.

From Kucha there were stories of a breed of 'dragon horses', the alleged progeny of lake dragons and wild mares. From Kushan came 'heavenly horses', said to be able to take one up among the celestial realm. Arabian steeds came from Bokhara and Samarkand in Transoxiana. The short, sturdy Mongolian pony was a comparatively common breed in China, but capable of travelling long distances under adverse conditions.

Successive Chinese dynasties used imaginative methods to ensure a steady supply of war chargers and post-route horses to stock the imperial stables. The more devious strategies included political intrigue, marriages of Chinese princesses to distant rulers, and the detention of sons of chieftains for 'education' in the Chinese capital. In the mid-seventh century, a marriage was arranged between a Turkish khan and a Chinese princess for the price of 50,000 horses as well as numerous camels and sheep.

D uring the Sui and Tang dynasties, special frontier towns became centres of barter trade, where Chinese silk was exchanged for Central Asian horses. The Song and Ming courts even created a government monopoly on tea (an important barter item) to guarantee the means to meet the ever-growing demand for horses.

During the Tang dynasty, Uygurs and Tibetans were the main suppliers. In the mid-eighth century there was a minimum requirement of 80,000 cavalry horses to serve the 490,000 frontier troops, not to mention the number of steeds to combat domestic uprisings within China proper. When the Tibetans overran the Tang capital of Chang'an in 763 and occupied the main imperial pastures in western Gansu, the Tang government was forced to beg for assistance from the powerful Uygur Turks, shrewd businessmen who demanded 40 bolts of silk for one poor quality horse. In the late Tang, China had to barter one million bolts of silk for 100,000 horses annually, a heavy financial burden on a country already plagued with internal strife. The Tibetans slowly replaced the Uygurs as the sole horse suppliers.

Horses as well as the spoils of war were inevitably part of any tribute mission to China. Horse hides and tails—even the penis of a white horse— were highly valued gifts. Hides were made into saddle cloths, coracle-boats and even armour.

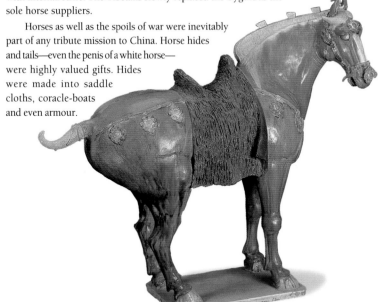

Tri-colour pottery horse (Tang dynasty, 618–907 AD), unearthed at the tomb of prince Yide, Qian County, Shaanxi Province

Decorative horse tails were affixed to sword sheaths or, as with the Mongols, to military banners and standards. Mixed with honey and wine, the dried penis of a white horse was said to restore virility.

The finest animals were assigned to the imperial stables near Chang'an to be groomed as mounts for royal hunting forays, palace guards or for courtiers as a form of political favour. Polo had been introduced to Central Asia during the Tang dynasty and was a popular sport among aristocrats. During the reign of Xuanzong (713–742) exquisitely caparisoned horses were trained to dance to music and perform for the emperor's birthdays.

Chinese literature, sculpture, painting and music glorified the beauty and stamina of these invaluable beasts. A renowned painting shows the legendary exploits of the Eight Bayards of Emperor Mu of the Zhou dynasty, which carried him a thousand *li* (500 kilometres) a day on his visit to the sacred Kunlun Mountains in southern Xinjiang, where the emperor had his legendary encounter with the goddess Queen Mother of the West. The grace and strength of the Han-dynasty charges were commemorated in stone sculptures placed before the imperial tombs. Poems and songs were composed to the Six Steeds of Emperor Taizong (627–650) that bravely carried him into battle, especially his famed red roan, which survived five arrows in a charge.

During the Yuan dynasty, the insatiable Mongol demand for horses, needed for maintaining their fast and efficient pony express system serving all of Central Asia, was easily met within the wide expanses of the Mongol Empire. The succeeding Ming dynasty, however, was forced to establish a special Horse Trading Office in Shaanxi Province, with branches in Hami and Dunhuang.

Pottery warrior figure on horseback (Weastern Han dynasty, 206 BC–8 AD), Unearthed in 1965 at Yangjiawan, in Shaanxi Province

HUOCHENG COUNTY

 ifty kilometres (30 miles) northwest of Yining is Huocheng County and its several historical monuments. The land surrounding the county seat is cultivated with fields of purple lavender, wheat, maize, hops, vegetables, sunflowers and other oil-yielding plants. A sand-burrowing land tortoise is unique to this area.

In the small farming township of **Huiyuan**, 30 kilometres from Yining on the road to Korgas, is a three-storey Drum Tower dating from 1883, which stands at the main intersection of this dusty town. It was part of a small garrison town for Manchu troops, but all that remains beside the Drum Tower are sections of the city wall, a few rooms of the old Yili military headquarters and a garden with four oak trees planted by Lin Zexu. It was his stringent anti-opium policies in Guangzhou that led to the First Opium War in 1840. Commissioner Lin was exiled to the Yili region in 1842, where he is fondly remembered for constructing irrigation canals and opening up wasteland to agriculture. The 'old' city of Huiyuan, on the steep bank of the Yili River, seven kilometres (four miles) west, was built in 1763 as a garrison town for some 20, 000 Manchu troops. But it became partly inundated when the river changed course and was abandoned for the 'new' town. The site is now farmed by Uygurs, but long sections of the city wall remain.

North of the town of Qingshuihe (where the road forks westwards to the CIS border and northwards to Sayram Lake) is a turn off to the village of **Masar**. In this village stands the lovely turquoise-, purple- and white-tiled Persian-style **Tomb of Telug Timur**, who was Khan of Mogholistan (part of the Chaghatai Khanate) from 1347 to 1364. He was decisive and energetic, and his circumcision and conversion to Islam, along with 160,000 followers, marked a religious turning point for the mainly Buddhist and shamanist herdsmen of the region. His military exploits took him as far south as the Hindu Kush. Telug Timur also named as his son's adviser the young Tamerlane, a fact which inaugurated the latter's meteoric rise to power.

The high-arched entrance to the tomb is inscribed in Arabic; the tiles and decorations on the lower section of the facade are gone, baring the bricks. Inside are two small ante-rooms, and a series of niches supports a high, domed ceiling. Two memorial caskets stand in the centre, around which pilgrims kneel while praying aloud. An inside staircase leads to the narrow circular corridor on the upper floor and then up to the roof, where there is a view across a low mountain range marking the border. The smaller, simple white tomb of Telug's sister stands alongside.

SAYRAM LAKE (SAILIMU HU)

The poplar-lined road to Urumqi winds through Huocheng County for about 180 kilometres (112 miles) before reaching the foothills of the Heavenly Mountains and Sayram Lake, some 2,000 metres (6,600 feet) above sea level. This stunning and peaceful lake is on the border of the **Yili Kazakh** and **Bortala Mongolian Autonomous Prefectures**. The lake measures 90 metres at its deepest point, and although the water is salty, it freezes over in winter. In summer the mountain slopes and wide grassy fringes support the yurts of **Kazakh** and **Mongolian** herdsmen who bring their horses, cattle, sheep and camels to graze. Wild strawberries, mushrooms, small yellow irises and other grassland flowers are trampled underfoot each July, when 3,000 or more Kazakhs hold a outdoor *nadam* for six days, much like a summer fair with horse-racing, sheep-tossing, wrestling, 'girl-chasing' riding competitions and much feasting.

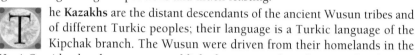he **Kazakhs** are the distant descendants of the ancient Wusun tribes and of different Turkic peoples; their language is a Turkic language of the Kipchak branch. The Wusun were driven from their homelands in the Hexi Corridor but became an established power in the Yili region by the first century BC, when Chinese envoy Zhang Qian courted them (see Special Topic on page 94). Kazakhs have traditionally been divided into four main clans, to which smaller clans owed allegiance, and were led by *begs* chosen for their strong leadership skills. As many as three generations live in a single yurt, hung with embroidered curtains to create more rooms for privacy. Families rarely split up, for it takes many hands to tend the large herds of sheep and horses. Following the birth of a Kazakh child, the mother names her baby after the first thing that comes into her mind when she leaves the yurt on the second day, resulting in many beguilingly simple Kazakh names. The mobile Kazakh children are formally educated in one of three ways: roving schools that follow the nomadic households; horseback schools, where a teacher rides out to a group of children or they to him; and boarding schools for the older students. Most Kazakhs finish their education at 15 years of age. There is a small country guesthouse beside the lake.

URUMQI (WULUMUQI)

Urumqi (meaning 'Beautiful Pastures' in Mongolian, but today a misnomer) is the capital of the Xinjiang Uygur Autonomous Region. It is the political, economic, scientific and technological centre of Xinjiang, and one of the least interesting cities in the region. Urumqi's industrial plants, educational institutes and commercial activities are the hub of Xinjiang's economy. It is the regional centre for road, rail and air communications and is inhabited by 1.5 million people. Urumqi is the most

modern and least Muslim city in Xinjiang; it was settled relatively recently and did not play a role in early Silk Road trade.

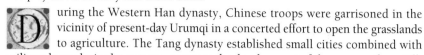uring the Western Han dynasty, Chinese troops were garrisoned in the vicinity of present-day Urumqi in a concerted effort to open the grasslands to agriculture. The Tang dynasty established small cities combined with military barracks in the area to encourage the development of the new northern Silk Road. In 1767, a city was established on the east bank of the Urumqi River, settled by Chinese soldiers and exiles, and given the name Dihua in 1762. Dihua in Chinese means 'to enlighten and civilize', which appeared to be the attitude of the Qing-dynasty rulers towards the local minorities. The town grew in importance with the opening of silver and lead mines as well as Emperor Qianlong's military expansion into the Junggar region. An independent Muslim rebellion swept through the city in 1864, led by Tuoming, who declared himself the 'Pure and True Muslim King', but was soon defeated by Yakub Beg's Kashgarian troops in Kucha.

Dihua was declared the capital of Xinjiang Province in 1882. It became a city of spies and intrigue, where the governors were virtual warlords and succession to the post was frequently contested with violence. Dinner parties were infamous stages for overthrowing contenders for power. In 1916, Governor Yang Zengxin invited all whom he suspected of disloyalty to a banquet and while he ate heartily and the military band played on, his dinner guests had their heads severed one by one. At another banquet in 1928, the governor himself and several officials were executed in a hail of bullets. The new governor and the Russian consul rode through the city in an open carriage escorted by 40 mounted Cossacks. Soviet Russian influence became all-pervasive.

Foreign Devils on the Silk Road by Peter Hopkirk is an excellent account of the race for buried archaeological treasures in the early 20th century. In it Hopkirk records Albert von Le Coq's first experience in Urumqi in 1904:

> ne of the first things they witnessed on arrival was a particularly cruel form of execution in progress in the town's main street. The victim was incarcerated in a specially built cage known as a *kapas*. His head, firmly secured, stuck out of the top, while his feet rested on a board. The latter was gradually lowered, day by day, until on about the eighth day his neck finally broke. The traffic went on as usual past this barbaric apparatus. A melon dealer sits surrounded by his fruit, totally unperturbed by his neighbour's dying agonies.

The city (also called Hongmiaozi or 'Red Temple' by locals) was divided into three: a Chinese walled city, a native walled city and a Russian refugee settlement. The latter was home to poverty-stricken refugees—their houses clustered about the Russian Consulate-General and an Orthodox church—and a hive of intrigue between

Sayram Lake in Yili

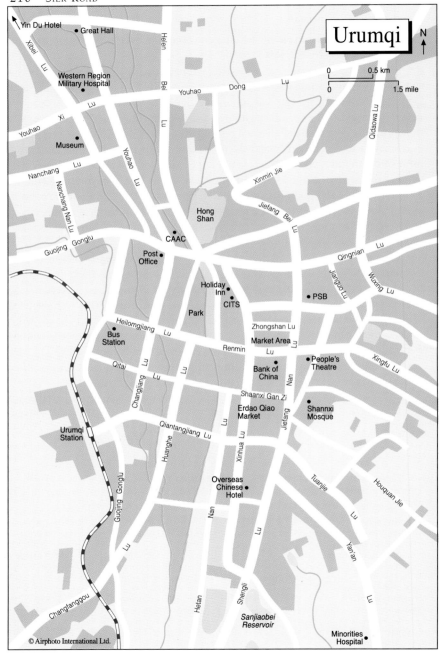

Urumqi

N

0   0.5 km
0   1.5 mile

Yin Du Hotel
Great Hall
Western Region
Military Hospital
Xibei   Lu
Helen
Bei
Youhao
Dong   Lu
Qidaowa Lu
Youhao   Xi
Lu
Museum
Nanchang
Lu
Youhao
Lu
Nanchang Nan Lu
Xinmin Jie
Jiefang   Bei   Lu
Hong
Shan
Guojing   Gonglu
CAAC
Post
Office
Qingnian   Lu
Wuxing Lu
Holiday
Inn
CITS
PSB
Jianguo Lu
Park
Zhongshan Lu
Heilomgjiang   Lu
Bus
Station
Market Area
Lu
Renmin   Lu
People's
Theatre
Xingfu Lu
Qitai
Changjiang
Lu
Lu
Bank of
China
Nan
Shaanxi Gan Zi
Erdao Qiao
Market
Jiefang   Lu
Shannxi
Mosque
Urumqi
Station
Qiantangjiang Lu
Huanghe
Xinhua Lu
Overseas
Chinese
Hotel
Nan
Tuanjie
Houquan Jie
Guojing Gonglu
Lu
Lu
Hetan
Shengli
Yan'an
Lu
Changfanggou
Sanjiaobei
Reservoir
Minorities
Hospital

© Airphoto International Ltd.

Red and White Russian factions. Rain turned the rubbish-strewn streets into mud pits so deep that, according to Sven Hedin, writing in the 1920s: 'During our stay two horses were drowned and even children are said to have perished.' Like China's customs office, the postal service was run by foreigners. Mail took 45 days to get to Beijing but only 28 days to London, carried first by couriers and then by Russian trains. Urumqi was linked to Beijing by telegraph, but the Muslim rebellion that enveloped Xinjiang in the 1930s destroyed the line. The rebellion also frustrated the attempts of the Eurasia Air Line (a Sino-German enterprise) to run regular flights from China to Europe via Urumqi.

In 1935, Soviet troops were invited by Governor Sheng Shicai to help quell Ma Zhongying's Muslim rebellion: aid included a five-million-rouble loan, weapons and advisers. In exchange the Russians were granted exclusive trading, mineral and petroleum rights. Strong Russian influence was evident after 1949 and continued until the Sino-Soviet split in 1960.

Urumqi stands at 900 metres (3,000 feet) above sea level, just below the northern foothills of the **Heavenly Mountains (Tian Shan)**. The snow-clad **Bogda Peak**, 70 kilometres (40 miles) to the east, dominates the skyline on clear days. Urumqi's population is mostly Han, but includes Hui, Uygur, Kazakh, Manchu, Mongol, Xibo and Russian minorities as well. The city is developing rapidly and has set up joint-venture projects with numerous foreign firms; the Urumqi-Moscow railway opened for passengers in late 1991.

SIGHTS

rumqi's main streets are wide and tree-lined, along which open water channels help cool the air. The skyline is changing rapidly with high-rise construction. In the last few years emphasis has been placed on Uygur-style architecture, notable examples being the Great Hall opposite the Kunlun Hotel and the Minorities Hospital on Yan'an Lu. There are a few handsome Russian-style buildings, with green corrugated-iron roofs, stucco facades painted blue, yellow and white, and classically columned porticoes dating from the 1950s. A particularly attractive example is the Western Region Military Hospital on Youhao Lu.

The city has well over 100 mosques, many built after 1978, when the Communist Party adopted a more relaxed attitude towards religion. The largest is the **Shaanxi Mosque**, on Heping Nan Lu, just southeast of the People's Theatre on Nanmen Square. Built during the Qing dynasty with money contributed by Muslims in Shaanxi Province, this Chinese-style mosque is a brick and wood structure with an elaborate, green-tiled roof topped with the Islamic crescent. The prayer hall, with large red pillars and painted eaves, can accommodate up to 500 for religious services. Outside the mosques, vendors offer copies of the Koran and holy commentaries printed in Arabic.

YANGHANG MOSQUE

Also known as the Tartar Mosque, and standing at the southern end of Jiefang Lu, this huge complex of 3,000 square metres, was built in 1897 with private donations from the Tartar community. The dome is a Tartar-style octagonal pyramid adorned with a crescent and wood-and-brick geometric carvings, since Islam strictly prohibits the use of idols or animal figures in its religious artwork. This mosque is the main centre of worship for Muslims in Urumqi, containing classrooms for teaching the Koran and dormitories for the imam.

SOUTHERN MOSQUE

This was moved in 1919 to its present location in the Erdao Qiao Market area on Jiefang Lu. The convex-shaped prayer hall has two layers of raised eaves covered with glazed tiles above a colourfully painted panel. Two walls of the passageway leading to the prayer hall are decorated with carved orchids, plums, bamboo and lotuses. The compound includes a washing room for use before prayers.

More than 20 seminaries throughout the city train young men from the age of 16 to become *ahuns* (teachers) and translators of Islamic scriptures. One Russian Orthodox and four Christian churches hold regular services.

STREET LIFE

 Xinhua Lu is a busy shopping street with modern department stores and offices. The shops along Jiefang Bei Lu are typical single-storey Chinese stores selling everyday merchandise, whereas the southern section of the street, Jiefang Nan Lu, has a more distinctive Uygur atmosphere, with mosques and traditional markets. This is a good area for experiencing Uygur city life—carpet sellers display vividly-coloured Hetian wool rugs and felt mats, and bootmakers labour on the knee-length leather boots worn by Uygur men and Kazakh women. The delicious aroma of fresh-baked nan bread emanates from bakeries. Milliners display the broad, flat caps that are an indispensable item in every Uygur's outfit. Animal skin traders and black-market money changers bargain along the street.

Traditional covered markets are found all over the city; one of the largest is **Erdao Qiao Market** off Jiefang Nan Lu. Stacks of colourful silver and gold filigree gauze cloth from Pakistan, traditional Uygur *aidelaixi* silk and Chinese cotton is sold from small, privately-owned stalls. Food stalls sell yellowish chunks of fatty lung served with a piquant sauce, cold spicy noodles with dried beancurd, boiled sheeps' heads and roasted meats. *Shashlik* vendors have a constant stream of customers for spicy sticks of barbecued mutton, fat or liver. Uygur families bargain for wall or *kang* (heated sleeping-platform) carpets, and Pakistani traders bustle around yelling and making deals. Tinkers make kettles, boxes, moulds and water holders, and sell traditional Yengisar knives. Modern Pakistani house music blares from tape players.

On Sundays, crowds of young people gather at the entrance to admire, buy and sell Japanese and Chinese motorbikes.

Another market stands at the northern end of Jiefang Bei Lu, opposite the shaded roundabout where old men 'walk' their caged birds on Saturday afternoons. A larger market is beside the main Post Office, near Hongshan Park, and has a section devoted to traditional Uygur medicine, which, apart from herbs and minerals, includes dried lizards, animal foetuses, birds of prey and antlers, each emitting its own unique smell.

During the summer months melon vendors set up tents around the city and do brisk business amidst enormous piles of Hami and watermelons.

Pᴀʀᴋs ᴀɴᴅ Hɪʟʟs

rom **Red Hill** (**Hong Shan**), 910 metres (3,000 feet) high, on the east bank of the Urumqi River, there is a panoramic view of the city. The reddish-brown hill is dotted with small pavilions and the nine-storey grey-brick **Zhenglong Pagoda** (**Pagoda to Suppress Dragons**), which figures prominently in the folklore of Urumqi. In 1785 and 1786 the city suffered from severe river flooding caused, it was rumoured, by a big red dragon that had settled here, turned into a mountain and was clawing its way towards the opposite Yamalike Hill. If the two mountains joined, the Urumqi River would be blocked and drown the city. So in 1788, Governor Shang An built two pagodas to placate the dragon, one on the dragon's head, Red Hill, and the other on Yamalike Hill. There were numerous other pagodas built on Hong Shan, which became a holy Buddhist centre; however, many were burnt down by the warlords who later ruled the city.

Large shady trees, Mirror Lake (Jian Hu) for boating (nowadays motorized inner tubes), and ornamental pavilions and halls make up **Hongshan Park**, more recently known as the People's Park, a cool, pleasant spot to relax in or stroll around. Construction of the park began in 1883; the lake was dredged in 1918 by a Xinjiang warlord who added the 'Hall of the Red Phoenix Crying in the Morning Sun', modelled after the Palace Museum in Beijing. Families of three or four generations come for lavish picnic feasts on Sunday afternoons. There is also a small zoo and a children's amusement park.

Xɪɴᴊɪᴀɴɢ Rᴇɢɪᴏɴᴀʟ Mᴜsᴇᴜᴍ (Xɪɴᴊɪᴀɴɢ Bᴏᴡᴜɢᴜᴀɴ)

This museum is now closed for extensive renovation until 2005 or later. Located on Xi Bei Lu, the museum is housed in a large building constructed in 1953, an attractive mix of Uygur and Russian styles. A green-tiled dome tops the main hall, while an enormous mural relief on either side of the entrance depicts flying apsaras (celestial nymphs) who dance and celebrate above and below the gothic pillars. There are two permanent exhibitions in the museum: one (north wing) focuses on archaeological treasures from the Silk Road, and the other (south wing) on Xinjiang's minority

(following pages) Horses graze below Bogda Peak, in the Heavenly Mountains near Urumqi

cultures. Although the Silk Road exhibit is very good, little attention is paid to dating the exhibits, the lighting is poor (you have to insist that the lights are turned on), and most captions are in Chinese and Uygur only.

ragments of silks, brocades, embroideries and wool carpets, wooden utensils and simple pottery—all Han-dynasty pieces taken from the sites of Loulan and Niya—are on display. From the Northern and Sui dynasties are samples of silk weaving from Hetian and Turpan, with Central Asian tree and animal patterns, as well as wooden slips with Buddhist scriptures in Brahmani and Guici scripts. A pair of brocade shoes, exquisite silks and hempen cloth documents from the **Astana Tombs** near **Kharakhoja** date from the Tang dynasty, as do specimens of grains, nuts, dried fruits, and nan (stamped with the same pattern used today), painted wooden figures, pottery tomb guards, Buddha heads in the Gandharan style, and a pair of metal eye shades. There are also Qing-dynasty gold and brocade hats belonging to the Hami kings, embroidered robes, cloth-printing moulds and wonderful silks from Hetian. A display of well-preserved 3,000-year-old corpses from Cherchen, Loulan and Hami completes the exhibition.

The minority-cultures exhibit includes full-scale models of a Uygur house and different styles of yurts—the large cloth tents with wooden frames used in the grasslands by the Kazakhs, Kirghiz and Mongolians. Clothing, household utensils, handicrafts, hunting accoutrements and musical instruments of the many Xinjiang minorities are included in the exhibit. A temporary display behind the bookshop houses large copies and photos of the remaining wall paintings at Bezeklik, Kizil and Kumtura.

The museum bookshop is quite good, containing many references on Xinjiang minorities and Buddhist cave temple art, as well as copies of artefacts and murals, minority carpets and jade. Take city bus number 2 from the train station.

URUMQI PRACTICAL INFORMATION

This is a sprawling industrial Chinese city. Local buses are convenient and walking in the market areas can be interesting. Normal business hours are 10 am–2 pm, 4 am– 8 pm, Beijing time.

TRANSPORTATION

Daily flights to/from Beijing, Guangzhou, Xi'an, Aksu and Kashgar, Yining and Korla; twice-daily to Shanghai; four flights a week to/from Lanzhou and Hetian; three flights a week to/from Dunhuang (daily in peak season), Altai and Qiemo. International flights: four flights a week to/from Almaty. There is a once a week service to Moscow with Xinjiang Airlines. If you take this flight, a visa is needed for Russia. Aeroflot services have stopped. Daily trains operate to/from Beijing, Shanghai, Xi'an, Korla and Lanzhou (and points in between). Trains operate between Almaty and Urumqi via Aktogay–Dostyk (Kazakh border post) and Lankol (Chinese border post). Daily buses operate to/from Korla, Kucha, Aksu, Kashgar, Hetian and Yining; several per day to Turpan (sleeper buses now run on the longer-distance routes). For flight schedules go to www.linktrip.com/silkroad/xinjiang/fs_xijg.htm, and for trains www.linktrip.com/silkroad/xinjiang/ts_xijg.htm.

ACCOMMODATION

Hongfu Hotel

26 Huanghe Rd. Tel: (0991) 588 1588; fax: (0991) 582 3188;
email: hf-hotel@mail.xj.cninfo.net; website: www.hongfuhotel.com.cn
新疆鸿福大酒店 黄河路 26 号
Five-star hotel with 349 rooms and all luxury amenities located in city business district.

Yin Du Hotel

39 Xibei Rd. Tel: (0991) 453 6688; fax: (0991) 451 7166;
email: yindu@yinduhotel.com; website: www.yinduhotel.com
银都酒店 西北路 39 号
Five-star hotel north of city centre in busy business district, with 253 rooms and all modern facilities.

Hotel World Plaza

2 Beijing Nan Lu. Tel: (0991) 383 6400; fax: (0991) 383 6399
新疆环球大酒店   北京南路 2 号
Four-star facility, conveniently situated in the centre of the prosperous and pioneering business district of Beijing Road close to the Urumqi Economic and Technological Developing Zone. Within easy access of the railway station and the airport.

Holiday Inn Xinjiang

168 Xinhua Bei Lu. Tel: (0991) 281-8788; fax: (0991) 281-7422
新疆假日大酒店   新华北路 168 号
Four-star hotel located in the centre of the city; business centre; health spa and gym, Western, Muslim and Chinese restaurants; banquet and meeting facilities for up to 200 people; airport and station pick-up.

Overseas Chinese Hotel (Huaqiao Binguan)

Xinhua Lu. Tel: (0991) 286 0793; fax: 286 0298
华侨宾馆   新华路
Three-star hotel located south of the city centre; clean and comfortable rooms popular with visiting Central Asian relatives; Muslim restaurant, café and disco; Aeroflot and CTS on the grounds.

FOOD AND DRINK

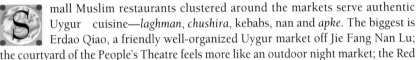

mall Muslim restaurants clustered around the markets serve authentic Uygur cuisine—*laghman, chushira,* kebabs, nan and *apke.* The biggest is Erdao Qiao, a friendly well-organized Uygur market off Jie Fang Nan Lu; the courtyard of the People's Theatre feels more like an outdoor night market; the Red Flag Covered Market (Hongqi Lushi Chang) that connects Renmin and Zhongshan Lu is a lively fruit and vegetable market lined with restaurants. Sichuan and other Chinese restaurants can be found on Renmin Lu, around the bus station and opposite the Red Flag Covered Market. Grapes and melons from Turpan and Yili peaches begin to arrive in late July.

SOUTHERN PASTURES (BAIYANG GOU)

Seventy-five kilometres (46 miles) south of Urumqi is White Poplar Gully, in the **Southern Mountains** (a spur of the **Heavenly Mountains**). Through this narrow verdant gully, screened by snow-capped peaks and dotted with tall dragon-spruce trees, runs a mountain stream, and at the far end is a 20-metre-high (65-foot) waterfall. Between May and October, **Kazakh** families move their yurts into the area to graze their herds. Horsemen offer rides to tourists, and you can visit their yurts, drink milk tea, watch horse-racing and traditional Kazakh dancing. Buses leave Hongshan Park in the morning and return late in the afternoon.

HEAVEN LAKE (TIAN CHI)

he three-hour road journey to this azure lake, 110 kilometres (68 miles) east of Urumqi, ascends into the foothills of the Heavenly Mountains, where Kazakh families pitch their yurts in summer and graze their herds of horses, sheep and cattle. The picturesque drive winds higher to almost 2,000 metres (6,500 feet) above sea level before it reaches the lake, which is surrounded by alpine meadows and rugged snow-capped mountains densely covered in fir, pine and cypress. Amidst fields of wild flowers grow morrel mushrooms, wild peppermint and rhubarb, while higher up the mountain are edelweiss and the rare, creamy Snow Lotus (*Saussurea involucrata*), which blooms in July. Larger than a normal lotus flower, the plant grows from rock crevices and is believed to have magical powers, which often figure in Chinese kung-fu stories. Its dried pistils, marinated in wine, are popularly believed to relieve arthritis, rheumatism and menstrual cramps. In 985 BC, legend has it that Emperor Mu of the Zhou dynasty attended a banquet at Heaven Lake as the guest of the fairy goddess Queen Mother of the West.

Waterfall at White Poplar Gully near Urumqi

Most tourists just go for the day, take a boat ride on the lake, have lunch at the lakeside restaurant and ride or walk along the mountain paths. However, it is more rewarding to stay overnight, since the area is significantly more quiet and calm after the tour buses leave in the late afternoon. It is possible to hike or ride up on horses to the snow line or glaciers, where the wilderness is stunning and pristine.

Travellers can stay in one of the many yurts owned by locals, with a mat on the floor and a bowl of hot fresh milk in the morning. The farther away you go, the less likely you are to see other tourists. Be forewarned that the yurts do not have washing or toilet facilities. The Tianchi Hotel has small chalet-like rooms overlooking the lake, which are quite expensive. Buses leave daily from the bus station and the Hongshan Park in Urumqi.

ANCIENT CITY OF WULAPO

uins of this Tang-dynasty city lie about 20 kilometres (12 miles) south of Urumqi near the Wulapo Reservoir. In ancient times, the city controlled the route to Turpan and southern Xinjiang. Its walls are about seven metres (23 feet) high in some parts, and the remains of the corner towers are evident. An earthen wall divides the city into two sections, and there exist traces of courtyards in military configurations. The site is strewn with pottery sherds. Access is by taxi or hired car.

URUMQI TO TURPAN

With the new highway now open, buses run daily between Urumqi and Turpan and take about two hours; cars take ninety minutes. Nobody takes the train anymore for this short sector. Before, trains stop at **Daheyan**, the railway station for Turpan; then passengers must take a bus the rest of the way, about an hour's journey. The railway line and the road criss-cross each other through a flat landscape of low shrubs and pebbles, with Bogda Peak of the Heavenly Mountains to the north and a lower spur to the south. Beyond a large salt lake is the town of **Dabancheng**, where buses sometimes stop at the lively Peasant-Farmers Market. The ladies of old Dabancheng were made famous by an Uygur folksong praising their beautiful long plaits. Beyond the town are the ruins of a fort built in 1870 by Yakub Beg of Kashgar and destroyed soon after by the Qing-dynasty army that was sent to put down the rebellion.

From Dabancheng the road begins its descent into the Turpan Depression, leaving the railway and weaving through the rocky White Poplar Gully. Across the *gebi* desert (meaning stony and not to be confused with the Gobi Desert of Mongolia) run the famous underground water channels or *karez* that irrigate the rich oasis of Turpan. Traceable by the mounds of earth at their openings, these lines of connected wells stretch from the mountains to the oasis.

XINJIANG'S SUPERLATIVES

aken from a *General Survey of Xinjiang*, a guide published by the Chinese Foreign Languages Press in Beijing, this list enumerates some of the region's lesser-known accomplishments.

- Urumqi is the farthest city from the sea in the world, at a distance of 2,250 kilometres.

- Kucha County averages 180 sunny days per year while Turpan County averages 299 rainless days per year.

- On July 25, 1962, Turpan recorded a ground temperature of 76.6°C and on January 27, 1969, Yining registered 94 centimetres of snowfall in one day.

- On average, each person in Xinjiang eats more than 100 kilograms of fruit and sweet melons per year.

- The highest road in the world (more than 5,000 metres above sea level) runs from southern Xinjiang over the Kunlun Mountains into northern Tibet.

- Xinjiang's underground *karez* irrigation system totals some 5,000 kilometres.

- Xinjiang has the largest forests of wild apple trees and the best strains of walnuts in China.

- Pastures in Xinjiang have the best alfalfa and hops in China.

- China's only wild camel reserve is located in the Altun Mountains.

- Xinjiang's beaver and swan reserves are the first of their kind in China.

(following pages)'The funnel' in the Altun Nature Reserve, an area to the west of Dunhuang, closed to all but a privileged few

A COMMON LANGUAGE

am still hurrying to the mosque when a dark, narrow shop, with caps of all kinds displayed by its doorway, catches my eye. I stop: I will need a cap to protect myself in Tibet from the rays of the sun. The interior of the shop is dingy. A sewing machine is clattering anciently away. Moons of cloth, strips of plastic, bobbins of thread, circles of cardboard lie on the floor, or on shelves, or hang from nails in the door. An old, bespectacled, bearded man, sharp-featured and dark, sits inside the shop talking in Uyghur to a boy of about twelve. When I enter, he addresses me in Uyghur. I shrug my shoulders. He repeats his sentence, but louder this time.

'I don't understand,' I say in Chinese.

He understands this, but not much more, in Chinese. 'Hussain!' he calls out in a thin and authoritarian voice.

Hussain, who must have learned Chinese at school, asks me what I want.

'A cap. Maybe one of those,' I say, pointing at blue cloth caps hanging by the door. 'How much are these?'

The boy speaks to the old man, who holds up three fingers.

'Three yuan. Are you travelling through here? Where are you from?'

'Yes,' I answer, as I try on a couple for size. 'I'm from India. This one fits. I'll buy this one.' I take out a five yuan note.

'Yindu!' exclaims the boy. He exchanges a few excited words with the old man, who peers at me over his spectacles in annoyed disbelief. The boy runs out of the shop.

'Yes, Yindu. Hindustan,' I say, hoping to convince the old man. In a flash of inspiration, I pull out my pen and write 'Hindustan' on the palm of my hand, in Urdu.

The old man readjusts his spectacles, catches hold of my wrist tightly and peers at the writing. Urdu and Uyghur share the Arabic script; as he reads it his face lights up.

'Ah, Hindustan! Hindustan!' This is followed by a smiling salvo of Uyghur. He hands me three yuan in change.

'But the cap costs three yuan,' I say, handing him back the extra yuan, and raising three fingers.

He refuses to take it, and I refuse to do him out of a yuan. Suddenly, with an exasperated gesture, he grabs the cap from off my head and begins to rip it apart. I am horrified. What is he doing? What have I done? Have I insulted him by refusing his gift? Fifteen young boys suddenly appear at the door with Hussain at their head. They gather at the open entrance in a jigsaw of heads and gaze unblinkingly at the man from India. They are all speaking at once, and I am even more concerned and confused than before.

The old man shouts 'Hussain!' There is silence in the shop. He then fires rapid sentences off at me, which the boy translates.

'My father says he will make the stitching firmer for you because you will be travelling a long way.'

With a few strong pulls of the needle and a few minutes at the sewing machine, the old man, now intent on his work and paying me not the slightest attention, stretches and stitches the cap into a tougher form. With a restrained smile, and a faint snort of satisfaction, he stands up to put it back on my head, gently, and adjusts it to the correct angle. He says a few more words, but I am too moved by his kindness to think of asking Hussain for a translation. As I nudge past the fifteen spectators at the door, I turn to say 'salaam aleikum', knowing that he will understand this.

Vikram Seth, From Heaven Lake, 1983

TURPAN (TULUFAN)

ne of the town's earliest names, Huozhou ('Land of Fire'), was derived from the intense summer temperatures, over 40°C (or 104°F) between June and August. Yet another appellation, 'Storehouse of Wind', refers to the blustering winds that often whip through the town for several hours in the afternoons. The winters here are also extreme, –10° to –15°C (or 14° to 5°F). Turpan is principally an agricultural oasis, famed for its grape products—seedless white raisins (which are exported) and wines (mostly sweet). Turpan is located in a depression, some 80 metres (260 feet) below sea level and the climate is extremely dry. Nearby **Moon Lake**, at 154 metres (505 feet) below sea level, is the second lowest continental point in the world after the Dead Sea.

Along with other southern Xinjiang cities, Turpan claims longevity records, with many people over 100 years of age. Locals believe that the climate, drinking milk and eating grapes are the main factors. Two-thirds of Turpan County's population of 190,000 is Uygur.

In 108 BC, Turpan was inhabited by farmers and traders of Indo-European stock who spoke a form of Tokharian, an extinct Indo-Persian language. Whoever occupied the Turpan oasis commanded the northern trade route and the rich caravans that passed through annually. In the Han dynasty control over the route went back and forth between the Xiongnu and Chinese. Until the fifth century, the capital of this kingdom was at Jiaohe (Yarkhoto).

The House of Qu, a Buddhist Han Chinese dynasty, ruled Turpan from the beginning of the sixth century. During the Northern Wei dynasty the capital of **Gaochang (Kharakhoja)** was established here by the Loulan people who sent tribute to the Tang court in Chang'an, maintaining diplomatic relations with 24 sovereign states. Qu Wentai was so aggressively hospitable to the Buddhist monk, Xuan Zang, and so eager for him to stay and teach the people of **Gaochang** that after a month's delay, the monk resorted to a three-day hunger strike to secure permission to continue his pilgrimage to India (see Special Topic on page 97). The Khan of the Western Turks later urged Qu Wentai to prevent Silk Road merchants from travelling eastwards, which prompted Emperor Taizong to send an expeditionary force to Gaochang. Its approach caused Qu Wentai to die of fright, and it was left to his son to surrender in 640. In their campaign to pacify the west, the Chinese established a protectorate-general to watch over the region. Turpan's cotton cloth, alum (used in paper making), Glauber's salt and fresh 'mare's-nipple grapes' were traded in Chang'an. During the Tang dynasty Turpan introduced China to the art of making grape wine.

W hen the northern Uygur Empire disintegrated, the nomadic tribes dispersed, and some established an independent kingdom at **Gaochang** around 840. The Indo-European natives were absorbed by the Uygurs and a rich, intellectual, highly artistic, religious culture developed. Buddhists, Manichaeans and Nestorians lived together harmoniously and religious art flourished in the cities and monastic caves; religious literature was translated into the numerous languages and scripts used at that time. The **Gaochang** state continued to exist well into the 13th century, when the Mongols swept through Central Asia. After the death of Genghis Khan, Turpan became part of the Chaghatai Khanate known as Uyguristan.

Marco Polo observed in the 13th century that the people of Turpan 'declare that the king who originally ruled over them was not born of human stock, but arose from a sort of tuber generated by the sap of trees, which we call *esca*; and from him all the others descended. The idolaters [Buddhists] are very well-versed in their own laws and traditions and are keen students of the liberal arts. The land produces grain and

'Uygur Princes' wall painting, Bezeklik, Temple 9, ninth century AD

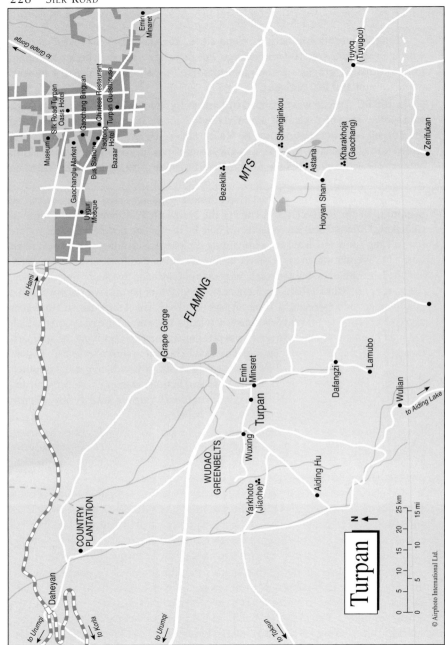

Emin
Minaret

to Grape Gorge

Silk Road Turpan
Oasis Hotel
Gaochang Binguan
Chinese Restaurant
Turpan Guesthouse
Jiaotong
Bazaar Hotel
Museum
Gaochanglu Market
Bus Station
Uygur
Mosque

Tuyoq
(Tuyugou)

Shengjinkou

Zerifukan

Kharakhoja
(Gaochang)

Bezeklik

MTS

Astana

Huoyan Shan

FLAMING

Grape Gorge

Emin
Minsret

Turpan

Dafangzi

Lamubo

Wulian

to Aiding Lake

to Hami

Wuxing

WUDAO
GREENBELTS

Yarkhoto
(Jiaohe)

Aiding Hu

COUNTRY
PLANTATION

Daheyan

to Urumqi

to Korla

to Urumqi

to Toksun

N

25 km

15 mi

20

10

15

5

10

5

0

0

Turpan

© Airphoto International Ltd.

excellent wine. But in winter the cold here is more intense than is known in any other part of the world.'

At the end of the 14th century, the Uygurs in the Turpan area were forcibly converted to Islam by an heir to the Chaghatai Khanate loyal to Tamerlane the Great. During Turpan's period of aggression towards the neighbouring oasis of Hami, the Chinese refused entry to all trade caravans from Uyguristan and expelled Uygur traders from Gansu Province. However, the Ming dynasty maintained good relations with Turpan, which supplied a special dye vital to the production of the famous blue-and-white Ming porcelain.

The Islamic inhabitants of Turpan rebelled against the domination of the Buddhist Oirat Mongols, and with Hami, joined in the Qing dynasty's Junggar campaign against the Oirats. In 1861, Turpan rebelled against the Chinese garrison troops and joined in Yakub Beg's revolt.

Sir Francis Younghusband, journeying through Turpan in the 1880s, noted that it 'consists of two distinct towns, both walled—the Chinese and the Turk, the latter situated a mile west of the former. The Turk town is the [more] populous, having probably twelve or fifteen thousand inhabitants, while the Chinese town has not more than five thousand at the outside.'

In the early 20th century, many Western explorers and archeologists were attracted to Turpan's ancient cities and Buddhist caves. The German Albert von Le Coq's first expedition in 1902–1903 yielded nearly 2,000 kilograms (two tons) of treasures, which he transported back to Europe; on his second expedition a year later, he shipped off 103 crates. The other two German expeditions yielded 128 and 156 boxes respectively. The British archeologist, Sir Aurel Stein, mopping up after von Le Coq in 1915, loaded over 140 crates onto 45 camels and dispatched the antiquities to Kashgar. Incalculable damage was done to these monuments by the Uygurs themselves, who had by now become ardent Muslims and defaced most of the beautiful artwork that remained.

The main crops grown in Turpan are wheat, sorghum, cotton, grapes, peanuts, melons and vegetables. There are several communally-owned industries, the main ones being coal and chemical production; smaller ones include dried fruit, wines and fruit juices.

SIGHTS

CITS offers daily sightseeing tours to Turpan's various sites and prices are rated according to the number of persons. Most visitors simply arrange day trips with the private mini-van operators lurking outside the Turpan Guesthouse, which are cheaper and fairly reliable.

Turpan's verdant growth of poplar and fruit trees, vineyards and lush cultivated fields form a striking contrast to the surrounding desert. Cable and French wrote in

(following pages) Emin Mosque at Turpan, constructed in 1778

the 1930s: 'Turpan lies like a green island in a sandy wilderness, its shores lapped by grit and gravel instead of ocean water.' The annual Turpan Silk Road Grape Festival takes place in late August; for one festive week the streets are lined with grapes from all over the county, and people from over 30 cities in the northwest provinces and Tibet serve regional delicacies and wear traditional clothing.

I n the dusty streets of the town, spacious houses with shady courtyards and cool underground rooms for sleeping or storing produce accommodate the large Uygur families. Either attached to the house or nearby is a high open mud-brick room used for drying grapes. After 40 to 50 days the raisins are ready for market, where they are sold for better prices than fresh grapes.

The town itself is not large, and the main tourist hotels are a few minutes' walk from the bazaar and shops. The streets of Turpan are being trellised with grapevines; several streets are already thus shaded, which has a delightful cooling effect.

The two-storey covered section of the bazaar contains stalls selling cloth, hats, clothing, Yengisar knives, bright embroideries and bolts of cloth. Boots, shoes and miscellaneous merchandise are displayed on beds. The bazaar continues further back, teeming with vegetable and fruit sellers, dried fruits and nuts, carpet dealers, bakers and small private food stalls. A thirst-quenching, cold summer drink made up of cold water and the juice of rehydrated peaches or apricots (known as *bingshui*) is ladled from refrigerated tins; an ice slush, sold in small shot glasses, is also popular. Sunday is the busiest market day but the rest of the week is active as well.

On the south side of the main street, a short walk west of the bazaar, is the **Uygur Mosque**, built in 1983, its six minarets surmounting a green-and-white mirrored facade. Opposite stand several new Islamic-style buildings, including the hospital and the teacher's training college.

B etween July and September each year, hundreds of people come from all parts of Xinjiang to take the sands—a traditional Uygur treatment for rheumatism. At the Shabo Sand Mound, patients lie under makeshift tents, covering themselves with the hot desert sand (70°–80°C, or 150°–170°F) several times a day to relieve their aches and pains. Treatment is supervised by a local Uygur medical centre. Visits by foreigners can be arranged through CITS.

TURPAN REGIONAL MUSEUM (TULUFAN BOWUGUAN)

The new museum is located on Gaochang Lu just north of the market and houses a collection of artefacts from the Turpan area—paper fragments, porcelain, weapons, implements, silks and earth and wooden figurines unearthed from Kharakhoja, Jiaohe and Astana. An extensive display (copies and photos) of wall paintings found in the Kizil region clearly depicts the evolution of style from Gandharan to Guici to Han. Five naturally preserved corpses from the Astana Tombs are also on display.

Emin Minaret (Su Gong Ta)

This minaret two kilometres (just over a mile) east of the city is one of the architectural gems of the Silk Road. Started in 1777 at the behest of the ruler of Turpan, Emin Khoja, it was completed in 1778 by his son Suleman, for whom it is also called Su Gong (Prince Su) Minaret. The circular tower is 44 metres high and was designed by a Uygur architect called Ibrahim. The plain sun-dried bricks taper skywards in geometric and floral patterns. There is a good view of the area from the second-storey balcony above the mosque but visitors are no longer permitted to climb the steps in the minaret itself. The adjoining mosque has a beamed ceiling supported by simple wooden pillars and a domed sacred area. Nearby you can walk or ride a bicycle; the road leads past mud-brick houses and bakeries, vegetable plots, a stream and finally the vineyards surrounding the minaret.

Karez

 he ancient *karez* irrigation system is comprised of a series of wells and linking underground channels that uses gravity to bring ground water to the surface, usually far from the source. Glaciers in far-off mountains feed into streams and rivers contained by the *karez* system. Ancient oasis towns depended on this irrigation for survival, and if neglected or abandoned, the desert would reassert itself and the towns would dry up and die. As the glaciers gradually shrank over the centuries, the streams they fed likewise diminished, resulting in less or no water flowing to the dependent oasis towns. Many Silk Road towns, including Yotkan, the original site of Hetian, were abandoned because their life-support system had disappeared.

In Turpan County there are more than 470 systems, totalling over 1,600 kilometres (1,000 miles) of tunnels. The longest measures over 40 kilometres (25 miles). Wells begin at the base of the mountains, tapping their subterranean water. The tunnels slope less than the contours of the geographical depression, so that the water reaches the oasis close to ground level, where surface canals distribute it. Keeping the underground channels unclogged is an ongoing task, as the mounds of earth beside each well shaft indicate. Two men and a draught animal work as a team—one man is lowered down the shaft to clear the tunnel and the buckets of mud are hoisted to the surface by a rope haltered to the animal. The *karez* channels of Turpan and Hami have a history of more than 2,000 years. Although the Chinese claim it as their own, the *karez* system first appeared in ancient Persia and probably came to Xinjiang from the west.

Grape Gorge (Putao Gou)

Grapes were introduced to Turpan over 2,000 years ago, including the green, elongated 'mare's-nipple' (*manaizi*) variety. Together with Turpan melons and

Ruins of the ancient city of Jiaohe, near Turpan

wines, they formed an essential part of the kingdom's tribute to the Tang imperial court at Chang'an, where the fruit arrived fresh and tender, transported in lead-lined boxes packed with snow from the Heavenly Mountains.

Lying at the base of the western end of the **Flaming Mountains**, in a green valley 12 kilometres northeast of the oasis, is a pleasant public park with vineyards and fruit trees. There are trellised walkways overhung with bunches of grapes, and patios with tables for relaxing and eating the grapes and melons. A small, tart grape first comes

out in mid-July, followed by the 'mare's-nipple' and the red and black grapes in August. Mulberry, fig, apple and pear trees also bear fruit in season. Running at the foot of the mountains is a spring; the cool water is safe to drink and refreshing.

The trip to Grape Gorge is a good day trip by bicycle if you leave early enough to avoid the intense afternoon sun. A small road leads through mud-brick villages, several mosques and cemeteries surrounded by fruit-drying houses. There is a winery located in the valley as well.

Ancient City of Jiaohe (Yarkhoto)

The ruined city of Jiaohe is just ten kilometres (six miles) west of Turpan (accessible by bicycle), in the Yarnaz Valley, perched atop a narrow terrace like an island above two rivers—the city's Chinese and Uygur names both mean 'confluence of rivers'. The cliffs rise more than 30 metres above the riverbeds, forming a natural defence.

Jiaohe was the capital of the State of South Cheshi, one of the 36 kingdoms of the Western Region during the Han dynasty. The city was developed by a general appointed to administer the entire Turpan area. It proved to be an effective fortress when troops and peasants took refuge from raiding bands of Xiongnu horsemen. From the Wei to the Tang dynasty, Jiaohe was under the jurisdiction of the Gaochang Kingdom. Between the mid-eighth and mid-ninth century the city was occupied by Tibetans, and was subsequently under the control of Gaochang. Jiaohe reached its cultural peak under the Uygurs in the ninth century. The city was largely destroyed by Mongol rebellions and was gradually abandoned after the Yuan dynasty.

 he remains are Tang dynasty, a period when the population numbered more than 5,000. They stretch for 1,700 metres (1 mile) from north to south. A central watchtower overlooks the main street. A Buddhist monastery complex stands in the city centre. Inside the monastery are the remains of several headless Buddha statues in niches, a dagoba and monks' cells. The west side of the main road was the residential area, and to the east were government buildings and a prison. At the far northern end stand the walls of a Buddhist dagoba and tombs.

The layout of the city is still clear among the dusty ruins. High adobe walls, once enclosing private homes, face the street and side-lanes. Like the streets, the courtyards were dug below the surface, the living quarters hollowed out of their sides. Little wood was used except for doors, windows and ceilings. Among the eroded remains are bread ovens and wells. The view over the steep gorges where the rivers once ran is breathtaking, and the green valley below contrasts with the brown ruins of the city. Jiaohe was partly excavated in the 1950s, and brought under the protection of the state in 1961.

The Ancient City of Gaochang (Kharakhoja)

The impressive ruins of the ancient city of Gaochang lie 47 kilometres (29 miles) southeast of Turpan. Built in the second century BC as a garrison town, it became the capital of the Kingdom of Gaochang under the Han house of Qu. By the seventh century it held sway over 21 other towns. The practice of Buddhism led to the establishment of many monasteries, temples and large religious communities, and the monk, Xuan Zang, taught in this city for several months amidst paintings and statuary in Graeco-Buddhist Gandharan style. A Confucian college taught the classics of Chinese ethics. In the ninth century, the Uygurs established their Kharakhoja Kingdom here, bringing with them Manicheanism, which flourished alongside Buddhism and Nestorianism. Manuscripts have been discovered here, including beautifully illuminated Manichaean scriptures. The city was destroyed around the 14th century, during a period of warfare lasting 40 years.

aochang consisted originally of three parts: the inner and outer cities, and a palace complex. The palace, which was guarded by 900 soldiers, had 12 gates. Nothing remains of it today, but inside the huge city walls, amongst the acres of ruins, are the Bell Tower and the temple area, and a few traces of Buddhist paintings are still visible in the niches and on the walls.

German archaeologists from the Ethnographic Museum of Berlin, Professors Grunwedel and von Le Coq, dug extensively here and found superb floor mosaics, frescoes, statuary and manuscripts. A Nestorian church was discovered outside the walls of the old city, containing a Byzantine-style mural possibly depicting a Palm Sunday service. The Germans also discovered an underground room with the thousand-year-old corpses of more than 100 violently murdered Buddhist monks, thought to be the victims of religious persecution.

Von Le Coq's discovery of a six-foot-high fresco depicting Manes, the founder of Manicheanism, proved that Gaochang had been a flourishing Manichean community in the mid-eighth century. This ancient religion was founded by Manes around 242 AD in Sassanian Iran, but met with intense hostility from Zoroastrians and later Christians in Northern Africa and Muslims. Manes died in jail in 274 or 276 and his converts were persecuted; consequently, there are no written records or religious texts of this faith anywhere else. Some 500 Manicheans fled east to Samarkand and founded a community. The religion and its art were subsequently transported along the Silk Road, assimilating Buddhist influences (particularly those from Persia and Gandhara) by the time it reached Gaochang. Von Le Coq's discoveries included Manichean manuscripts done on leather, silk, paper and parchment, frescoes, and hanging paintings done on cloth, all revealing strong Persian influences. The manuscripts helped illuminate facets of this little-known faith.

uch of Gaochang has been destroyed by locals and the site only vaguely resembles a town. The soil of the old walls is rich, and peasants have carried off large quantities over the centuries to fertilize their fields. Farmers believed that the bright pigment of the wall paintings was excellent fertilizer. Beams and wood have been carted off to be used as fuel. Cable and French noted: 'Destruction of the buildings had been going on for a long time, and we saw farmers at work with their pickaxes pulling down the old ruins and probably destroying many relics in the process.' Anti-Buddhist feeling was another cause of the destruction.

(following pages) Bezeklik Thousand Buddha Caves, near Turpan

Many wall paintings of the Buddha in human form were slashed and the eyes picked out by fearful Muslims. 'For the belief still exists,' wrote von Le Coq, 'that painted men and animals, unless their eyes and mouths at least had been destroyed, come to life at night, descend from their places, and do all sorts of mischief to men, beasts and harvest.' One tragic story relates how a Muslim peasant came across a library of illuminated manuscripts and simply threw them into the river, worried that his mullah would find him with blasphemous material.

At the entrance to the city, horse and donkey carts offer rides to the partially repaired temple, roughly two kilometres out on a track that winds through indistinguishable dirt mounds and the remains of the city wall.

ASTANA TOMBS

 n this Tang-dynasty burial ground, 40 kilometres (25 miles) southeast of Turpan, the imperial dead of Gaochang were buried. The dry climate preserved the bodies and artefacts perfectly, and the custom of wrapping corpses has yielded a rich variety of silks with Chinese and Middle Eastern designs. The Xinjiang Regional Museum in Urumqi has a fine collection of relics from Astana. Painted stucco figurines have revealed such aspects of daily life as traditional costumes, customs and riding accoutrements. Samples of grains, breads, pastries and dumplings placed in the graves gave insight into their diet. Von Le Coq excavated the site in the early 1900s and found a buried box of Russian matches made in 1890—proof that a tsarist expedition had been there before him. He was followed by Sir Aurel Stein in 1915. The Chinese carried out extensive excavations in 1972 and 1973.

Three of the tombs are open to the public. A steep, narrow passage leads down about 16 feet into a small dark chamber. Two contain faded, simple paintings: in one, auspicious birds; in the tomb of the Tang-dynasty General Zhang Xun and his wife (now encased in the Turpan Regional Museum), four murals depicting Jade Man, Gold Man, Stone Man and Wooden Man—all symbols of Confucian virtues. The third tomb contains the mummies of a woman and a man, in whose mouth a Persian coin was found. These well-preserved bodies have extremely long hair and fingernails, which continued to grow for many years after their death.

BEZEKLIK THOUSAND BUDDHA CAVES

Tucked away in the Flaming Mountains, at a breathtaking site high above the Murtuk River gorge (56 kilometres, or 35 miles, northeast of Turpan), are 67 caves dating from the Northern and Southern dynasties (317–589) to the Yuan dynasty (1279–1368). Bezeklik was an important centre for Buddhist worship under the Xizhou Huigu government, which built the royal temple of the King of Huigu at the site. The caves are well-hidden and rest on a long ridge overlooking a valley where the monastery was located. Originally access was via a winding pathway to the cliff top, and a steep stairway led down to the monastery 30 feet below. Some of the temples were hewn into the rock face, others constructed of sun-dried bricks—a unique feature of Bezeklik.

In the Uygur language Bezeklik means 'place where there are paintings'. The caves were excavated at the beginning of this century by the Germans von Le Coq and Grunwedel, who found them filled with sand. They first dug away at the entrance and found six huge portraits of Buddhist monks. The thousand-year-old murals inside the caves were in superb condition, their colours rich and fresh; some showed Indian monks in yellow robes, their names inscribed in Brahmi script; others were clad in the violet robes of East Asia. They found huge portraits of Buddhas at different periods throughout history, and figures of foreigners presenting gifts to the Buddha, including Indian princes, Brahmins, Persians, and a stranger with red hair and blue eyes. The central shrine had frescoes depicting the legends of Indian gods and mythical demons; in each corner of this temple was one of the Guardians of the World. The Germans also found life-size painted stucco statues of Buddhas, disciples and guardians.

Von Le Coq and his associate, Theodor Bartus, set to work removing as many of the best murals as they could, sawing through the stucco and straw surfaces. Crated and transhipped to Europe, the murals were housed in the Ethnological Museum in Berlin. Allied bombing during the Second World War destroyed some of them, and the remainder are on display in the Museum of Indian Art in Berlin. A few large, beautiful murals from Bezeklik are kept in the Hermitage Museum in St Petersburg.

Sadly, most of the cave paintings are now in terrible shape and very little is visible, most having been defaced by Uygur Muslims. But Bezeklik is still worth visiting for a view of the cliffs and the valley in the heart of the Flaming Mountains. A few good fragments do remain in Caves 16, 17 and 33 but make sure the attendant unlocks these for you. Near the mouth of the valley are the Shengjinkou Thousand Buddha Caves, but absolutely nothing of interest remains.

Tuyoq (Tuyugou)

 This peaceful, ancient village is situated 70 kilometres east of Turpan in a lush gully carved into the Flaming Mountains. It is surrounded by vineyards and famous for its oval-shaped seedless grapes, the raisins of which are well known in Beijing. Albert von Le Coq discovered the ruins of Buddhist cave temples here in 1905, 'clinging like a swallow's nest to the almost perpendicular slope of the mountainside'. These caves are thought to be the oldest in the Turpan area and date from the fourth century. Part of the monastery perched atop one of the cliffs fell into the gorge in 1916 during an earthquake. Von Le Coq found a monk's cell, with Persian architectural influences, containing numerous eighth- and ninth-century religious texts and beautiful embroideries.

The famous Uygur legend of Tuyoq concerns six pious Muslims who sought refuge in the caves. According to the myth, when an imposter tried to pose as Allah these six men, who were determined to test the power of this supposed deity, witnessed his fear upon meeting a black cat on the way to the mosque and knew immediately that he could not be their true god. The denounced Allah tried to kill the faithful Muslims but they fled to the caves of Tuyoq and a spider spun a web in the doorway to conceal the cave while two pigeons stood guard. Because of the extreme piety of the six men, a trip to the mosque in Tuyoq is considered 'half as sacred' as the pilgrimage to Mecca, and is rewarded with the title of 'half a hadji'.

Tuyoq is a beautiful, timeless village with a friendly Auger community. The mosque is on the road cutting between the lush vineyards up to the cemetery, behind which runs the gorge and the caves; its dome is visible behind the green valley and mud-brick houses. Behind the mosque is a stream where children swim and yell while old men stroke their long beards and eat melons in the shade. The caves are located one kilometre upriver in the gulley. Over 40 have been carved into the soft dirt and rock surrounding the gully, amidst verdant vineyards and the rugged backdrop of the Flaming Mountains. Only nine caves contain traces of frescoes, three of which are locked. Viewing the caves without the help of ropes or ladders can be challenging (just follow the lead of the local children who make the climb barefoot!). CITS needs a one-month notification in order to arrange a visit; however, there is an afternoon bus that returns the following morning. Although there are no lodgings, you will assuredly be welcome to spend the night with an Uygur family.

FLAMING MOUNTAINS (HUOZHOU SHAN)

These red sandstone hills run along the northern edge of the Turpan Depression, beginning just northeast of Turpan. The range is 100 kilometres long and about 10 kilometres wide. When the sun's rays beat down in mid-afternoon, the hillsides appear to be engulfed by tongues of fire, and the reflected heat is intense. In the famous 16th-century Chinese allegorical novel *Journey to the West* by Wu Cheng'en, Xuan Zang and his bizarre companions, Pigsy, Monkey and Sandy, attempted to cross them but could not penetrate the flames. Monkey procured a magical palm-leaf fan from Princess Iron Fan, wife of the Ox Demon King, and waved it 49 times, causing heavy rains to fall and extinguish the fire. The locals now add that, while attempting to cross the Flaming Mountains, Monkey burnt his tail, and ever since then all monkeys have had red bottoms.

MOON LAKE (AIDING HU)

This lake 55 kilometres (34 miles) southeast of Turpan, in the heart of the Turpan Depression, is a most dismal place, a salt puddle at the bottom of the second lowest continental basin in the world, 154 metres (505 feet) below sea level. The surface of the lake is completely encrusted with an ice-like layer of salt, and its shores are like quicksand. Glauber's salt—used in detergents and as a diuretic—is manufactured here in a factory employing 3,000 people. In the winter the lake freezes over, and trucks move out onto the surface collecting frozen salt to dump into troughs beside the lake; there it melts in the searing summer temperatures, which can reach 65°C (150°F). Many of the workers were sent here during the Cultural Revolution (1966–1976) from the rich, green provinces of Zhejiang, Sichuan and Guangdong and have been here ever since. Several Han-dynasty beacon towers loom over the lakeside.

Turpan Practical Information

The population of Turpan County is roughly 400,000—72 per cent of which is Uygur. The town itself is not large, and the main tourist hotels are a few minutes' walk from the bazaar and shops. The streets of Turpan are trellised with grapevines and provide hazy green shade; beware, it is a Rmb15 fine for picking the enticing grapes that hang in large bunches just a few feet above. Although Turpan is a small town and easy to walk around, donkey carts and three-wheeled taxis can be hired for trips within the oasis. Check out www.passplanet.com/china/cw/turpan.htm for chatty information about Turpan.

Transportation
Hourly buses to/from Urumqi and Daheyan, the closest railhead on the Lanzhou-Urumqi line; daily buses to/from Hami and three times a week to/from Kashgar (and points in between). The bus station is opposite the bazaar, next to the Jiaotong Hotel.

Accommodation
Water is often rationed during the dry summer and hotels are forced to limit its use (showers) to a few hours in the afternoon or evening.

Silk Road Turpan Oasis Hotel (Luzhou Binguan)
41 Qing Nian Lu. Tel: (0995) 522 491; fax: (0995) 522 768 (Hong Kong booking), tel: (852) 2525 3661; fax: (852) 2537 3790);
email: webmaster@the-silk-road.com; website: www.the-silk-road.com
绿州宾馆　青年路 41 号
A three-star hotel of Islamic-style architecture with air-conditioning and many other Western amenities. Nice gardens with a grape arbour; excellent Muslim restaurant with Uygur singing and dancing nightly. Western and Chinese restaurants.

Turpan Guesthouse (Tulufan Binguan)
Qing Nian Lu. Tel: (0995) 852-1416; fax: 852-3262
吐鲁番宾馆　青年路

Old guesthouse with new wings; extremely relaxed atmosphere, especially in the social beer garden; Uygur singing and dancing nightly during the tourist season; bicycle rental and tours to the sights.

Jiaotong Hotel (Jiaotong Binguan)
Next to the bus station. Tel: (0995) 853 1320
交通宾馆　交通路
Close to the liveliest area of the town. Air-conditioned rooms; better than average Chinese accommodation; Muslim restaurant.

Food and Drink

 asty Uygur dishes can be found in many of the small restaurants and teahouses throughout the bazaar and Gaochang Lu market—*laghman*, *chushira*, *samsa*, kebabs and nan as well as the Sunday treat of *poluo* and *manta*. Cold flat rice noodles in a garlic/vinegar sauce make for a particularly satisfying meal during the intense midday heat. In the mornings, fresh milk and yoghurt is sold on the streets and in the bazaar. Aside from *chai*, liquid refreshment includes *bingshui*, fruit juices (manufactured in Turpan) and a sweet ice slush; ice cream and popsicles are eaten all day long. Xinjiang *pijiu* is of fairly poor quality, more like soda water with a barley aftertaste (try the watermelon cider). One of the local specialities is salt fish, a dried fish encrusted with mud and salt harvested from the beds of the surrounding lakes once they begin to evaporate in early summer. There are several Chinese restaurants with English menus just east of the main roundabout in the centre of town.

With over 30 communes in Turpan County, fresh fruit is always available in the markets and along the streets: apricots, grapes, peaches, mulberries, pears. Aside from the common watermelon, some of the more popular varieties of sweet melons include the exportable Hami *gua* (a large netted green melon with orange meat resembling a cantaloupe in taste and a watermelon in texture), the sweet Minzu *gua* (a smooth-skinned melon with green meat like a honeydew), and the fragrant Tang *gua* (a black-striped yellow melon; the inside is green with an orange tint to the pulp).

Turpan to Korla

The northern Silk Road was still a dirt track until it was tarmacked in the 1970s. It weaves southwest from Turpan to the small oasis township of Toksun, which is sustained by the waters of the Baiyang and Ala streams. Soon the road enters the most dangerous stretch of its 1,500-kilometre (930-mile) run to Kashgar. **Dry Ditch (Gan Gou)** is aptly named. For 60 kilometres (37 miles) the road winds through the gorge of this barren spur of hills coloured blue, ochre, brown and grey. The surface of the road is in poor condition, washed away by the frequent flash-floods that sweep down the naked hillsides with amazing force and suddenness.

I n *Journey to the West*, the angry husband of Princess Iron Fan, the Ox Demon King, aims to obstruct Xuan Zang and company by casting down his long waistband, which turns into this dry, perilous gulch. The god of the Flaming Mountains, however, comes to their rescue by scattering pearls along the way, which turn into delicious, thirst-quenching fruit—the grapes of Turpan.

At **Kumux (Komishi)**, the far end of **Dry Ditch**, drivers of south-bound trucks carrying oil from the Karamai oilfields, agricultural machinery, fertilizer, drums of bitumen and rubber tyres take a breather following their ordeal, while drivers of north-bound vehicles loaded with rope, reed matting and timber fill their radiators with water in anticipation of the difficult stretch that lies ahead.

The hilly pass of **Elm Tree Gully (Yushu Gou)** marks the border between the Turpan District and the **Baiyingouleng Mongol Autonomous Region**. 'Protect trees!' exhorts a roadside sign, but there is not a tree in sight, just the ubiquitous camel thorn.

Some distance before the town of **Yanqi**, soda-whitened marshes, tall grasses and grazing cattle indicate the proximity of the vast **Baghrash Lake**. Today, Yanqi is only a county seat in the Yanqi Hui Autonomous County, where one of the main industries is the production of reed screens for fencing and roofing. But historically it was the very important oasis of **Karashahr** (Black Town), which in AD 11 revolted against Han domination by murdering the Chinese protector-general. The revolt was ruthlessly stamped out by the Han-dynasty general, Ban Chao, who sacked the town, decapitating 5,000 inhabitants and carrying away 15,000 prisoners and 300,000 head of livestock.

By the Tang dynasty, Karashahr was the capital of the Buddhist Kingdom of Agni (a Sanskrit word referring to the God of Sacrifice or Burnt Offerings), whose king, the monk Xuan Zang noted, was boastful of his military conquests, but whose people were 'sincere and upright'. Xuan Zang further observed that 'the written character is, with few differences, like that of India. Clothing is of cotton or wool. They go with shorn locks and without head-dress.' Karashahr was the northernmost point of the Tibetan occupation of Xinjiang in the seventh century. Its Indo-European Tokharian population was gradually absorbed by the Uygurs after the ninth century. The mighty Tamerlane sacked the city in 1389.

Sven Hedin described Karashahr as 'the chief commercial emporium in that part of Chinese Turkestan' and 'the dirtiest town in all Central Asia . . . consisting of a countless number of miserable hovels, courtyards, bazaars, and Mongol tents, surrounded by a wall'. The British diplomat, Sir Eric Teichman, noted in the 1930s that it was 'not a Turkic but a Chinese-Mongol city'. The **Torgut Mongols** of Karashahr were famous for breeding the best horses in all of Turkestan; they were hardy and capable of covering 300 kilometres (185 miles) a day.

Twenty-four kilometres (15 miles) east of Yanqi lies the largest lake in Central Asia, **Baghrash Lake (Bositeng Hu)**, with a surface area of 1,000 square kilometres. It is fed by the **Kaidu River** and is a source of the **Konche (Peacock) River**, which flows right across the northern wastes of the Taklamakan Desert to Lop Nor. During the summer months Mongol fishermen construct makeshift shelters along the shore and fish the waters from boats, but it is a poor living. Legend tells that the lake once swarmed with water snakes, which attempted to bar the way to Xuan Zang. With a flap of his long sleeves he ordered them all back to the lake and turned them into fish. There are 16 small lakes in the vicinity, one of which is a breathtaking mass of pink and white water-lilies in the summer.

A number of ancient Silk Road ruins are scattered around the area, including the earth-rammed walls of a city dating from the Han dynasty. Within are large grassy mounds yet to be excavated. There are plans to excavate the remains of two large Tang-dynasty Buddhist temples about 20 kilometres southwest of Yanqi, which are said to have once quartered 1,000 monks. Nearby are the **Qixing Buddhist Caves**, but they were thoroughly depleted by Japanese, British and German archaeologists, and a brick factory in the immediate vicinity has further ruined the area. Faded fragments of wall murals survive in only six caves, the best of which is sealed and there is no attendant.

Beyond Yanqi the road crosses the Nanjiang Railroad and winds down to the city of Korla through low, ugly hills of rock and sand—a stark contrast to the green cultivated fields of Yanqi.

Korla

Korla is the capital of the **Bayinguoleng Mongolian Prefecture**, the largest prefecture in all of China, encompassing the eastern half of the Taklamakan Desert and extending to the borders of Tibet, Qinghai and Gansu. The entire area has a population of 800,000, the majority of whom are Han Chinese, with about 260,000 Uygurs, 40,000 Mongols and 1,000 Tibetans.

The Mongols of this region are the **Torgut** or **Kalmuck Mongols**, who migrated to Russia from the steppes of Western Mongolia in the 17th century and settled along the Volga River. Torgut cavalry units were incorporated in the tsarist armed forces to great effect, but 100 years later the Torguts decided to return en masse to Xinjiang. Their journey was fraught with disaster: they were pursued and harassed by Cossack soldiers and attacked by marauding tribes. By the time they reached the border, seven months later, only 70,000 were left—fewer than half of those who had set out. Emperor Qianlong (reigned 1736–96) received the Torguts hospitably, granting them grazing lands in the Karashahr and Yili regions of Xinjiang and presenting them with gifts of horses, sheep, cloth, tea and yurts. The Torguts wintered around the shores of **Baghrash Lake** and passed the summer in the valleys of the Heavenly Mountains, much as they do today.

I n 1934, Sven Hedin and his Swedish-Chinese motor expedition undertook a journey under the auspices of the Chinese Ministry of Railways to survey road links between Chinese Turkestan and China proper. At Korla they ran into the desperate Muslim troops of the young rebel, General 'Big Horse' Ma Zhongying. Their five vehicles were commandeered by the retreating soldiers, the expedition members were rounded up in a courtyard and their hands were tied as they awaited summary execution. General Big Horse spared the expedition, but held them under house arrest while he sped away in their vehicles southwest towards Kashgar, fleeing bombing by Soviet planes undertaken at the request of the Governor of Xinjiang.

Today, Korla's population of 400,000 (more than half of whom are Han) live by heavy industry and the export of such products as fragrant pears (the largest market for which is Hong Kong), tomato paste (bought by the Japanese) and Korla cotton. Oil exploration conducted with American and Australian expertise is underway in the Taklamakan Desert south of Korla. There are no historical sites worthy of note apart from the **Iron Gate Pass (Tiemenguan)**, seven kilometres (four miles) to the north, and the small Korla District Museum located in the centre of the city, where a few interesting mummies are on display. This Silk Road gateway, wedged between the mountains and the river, guarded the only ancient route connecting northern and southern Xinjiang. All that remains from the destruction wrought by the Cultural Revolution is a pile of bricks. There are plans to rebuild the huge iron gate.

Korla Practical Information

Though opened to foreigners in 1986 Korla, until recently, had little of interest to offer visitors. But with the opening of the spectacular Tarim Highway, the oilfield access road which now crosses the heart of the Taklamakan (see Special Topic on page 320), Korla's strategic location at the northern edge of the desert is noteworthy.

Transportation

By road, rail or air: there are flights five times a week to Urumqi, twice to Kucha, and three times to Qiemo on the south side of the Taklamakan. Trains run all the way to Xi'an and beyond, and buses run to Urumqi and Turpan, across the top of the Taklamakan to Kashgar and beyond, and down the desert's eastern side to Qiemo and on to Hetian.

Accommodation

Available at the **Bus Station Guesthouse**, tel (0996) 207-6561, or in the centre of town at the **Bayinguoleng Binguan**, tel (0996) 202-2248, on Renmin Dong Lu, with Western and Muslim restaurants.

Food and drink

Available from street vendors and small restaurants that operate late into the night opposite the bus station.

THE UYGURS

he largest minority group in Xinjiang are the Uygurs, a Turkic-speaking people who number close to six million. They give their name to the vast Uygur Autonomous Region of Xinjiang but live, for the most part, south of the Heavenly Mountains, in the cities and farmlands of the Tarim Basin oases. The name *Uygur* means 'united' or 'allied'.

Their origins can be traced back to the early nomadic Turkic tribes, whose homelands lay south of Lake Baykal in present-day Buryatskaya. Legend states that the Turks are descended from the union between a boy and a she-wolf. Enemy soldiers killed the boy, and the she-wolf took to the mountains near Turpan, where she gave birth to ten boys. One of the wolf-boys married a human woman and produced the forebears of the Turkic tribe.

By the sixth century, the Turks were centred in the Altai Mountains and living as farmers and herdsmen. They were a growing power until the seventh century, when they split into the Eastern and Western Turkic Khanates. The Uygur Empire rose from the ashes of the Eastern Turkic Khanate in the eighth century, aided by their friendly relations with the Chinese. Uygur soldiers helped restore the weakened Tang dynasty during the An Lushan Rebellion of 755–763. The Kirghiz drove the Uygurs from their lands between 840 and 844, and the tribes divided: some settled in the Hexi Corridor and established kingdoms at Dunhuang and Zhangye; others moved westwards into the oases south of the Heavenly Mountains, then occupied by Indo-European peoples. The Uygurs eventually gained control of the Silk Road trade routes, supplying horses to the Chinese and establishing independent kingdoms. They abandoned shamanist beliefs, and first adopted Manicheanism, then Buddhism and finally, in the tenth century, Islam. The Uygurs heavily influenced the politics, economics and cultural affairs of the Mongols, and their alphabet was adopted as the basis for the Mongol written language.

After the fall of the Mongol Yuan dynasty, Xinjiang split up into khanates, with a great deal of fighting between the small feudal rulers. The Chinese regained control of the region in the 18th century during the Qing dynasty. In 1862, a Muslim rebellion led by Yakub Beg swept through the region. Yakub Beg, who claimed to be a descendant of

Tamerlane, first drove the Chinese out of Kashgar, establishing himself as ruler of Kashgaria in 1867, and then proceeded to conquer all of Xinjiang. He moved as far east as Urumqi, Turpan and Hami, recruiting local minorities along the way. Most Muslims disliked Beg as much as they disliked the Chinese, and his dictatorship was characterized by bloody massacres, the rape and pillage of towns, secret police and high taxes. Beg signed treaties with the British and Russians, as both powers wanted to establish strong relations with local rulers in an effort to extend their own area of control. In 1877, Yakub Beg was finally defeated by the Chinese, who re-established control of Chinese Turkestan, as it was then known.

In the early 20th century, northern Xinjiang was controlled by the warlord, Yang Zengxin, and a civil war erupted against the southern Muslims led by Ma Zhongying. The northern commander, Sheng Shizai, eventually won control of the region, instituting reforms, religious freedom and trade with the Soviet Union. By 1940, his dictatorship resulted in the murder of over 200,000 leftists. In 1943, Sheng alligned himself with Chiang Kai-shek's Nationalist government, which eventually drove him out of power.

In the 1950s and 1960s, the Communist government tried to stabilize the region and settled Han Chinese there in an attempt to dilute the volatile Muslim population and reduce the threat of Muslim uprisings. The Chinese consider Xinjiang a desolate, bleak region populated with barbarians, while the Uygurs antagonize and intimidate the transplanted Chinese. Intermarriage seldom occurs. Animosity towards the Chinese and Chinese rule was particularly strong when separatists attempted to prevent Xinjiang's incorporation into the People's Republic of China in the 1950s. There is still dissent—in 1986, China's first anti-nuclear protests were held in opposition to nuclear tests in the desert near Lop Nor. The Uygurs are a strong, proud people that defend their right to live under Islam.

The square mud-brick Uygur homes are comfortable and quite spacious. Rooms are heated in winter by a brick *kang*, a platform for communal sleeping. It is covered at all times by colourful wool and felt rugs, as are the walls, which have decorated niches for food and utensils. The villagers use their flat roofs for drying melon seeds and grain, and the many families who tend vineyards have an open brick-work drying

continues

room for grapes, either on the roof or in nearby fields. In an open courtyard, frequently shaded by trailing grapevines, or in a deep cellar under the house, families relax during the intense heat of the day.

The majority of Uygurs tend fields of wheat, maize, vegetables and melons, orchards of apricots, peaches, pears and plums as well as vineyards. Many engage in the sideline production of silk and carpets. In the cities they work as traders, restaurateurs, factory workers and civil servants. Ugyur secondary schools teach Chinese as a second language, Uygur history and Islamic religion. Chinese secondary schools do not teach Uygur and at most universities only Mandarin is used. The few Uygurs who attend university do so at either of the two institutes in Urumqi or the Foreign Languages Institute in Beijing, which also offers Arabic.

Muslim religious festivals are widely celebrated: in particular, the month-long *Ramadan* fast, which culminates in several days of festivities known as *Bairam* or 'Minor' festival, and *Korban* or 'Major' festival. *Korban* is the celebrated Muslim new year. In Kashgar, early morning services (6 am local time) can mean up to 10,000 people flooding the Aidkah Mosque, its courtyard and the central square, where spontaneous dancing moves throughout the day to the rhythms of the drummers and horn players perched on the roof of the temple. Children roam the streets in packs, the small ones with handfuls of candy and noisemakers, the bigger ones with holiday water pistols. Families who can afford it buy a sheep to be slaughtered on this festive day, and the whole family gathers for hours of feasting and celebration.

Weddings are merry occasions with music and dancing; an imam usually officiates and reads from the Koran. Until recently, national minorities were exempt from the one-child policy of the Chinese government, but efforts are now being made to introduce a limit of two children per family, being born at least three years apart—an extremely unpopular policy. Once polygamous, the Uygurs now conform to Chinese marriage laws but divorce is quite common in the countryside, as is early marriage.

Uygur dress is still quite traditional in the cities of Turpan, Kucha and Kashgar. The men wear three-quarter-length coats sashed at the waist over trousers tucked into high leather boots, and (though now more rarely) kaftans. The women wear full, unwaisted dresses of variegated colours, often of homespun *aidelaixi* silk, with heavy brown stockings; in earlier times their dress was more elegant. The more devout Muslim women still wear veils outside the house, but many women either cover their hair with a scarf or don the colourfully embroidered square *dopa* (cap), which is also worn by men and children. The velvet *dopas* are often beaded and couched in gold thread and, in earlier times, had distinct regional differences. Hats are now a question of personal preference and cost. Women enjoy wearing jewellery—red, blue or clear cut-glass earrings and necklaces. Unlike the Chinese, they also wear make-up and paint their eyebrows, linking them together in a single line. Long plaits are common, but unmarried girls traditionally wear their hair in ten or more braids.

Great importance is attached to etiquette. Upon entering a home you are expected to rinse you hands three times from water poured by the host from a ewer. In partaking of the *dastarkan*—a cloth placed on the floor and laid with fruits and nan—you should stand with the family with hands together, palms uppermost, as if holding the Koran, then pass them over your face in a downwards motion, a religious gesture of thanks and blessings. Forms of address are respectful and accord with the individual's status within the family. Older men stroke their beards in the Muslim sign of courtesy. The traditional greeting is *Es Salaam Aleikum* ('may peace be upon you'), the response being *Wa Aleikum Es Salaam* ('and upon you').

Uygurs have a rich tradition of storytelling, music and dance. Their folk instruments include the *dotar*, a two-stringed guitar, the *ravap*, a six-stringed mandolin, and the sheepskin tambourine. Their dancing is elegant, full of twirling and delicate hand movements. Their folk songs include themes of exile, poverty and love as well as humour. A popular folk hero, about whom numerous stories are invented, is the character Effendi (a Turkish creation) and his donkey. The tales are satirical and amusing; modern ones have Effendi setting out on his donkey to talk with Chairman Mao.

Manuscripts and treatises on Uygur medicine, which date back to at least the eighth century, include over 400 commonly used herbs and more than 200 prescriptions. A centre for Uygur medicine in Kashgar has been particularly successful in the treatment of skin diseases, especially vitiligo, known as 'the white wind sickness'. One treatment for this condition is a mixture of sugar, raisins, bird blood, mutton, grapes and Chinese medicine.

PEACHES, PAPER AND RHUBARB

he Silk Road was one of the great trade routes that, over the centuries, profoundly transformed the worlds of the East and West through the mutual exchange of products, skills and knowledge.

The expeditions of Zhang Qian (second century BC) and his successors were not simply political. They returned to the imperial court of China with new ideas and techniques and collections of unknown plants and minerals. The earliest products from the West were alfalfa and the grapevine—introduced, it is said, by Zhang Qian himself, though the art of wine making came later.

From Persia and beyond came delectable sugary dates, pistachio nuts, peaches, pears and walnuts, indigo dyes, purple mascara from the murex shell, fragrant narcissus (adopted by the Chinese as their auspicious New Year bloom) and oils of frankincense and myrrh. A Persian gift of an asbestos mat did nothing to clarify the nature of the material, which was believed to be the wool of a salamander.

From Central Asia came almonds, jade, lapis lazuli, Glauber's salt, cucumbers, onions and fine horses. From India came spinach, the lotus, sandalwood, pepper and the holy Buddhist peepul tree. Most important of all, came Indian cotton, which in the Song dynasty (960–1279) reached the Yangzi River heartland via the Turpan oasis. In return, the Indians gained the peach and pear from Persia via China, calling them 'Chinese fruit' and 'Chinese prince' respectively.

From China came millet, anise, green ginger, roses, camellias, peonies, chrysanthemums and cassia and mulberry trees.

The art of colour-glazing originated in the Roman Empire. It did not reach China until the fifth century, but was then adopted rapidly into the decorative arts. The beautiful glass of Rome also found its way by caravan to the East.

Paper making, invented by the Chinese, spread westwards following the defeat of the Chinese army at the Battle of the Talas River in 751, when the Arab victors captured Chinese artisans and set them to work in Samarkand. The knowledge of paper making reached Baghdad in 794, Egypt and Northern Africa in the tenth century, and from there spread to Sicily and Spain in the early 12th century. Moveable-type printing was invented in China in the 11th century using types made out of clay, and the first metal types appeared in Korea in 1234.

Foreign music, musicians and dancers heavily influenced the Chinese cultural scene, especially during the Tang, when envoys from the Western Regions introduced dancing boys from Tashkent, twirling girls from Samarkand, the flute, oboe and lute from Kucha, and musicians from Sogdiana. From Turkestan and India came dwarfs, contortionists, conjurers and fire-eaters to amaze and amuse.

A latecomer to East–West trade was wild rhubarb, which the Chinese had used for malaria, fevers and women's ailments in the 16th century. Europeans, too, found it efficacious for numerous complaints, and the demand for it grew. Central Asian traders purchased wild rhubarb from towns in the Hexi Corridor of Gansu and sold it to Russian officials of the Chief Apothecary Office founded by Peter the Great. There was even a special 'rhubarb road' that skirted the Caspian Sea. The Russian monopoly on the trade was abandoned in 1790, but the Chinese continued to believe that tea and rhubarb were essential to the foreign diet. During the opium wars of the 19th century the Chinese contemplated cutting off the supply of both, so that their British enemies would succumb to blindness and constipation.

BLOOD TIES

After an hour or so, our amiable bantering is interrupted by a loud bang. The Toyota lurches to one side and slows to a halt. All pile out to pinpoint the problem, which is not difficult: we have burst a front tyre, and it seems to have all but shredded itself in the process of stopping. There is silence while this sinks in, then someone remembers the spare wheel behind the back seat. A frenzy of activity breaks out; the stiff is removed from his position on the parcel shelf, and we open up the back of the vehicle. One by one the smiles disappear. There is no spare wheel; it has been left in Korla.

Minutes turn to hours. A lorry passes by, and a couple of army jeeps. One of the jeeps stops and we compare wheels, but they are not the same. Then, suddenly, from the north, we see approaching the unmistakable shape of a Toyota. Wild gesticulations from nine excited figures succeed in bringing it to a halt, and we explain our predicament.

The vehicle is carrying a spare wheel, but the Uyghur driver is reluctant to part with it for less than its full value, which is considerable. We bargain with gusto, offering all sorts of non-essential parts from our own vehicle in an attempt to beat him down. But our efforts are in vain. The man is about to drive off, and I have resigned myself to more waiting, when the conversation takes a surprising turn. His attitude visibly changes as it emerges that one of our passengers is engaged to his cousin. Kinship has been established! Instantly all monetary considerations are swept aside, and the man quickly hands over the precious wheel. Within minutes it has been fitted, hands have been shaken, and once more we are on our way.

John Pilkington, An Adventure on the Old Silk Road, 1989

Kucha (Kuqa)

ow scrub, very occasional trees, pink flowering shrubbery and, where there is water, tall grass punctuate the endless *gebi* expanse west of Korla on the rim of the Tarim Basin.

Kucha, the next major town, was the centre of the largest of the 36 kingdoms of the Western Regions. In the second century BC, Zhang Qian passed through on his way west. In AD 91, Kucha surrendered to General Ban Chao, who brought 50 Central Asian kingdoms under the suzerainty of the Chinese during his campaign against the Xiongnu. By the fourth century, the Kuchean Kingdom of Guici was an important centre for Central Asian trade and Indo-European culture. Trade routes running north to the Junggar Basin and south to Hetian across the Taklamakan intersected with the Silk Road at Kucha.

The city's most famous son was the linguist and scholar, Kumarajiva (344–413), who earned a place in Chinese Buddhist annals as the 'Nineteenth Patriarch of Buddhism'. Kumarajiva's father was Kashmiri, and his mother was the sister of the King of Guici. He received his education in Kashmir, returning eventually to Kucha as a respected teacher of Hinayana Buddhism. Among his disciples were grandsons of the King of Yarkand. In 383, Kumarajiva was taken to Liangzhou (modern Wuwei) in Gansu Province by General Lu Kuang, who had subdued the kingdoms of the Tarim Basin. There he lived for 17 years, gaining renown as a prolific translator of Buddhist manuscripts from Sanskrit into Chinese.

rior to accurate translations of Indian Buddhist philosophy, the Chinese thought this new religion was a foreign barbarian form of their own Taoism, partly because both religions strive towards a state of salvation, and partly because the Chinese were unable to understand the essential doctrinal differences. The Chinese language is ill-suited for the many subtleties and abstract reasoning in Buddhism that Sanskrit easily and gracefully accomplishes. Only after accurate translations appeared between the fifth and eighth centuries did the Chinese fully understand the nature of Buddhism. Still, the Buddhism introduced to China maintained only the simplest tenets of the religion; Chinese Buddhist sects of Chan (Zen) and Pure Land bear limited resemblance to Indian Buddhism.

During the Tang dynasty the kingdom reached its zenith as a centre of artistic achievement and cultural exchange. The wealth of the trade caravans subsidized the Buddhist monasteries, in which more than 5,000 monks worked and prayed, and where there are some of the finest examples of Gandharan frescoes. Kuchean music heavily influenced Chinese music: musicians and dancers from Kucha performed before the court at Chang'an, where their musical instruments (drums, lutes, reed-pipes) and notation were adopted.

hen Xuan Zang passed through the Kingdom of Kucha in the sixth century, there were two huge Buddha statues 27 metres high guarding the road. He wrote of Kucha's fabled dragon-horses, which despite their docility, were said to be offspring of lake-dwelling dragons and wild mares. Prior to 658, when the Chinese took control of the city, Kucha had its own style of painting, music and its own language. Archaeologist Paul Pelliot discovered Buddhist documents at Kizil that had been written in this lost, ancient Kuchean language.

The arrival of the Uygurs in the ninth century brought about the gradual absorption of Kucha's Indo-Europeans and their eventual conversion to Islam. Under the reign of the Mongols, Kucha formed part of the Chaghatai Khanate called Uyguristan and became embroiled in the power struggles and petty wars of neighbouring kingdoms, falling frequently under Kashgar's control.

In 1864, Kucha joined in the Muslim rebellion against the Qing dynasty and was incorporated in Yakub Beg's Kashgaria three years later. The Chinese regained control in 1877.

The archaeological free-for-all at the Kucha sites began in 1889, when local treasure-seekers discovered a strange tower, probably an ancient Buddhist stupa, containing the mummified corpses of sacrificed animals and several piles of dusty manuscripts. In 1890, Lt (later Sir) Hamilton Bower purchased a manuscript written on birch bark while in Kucha. Bower sent the manuscript to Dr Augustus Hoernle, an expert on Central Asian languages at the Asiatic Society of Bengal in Calcutta, who deciphered the script and dated the 'Bower Manuscript' to AD 500. The text was written in Sanskrit using the Brahmani alphabet, probably by Indian monks, and dealt with the subjects of medicine and necromancy.

This amazing find led to the freelance exploration of the ancient buried cities of the Taklamakan and a scramble for the treasures of the Kucha region. Japanese expeditions sponsored by Count Kozui Otani in 1902 and 1908 worked in the area. In 1906, von Le Coq was threatened by the Russian Beresovsky brothers during a squabble over sites. The French orientalist, Paul Pelliot, spent seven months here during the same period. Stein followed in 1908, then the Russian Sergei Oldenburg in 1910. Not much was left.

SIGHTS

Kucha is an Uygur city—only 24 per cent of its 83,000 inhabitants are Han Chinese. The old and new cities are divided by the remains of the old city wall, which once stretched eight kilometres (five miles) from east to west. The old city is a maze of narrow, unpaved alleys and high mud-brick walls; the new city is simple and functional, containing the usual tourist conveniences. The local economy centres on

The red sandstone hills of the Flaming Mountains to the northeast of Turpan

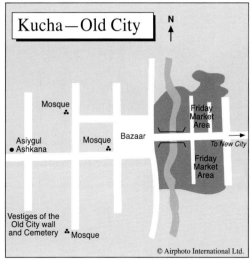

agriculture (wheat, cotton, maize, and such fruits as smooth-skinned apricots, rose-pink plums, sweet figs and grapes) and small factories producing cement, agricultural implements, carpets and other household necessities.

 he city comes alive on Fridays—bazaar day—when upwards of 30,000 people swarm in the streets and alleys of the old and new towns, carrying on a medieval Central Asian trading tradition in the heat and dust. Much of the bazaar takes place in the dried-up river bed and on surrounding banks, where hundreds of donkeys and horses wait tethered beside wooden carts. Uygur women, their heads covered with thick brown shawls and with their skirts hitched up to display stockinged legs and flowery bloomers, squat among their wares, aggressively selling home-dyed suede, wool for carpets, sheep skins, herbal medicines, dried fish, saddles and saddle bags, tasselled harnesses, farming implements, embroidered caps, cut-glass jewellery, scarves, haircuts, colourful felt rugs and thongs of neck leather. Entire sections of the market are devoted to silk and silk garments while small alleys are transformed into goat- and sheep-trading areas. Apart from vestiges of the ancient city wall, the old city contains Muslim cemeteries, several old mosques and narrow roads west and south of the main square that wind towards the surrounding fields and orchards.

The bridge over the river bed has two archways inscribed 'The Ancient Barrier of Guici'. Atop the Qing-dynasty mosque facing the river, the muezzin appears from a trap door to call worshippers to the mosque five times a day. White-bearded elders outside the mosque sell holy books and 'piddling tubes' for channelling children's urine through their layers of clothing, not to be confused with primitive wooden pipes. Under large, makeshift umbrellas, food stalls offer yoghurt, mutton sausage stuffed with rice, *shashlik*, boiled mutton and ice cream. Horsecarts and buses operate between the markets in the old and new cities. In the broad tree-lined streets of the new town is an agricultural market with fresh fruit and vegetables, grains and seeds, soft sun-dried apricots, and fresh mulberry and pomegranate juice. There is a Chinese outdoor dance hall with coloured lights and live music, where couples dance the tango, waltz and cha-cha to electronic rock and disco tunes.

In the summer, when apricots, peaches, pomegranates and figs are in season, tourists may visit a family fruit orchard southwest of the old city and experience traditional Uygur hospitality in the form of the *dastarkan*—a spread of nan and bowls of tea. For a nominal fee, visitors may pick their fill of fruit directly from the trees.

Kucha Mosque

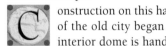onstruction on this handsome and imposing mosque in the northern part of the old city began in 1923. Its façade has two tall minarets, and the interior dome is handsomely niched in arabesque brick work. The large prayer hall, with its carved, inset ceiling and red, blue and green wooden pillars, is used for major Muslim festivals. Just to the west is a smaller mosque with honeysuckle roses in the courtyard, offering an excellent view of the old city and riverbed bazaar from the minaret. The mosques are closed to non-Muslims during prayer time.

Molena Ashidin Hodja's Tomb

A ten-minute walk from the Kucha Hotel is the tomb of an Arabian missionary who arrived in Kucha 600 to 700 years ago. One day he thoughtlessly killed a pigeon and the next day he dropped dead. His tomb is now a local shrine with an attached mosque; green tiles adorn the simple niched entrance-way. The sarcophagus, covered in white cloth, is inside a small hall of latticed wood. Strips of white cloth are tied to bare tree branches to indicate a holy site.

Kizil Thousand Buddha Caves

The Kizil Caves lie 75 kilometres (40 miles) northwest of Kucha in nearby **Baicheng County**. Access to the Caves is difficult unless you rent a car from a local travel agent. The caves, contain some of the best fresco fragments in Xinjiang. The main road out of the city, which eventually leads to Yining, passes through Salt Water Gully (Yanshui Gou), where the rock has been eroded by wind into weird, stark formations. A smaller road leads to the oasis and village of Kizil, and a dirt road branches off, winding down a steep pass that offers a spectacular view of the Kizil valley.

Of the 236 caves in this complex, 135 are considered intact, yet only 80 still contain fragments of wall paintings. No statuary remains. The earliest caves were hewn from the hillside in the third century, with the most artistically accomplished

(following pages) The Kizil Caves, 75 kilometres northwest of Kucha, contain some of the finest examples of Buddhist art in Central Asia. Begun in the third century, many remain inaccessible

ones coming later during the Tang dynasty. The cave temple complex was gradually abandoned with the spread of Islam to the Kucha region in the 14th century.

The Kizil Caves contained some of the finest examples of Buddhist art in Central Asia. The earliest wall paintings show Gandharan (Indo-Hellenistic) influences overlaid with Persian elements; there was no trace of Chinese influence in the Kizil Caves. Some 70 Buddhist fables from the Jataka stories are illustrated in the murals—the Pigeon King burns himself to attain nirvana, the Elephant King sacrifices himself to help the poor, and the Bear King donates food to help the starving; in Cave 38 the song-and-dance tradition of the ancient Kingdom of Qiuci is vividly represented by paintings of celestial musicians and dancers. Donors—usually wealthy merchants or royalty—are richly and colourfully painted, providing good examples of Guici dress. Most of what was left behind has been since defaced by local Muslims. Caves served different functions: some were for religious ceremonies, others for teaching sutras, and still others were living quarters. Murals were removed by foreign excavators in a neat patchwork, as the missing paintings reveal squares of the mud-and-stucco wall underneath.

f the numerous fin de siècle archaeological expeditions that came to Kizil, von Le Coq's probably made off with the most. He wrote upon his discovery of the caves that 'the pictures were painted on a special surface-layer, made out of clay mixed up with camel dung, chopped straw, and vegetable fibre, which is smoothed over and covered with a thin layer of stucco'. Using a sharp knife on the thin layer, von Le Coq cut the frescoes into pieces to fit the packing cases in which they were to be transported by cart, camel, horseback and train to Europe; now they are on display in Berlin.

Visitors may see only nine caves, of which six contain traces of frescoes, the others being completely bare. Photographers are charged a fee of Rmb200–800 per picture, depending on the size and quality of the fresco fragment. Lunch is available.

The site is attractive, with its thick groves of mulberry and poplar trees along the left bank of the Muzat (Weigan) River. Half a kilometre (a third of a mile) through an ever-narrowing gully behind the caves is the Spring of Tears, which flows from a semi-circular rock face. A local legend tells of the daughter of the King of Guici, the beautiful Princess Zaoerhan, who went out hunting one day and met a handsome young mason whose love songs won her heart. The young mason, who came to the king for permission to marry his daughter bearing all the presents he could afford, was harshly received by the king, who said: 'Since you are a mason carve out for me 1,000 caves. If you do not complete the task I will not give my daughter to you in marriage and shall punish you cruelly.' The young man went to the hills around the Muzat River and began carving out the caves. After three years he had completed 999 caves, but had worked himself to death. The princess went in search of him only to find his wasted body. She grieved to death; her endless tears fall to this day upon this semi-circular rock face.

Ancient City of Subashi

he extensive ruins of this ancient capital of the Kingdom of Qiuci lie 20 kilometres (12 miles) north of Kucha. They are divided by the Kucha River, which in flood cuts off access to the northern section. The city dates from the fourth century and includes towers, halls, monasteries, dagobas and houses. The ruins of the large Zhaoguli Temple date from the fifth century. A recently excavated tomb revealed a corpse with a square skull, confirming Xuan Zang's claim that in Qiuci, 'the children born of common parents have their heads flattened by the pressure of a wooden board'. The city was abandoned or destroyed in the 12th century. Access is by hired car only.

Kizil Kara Buddhist Caves

This small complex of 47 caves on a semi-circular bluff of barren rock 16 kilometres (ten miles) northwest of Kucha, was hewn between the third and tenth centuries. Fragments of frescoes remain in six of the caves: in cave 21, the repeated small Buddha images in black, turquoise and white are quite powerful, while on the ceiling at the back of Cave 30 are paintings, still well-preserved, of flying apsaras playing musical instruments. Nearby stands a lone mud-brick beacon tower from the third century, the original wooden struts still protruding from the upper section. Prior arrangements to visit these caves should be made through the FAO, as most of the caves are locked and there is no attendant. Original wood struts still protrude from the upper section.

Kumtura Caves

This famous site at the mouth of the Muzat (Weigan) River is 28 kilometres (17 miles) west of Kucha. A complex of 112 caves dating from the third to 14th century was extensively excavated by foreign archeologists. Unfortunately, the caves are not officially open to visitors; however, there are future plans to reopen them and build a museum at the site.

Kucha Practical Information

ucha is divided into the new city (*xin cheng*), where hotels and the bus station are located, and the old city (*lao cheng*), where the lively Friday market takes place. The locals are extremely friendly and curious, often inviting you to eat and drink with them.

Transportation

Flights three times a week to/from Korla and Urumqi (bookings at the Foreign Affairs Office); daily buses to/from Korla (continuing on to Turpan or Urumqi), Aksu, Kashgar and Hetian; buses to/from Yining several times a week (a spectacular journey

Grape vines growing on trellises above the courtyards of many houses in Xinjiang provide much needed shade during the hot summer months. Grapes were introduced to the region over 2,000 years ago, and together with a variety of melons, fill the markets during the late summer months

through the Heavenly Mountains and the Yili River valley). The bus station is at the eastern end of the new city.

ACCOMMODATION

The **Bus Station Guesthouse**
Tel (0997) 712-2682
Provides basic Chinese accommodation, communal toilets and no showers, adequate for travellers overnighting in Kucha.

Kucha Hotel (Kuqa Binguan)
Jiefang Lu. Tel (0997) 712-2844
库车宾馆　解放路
Secluded accommodation on the outskirts of the new city; Muslim restaurant; handicrafts and bookshop.

Silk Road Hotel (Si Lu Binguan)
Jiefang Lu. Tel (0997) 712-2901, fax 712-2602
丝路宾馆　解放路
Primarily geared for tour groups; next door to PSB; Muslim and Chinese restaurants.

FOOD AND DRINK
The Friday market in the old city is an orgy of food, fruit and drink. There are various small Uygur restaurants and teahouses that serve *laghman*, *samsa*, kebabs and nan—try the *chushira* at the Asiygul Ashkana, named after the friendly proprietor, just west of the old square. Local farmers stand beside mountains of melons and old market women sell fresh blackberries in natural syrup, which are exquisite when mixed with yoghurt or hand-churned *maroji*.

The night market area in the new city has many food stalls selling cold noodles and most other Uygur specialities, including *apke*. The Happy Sitar Restaurant on Jiefang Lu just opposite the market area prepares good Muslim dishes. For Sichuan and other Chinese flavours, try the small restaurants on the main road between the bus station and the new city.

TRAVEL AGENCY
The **Kucha FAO** (Waiban) on Wenhua Lu (tel (0997) 712-2022) opposite the Post Office functions as a tourist bureau; they can arrange for cars to the sites and provide for most other normal tourist services, but a hotel travel agent will be cheaper.

AKSU

he 262-kilometre (162-mile) journey from Kucha to Aksu takes between five and six hours by road. The area is frequently visited by light dust storms, generating an eerie, creeping fog around the base of sand mounds and the scattered ruins of the Han-dynasty beacon towers. Aksu lies at the base of barren yellow loess cliffs, its oasis stretching in a long green belt astride the banks of the Aksu River.

Neolithic artefacts from 5000 BC have been discovered in the Aksu area. By the first century BC, news reached the Chinese imperial court concerning the Kingdom of Baluka (as Aksu was formerly called), one of the 36 kingdoms of the Western Regions. Aided by the Xiongnu, the kingdom held out against a Chinese attack led by General Ban Chao, who finally marched upon the city in AD 78 and executed 700 inhabitants. Xuan Zang wrote of the kingdom in 629: 'With regard to the soil, climate, character of the people, customs and literature, these are the same as in the country of Qiuci. The language differs however a little. [The kingdom] produces a fine sort of cotton and hair-cloth, which are highly valued by neighbouring countries.'

In the mid-14th century, Telug Timur, Khan of Mogholistan, briefly made his capital in Aksu. Half a century later, an army led by Tamerlane the Great's grandson laid siege to the city, but by delivering the rich Chinese merchants to the troops in an effort to placate the Mongols, the people of Aksu ransomed themselves. Aksu was again the capital of Mogholistan during the reign of Esen-buqa (1429–1462) and a stage for murder and intrigue concerning the succession of the khanate. In the 1860s, Aksu became part of Yakub Beg's mighty state of Kashgaria; the city had joined the anti-Chinese rebellion and, like Kucha, was dominated by Yakub Beg, who had a fort on the bluff above the city. The Chinese re-established control a decade later.

ir Francis Younghusband, travelling along the northern Silk Road in the early 1890s, called Aksu 'the largest town we had yet seen. It had a garrison of two thousand soldiers, and a native population of about twenty thousand, beside the inhabitants of the surrounding district. There were large bazaars and several inns—some for travellers, others for merchants wishing to make a prolonged stay to sell goods.' Around the same time Sven Hedin stayed a few days in Aksu, noting fertile fields of grains, cotton and red opium poppies. Both he and Sir Aurel Stein enjoyed the warmth of local officials' hospitality and the cool of their fruit orchards. A less enchanted European traveller in the 1930s complained that 'the swarms of flies are denser [and] the smell of Moslem more concentrated and ranker than anywhere else', but conceded 'there are not many places where the temples are more wonderful or the gardens of the rich Moslems more beautiful'.

AKSU PRACTICAL INFORMATION

Han Chinese make up a majority of Aksu's 300,000 residents. There is little of interest for the modern tourist apart from a carpet factory and the bazaar; the buildings are uniformly grey concrete blocks devoid of any architectural merit.

TRANSPORTATION

There are air connections to Urumqi, Kashgar, and Hetian daily. A few buses start from Aksu, but most pass through en route between Kashgar and Korla or Urumqi.

ACCOMMODATION

Available either at the **Bus Station Guesthouse**, tel (0997) 212-3373, or in town at the **Aksu Binguan**, tel (0997) 212-3373, on Xin Jie Hua Lu in the western part of the city (dorm Rmb68 for three beds, double Rmb88–160).

AKSU TO KASHGAR

nce the green poplars of the Aksu oasis are left behind, the yellow void of *gebi* reappears. Truckloads of horses, mules and donkeys, and convoys of long-distance buses head towards Kashgar. Ranged along the highway are rocky mountains in startling shades of jade green, red, orange, ochre and maroon. Telephone poles mark the distance. A young Scandinavian traveller on the Urumqi-Kashgar route in the 1930s wrote: 'Out in the desert, up on the passes and in the narrow valleys—everywhere lie skeletons and skulls, grinning. Skeletons large and small, piles of bones and solitary femurs. Horse? Camel? Man? It is not easy to decide as you rattle past . . .' Mirages are common, and so are whirlwinds of sand, like dancing ghosts of the desert.

At the small town of **Sanchakou**, 214 kilometres (133 miles) southwest of Aksu, is a turnoff for **Bachu**, called Maralbashi in the records of 19th- and 20th-century European explorers. Sir Aurel Stein traced the wall of a fort and the structures of an extensive city, both long abandoned. A direct desert route along the Shache River linked it with Shache (Yarkand), a journey accomplished by Stein in 1908 in five days.

KIZILESU KIRGHIZ AUTONOMOUS COUNTY

orty kilometres before Kashgar is **Artush**, seat of the Kizilesu Kirghiz Autonomous County. Outside the town is the **Tomb of Satuq Bughra Khan**, the first ruler of Kashgar to convert to Islam. Legend tells how, while the young khan was out hunting one day, a hare he was pursuing suddenly transformed itself into a man. This apparition questioned the young man about his Buddhist beliefs and filled him with terror of the sufferings of hell. He convinced Satuq Bughra that by accepting the teachings of the Prophet Mohammed, he would unquestionably go to paradise, a place of wine, women and song. The boy unhesitatingly took the vow, and the wars against the Buddhist states of the southern Silk Road began soon after. He died in 955 and was buried here in what must have once been a grand tomb but was later destroyed in an earthquake; the present tomb is only 30 years old. The **Sulitanjiamai Mosque**, beside the tomb, has a larger prayer hall and in front is a tree-shaded pool, providing a peaceful, contemplative atmosphere for the old Muslim men who gather here.

The 120,000 nomadic **Kirghiz** who inhabit the Pamir, Heavenly and Kunlun Mountain ranges are of Mongol origin, but speak a Turkic-Altaic language. Many Kirghiz live across the border in Kirghizia. The Kirghiz were a fierce power in the ninth century and drove the Uygurs southwards from the Yenisei River region; by the 14th century they occupied their present highland pastures. In the last days of the tsarist empire, Russian peasants encroached on Kirghiz pasture lands, which led to violent reprisals by both sides, and many Kirghiz fled across the border into Xinjiang.

In the summer, Kirghiz herdsmen set up their yurts in pastures 3,700 metres (12,000 feet) above sea level, just below the glacier level; in the winter, quarters are set up in valleys at around 2,700 metres (9,000 feet). Their white yurts, called *ak-ois*, are described by the former British consul in Kashgar, Sir Clarmont Skrine, as 'looking like enormous button mushrooms on the wide meadow'. The *ak-ois* are furnished with felt rugs and large reed mats decorated with bold designs of dyed woollen thread.

The Kirghiz diet is simple and monotonous: curds, milk, sour cream, bread made from flour and mutton fat, sun-dried cheese balls, tea and *kumiss* (wine made from fermented mare's milk). This fare is supplemented by hunting and hawking, but livestock is rarely eaten. The killing of a sheep or goat is reserved for special occasions—marriages, funerals and festivals—when feasts of boiled meat are enjoyed.

All Kirghiz celebrations end in horse-racing, wrestling and *buzhashi*, rugby on horseback played with the headless carcass of a sheep or goat. After the animal is slaughtered by a respected elder, a young man, gripping a whip in his mouth, mounts his horse, grabs the sheep and rides off shrieking. Hundreds of riders join in the game trying to grab the sheep by the feet or any available part of its body. Whoever flings the carcass across the designated finish line wins a bolt of silk.

Kashgar's central Idkah Mosque

KASHGAR (KASHI)

Kashgar is at heart a medieval city, a vibrant Islamic centre within Chinese territory. It is the largest oasis city in Chinese Central Asia and 70 per cent of its population of over 300,000 are Uygur. Kashgar's importance derives from its strategic position at the foot of the Pamir Mountains, commanding access to the high glacial passes of the Silk Road routes into Central Asia, India and Persia. The weary trade caravans plodding west on the northern and southern routes met up at Kashgar, the desert hazards and demons finally behind them. Merchants bound for China thawed out after descending to Kashgar from the peaks of the Pamirs or the Karakorams, and exchanged their stolid yaks and exhausted packhorses for camels to convey their merchandise into the Kingdom of Cathay.

Kashgar's history spans over 2,000 years; the earliest references appeared in Persian documents referring to an alliance of Tushlan tribes, who founded their capital here. Kashgar was possibly the first of the Buddhist kingdoms of the Tarim Basin. In the second century AD, Hinayana Buddhism flourished here and continued to do so until the ninth or tenth century. During this period Indian and Persian cultural influences were strong. Xuan Zang noted that the Kashgaris had green eyes—perhaps a reference to Aryan origins—and that 'for their writing they take their model from India . . . . The disposition of the men is fierce and impetuous, and they are mostly false and deceitful. They make light of decorum and politeness, and esteem learning but little.'

In the first century AD, during the Han dynasty, China lost its power over the Tarim Basin. The great General Ban Chao was dispatched to subdue the wild kingdoms of the Silk Road that had aligned themselves with the Xiongnu against the Chinese. He took the kingdoms of Kashgar, Hetian and Loulan either by brute force or cunning strategy, installed pro-Chinese rulers and reopened the southern Silk Road to trade. Ban Chao remained in Chinese Central Asia for 31 years, crushing rebellions and establishing diplomatic relations with more than 50 states in the Western Regions. Accompanied by horsemen arrayed in bright red leather, he himself went as far west as Merv and made contacts with Parthia, Babylonia and Syria.

In the early seventh century, Kashgar recognized the suzerainty of Tang China, which garrisoned the city. However, the Chinese were soon forced to withdraw between 670 and 694, when Tibet expanded its territories throughout the southern oases of the Tarim Basin. Between the tenth and 12th centuries the Kharakhanid Khanate, a loose nomadic alliance of the Qarluq Turkic tribes, controlled the area between Bokhara and Hetian from its capital in Kashgar. The Sunni Muslim, Satuq Bughra Khan, was the first of the Kharakhanid kings of Kashgar; he and his successors carried on bloody jihads against the still-Buddhist kingdoms of Shache and Hetian. These battles, along with fierce Kharakhanid internecine struggles, disrupted the caravan trade, and East–West trade was increasingly forced to rely on the sea routes.

Marco Polo wrote in the 13th century that the Kashgaris 'have very fine orchards and vineyards and flourishing estates...[but] are very close-fisted and live very poorly....There are some Nestorian Christians in this country, having their own church and observing their own religion.'

Following the death of Chaghatai, who inherited the region from his father, Genghis Khan, there followed numerous succession wars. Only briefly during the mid-14th century, when Telug Timur had his capital in Kashgar, was a degree of calm and stability restored. But Tamerlane's armies were soon to lay waste to the Kingdom of Kashgaria.

In the 16th century, Kashgar came under the rule of a religious leader, or *khoja*, whose colleagues formed a powerful clique in Bokhara and Samarkand. A theological split saw the formation of two opposing sects, the Black and White Hats, which began a bloody see-sawing of power between Kashgar and Shache that ended only with Qing intervention two centuries later. The *khojas* attempted to return to power in Kashgar no fewer than six times, frequently backed by the Khokand Khanate and aided by Kirghiz nomadic horsemen, bringing fearful reprisals on the citizens. An unfortunate observer of the *khojas'* last attempt in 1857 was a German, Adolphus Schlagintweit, whose throat was cut because of his arrogant comment that the three-month siege of Kashgar would have taken his countrymen a mere three days.

ashgar was substantially fortified during the short but violent reign of Yakub Beg, who ruled Kashgaria from 1866 to 1877. This infamous boy dancer-cum-soldier from Khokand ruled most of Xinjiang, from Kashgar to Urumqi, Turpan and Hami, concluded treaties with Britain and Russia, and had the support of the Ottoman Empire. He was rumoured to have 300 wives and presided over a lavish court. In 1869, Robert Shaw, a British trader and unofficial diplomat, became the first Englishman to visit Shache and Kashgar, and was able to command two audiences with Yakub Beg, even though he was under virtual house arrest for the duration of his stay in the city. He wrote of Kashgar: 'Entering the gateway, we passed through several large quadrangles whose sides were lined with rank upon rank of brilliantly attired guards, all sitting in solemn silence so that they seemed to form part of the architecture of the building. . . . Entire rows of these men [were] clad in silken robes and many seemed to be of high rank judging from the richness of their equipment.' After a leisurely three-year advance on Chinese Turkestan, the 60,000-strong Chinese army of Zuo Zongtang suppressed the Muslim rebellions in Gansu and then moved southwest through the oasis towns, eventually ending Yakub Beg's rule in 1877. Yakub Beg fled to Kashgar where he died—rumoured to have either had a stroke or poisoned himself.

Gunnar Jarring, a Swedish diplomat and scholar who spent some months in the city in 1929, wrote:

> The city of Kashgar was surrounded by a massive wall about ten metres high and built of sun-dried brick with mud filling in the spaces between. On top it was wide enough for a two-wheeled cart. Communication with the outside world was through four great gates which were closed at dusk and reopened at sunrise. Inside the walls were bazaars, the large mosques, and dwellings for both rich and poor. The Chinese authorities were outside the walls, as were the British and Russian consulates, and the Swedish mission with its hospital and other welfare establishments. Outside there was green nature, sunshine and light; inside it was always half dark.

 s anti-Chinese Muslim rebellions broke out throughout Xinjiang in the 1930s, a pan-Turkic Islamic movement based in Kashgar declared an Independent Muslim Republic of Eastern Turkestan. Its flag (a white field emblazoned with a crescent moon and a star) flew over the walled city for two months in 1933. Chinese troops from Urumqi, aided by Russians, moved south in pursuit of Ma Zhongying and his rebel army. Ma held out at the Yangi Hissar (New Town) fortress of Kashgar for six months before mysteriously disappearing across the Soviet border in a truck he commandeered from the Swedish explorer, Sven Hedin.

The Kashgar prefecture administers 11 counties with a population of over three million. It is one of the main agricultural areas of Xinjiang, producing cotton, rice, wheat, corn, beans and fruit.

Sights

This fabled city is like a step back in time to an ancient Central Asian khanate; traditional rhythms of the traders, worshippers, bakers seem unchanged amidst the mud-brick walls, horse carts and bazaars. The old city is encircled by Russian-style administrative buildings erected in the 1950s and low concrete boxes from the 1960s and 1970s. An 18-metre-high (59-foot) steel-reinforced statue of Chairman Mao dominates the main street of the city. As its westernmost outpost, Kashgar is the heart of Uygur Islam in China.

The heart of the old city is the Idkah Mosque and the surrounding bazaar along Jie Fang Bei Lu and the alleys that extend east and west of the mosque. Uygur headdress is a kind of fashion statement and a wide variety of head coverings are available, including skull caps, 'thug' caps, prayer caps, fur-lined caps, and 'dunce' caps, as well as brown veils and colourful silk scarves for the women. Many young girls have the back of their heads shaved in a very modern cut designed for the heat of summer. Most older men tend to keep an extremely clean look; barbers set up throughout the bazaar

continued on page 277

A musical instrument maker in Kashgar

One of many characters that flock to Kashgar's Sunday market from the surrounding area

A sign outside a dentist's surgery graphically illustrates the proprietor's profession

The men of Xinjiang smoke a locally grown coarse variety of tobacco which they roll in the thin paper of pages torn from old books

THE SILVER SCREEN

t the Kashgar Odeon (or whatever name it went by) two films were currently being shown. One was advertised by pictures of the familiar 'Happy Peasant' variety, and that film might well have been about manure collectors. But there was no mistaking the second film. It was Dr No. We bought two tickets and went inside. The film had just begun.

The auditorium was not large by English standards, but was packed full. The audience consisted entirely of Uigur men and all were in a great state of excitement. It seemed not to matter that very few had seats, and had to sit on a floor glazed with spittle. Going to the cinema was clearly a great treat, and everyone was determined to enjoy themselves whether or not conditions were perfect, indeed whether they could see or hear anything at all. I assume this because the Uigurs can in fact have understood almost nothing of what was going on. The film had been dubbed out of its original English, not into Turki but into French, which cannot have aided comprehension greatly. And, although there were subtitles, this also did not greatly help. The Uigur subtitles were placed at the bottom of the frame, beneath those in Tibetan and Chinese, and because of a technical error in the projecting box, all of these had disappeared below the screen and now rested on the backs of the heads of the people in the front two rows. This same error also deprived Sean Connery and Joseph Wiseman of their heads, which were projected beyond the screen and could just be seen, along with everything else from the top of the frame, wildly distorted at the front of the hall.

Despite all these irritations, the Uigurs were tolerant. There was an excited murmur every time a character bent down and his face could be fleetingly glimpsed on the screen, and the Muslim audience behaved with remarkable restraint during the sex scenes. Even Ursula Andress coming out of the sea, enough to craze the most worldly-wise Western audience, failed to move the Uigurs to any really dramatic behaviour, although this may have been because none of the audience had ever seen the sea (Kashgar is further from it than any other town in the world) and so were distracted from the more inflammatory aspects of the sequence. It may also have had something to do with the fact that the more inflammatory parts of Ursula Andress's body had missed the top of the screen and could only be seen indistinctly (if hugely enlarged) on the far wall.

There was, in fact, only one scene in the film which really impressed the Uigurs. This was when James Bond wakes up to find a large and very hairy tarantula crawling up his crotch and making for his torso. There cannot be many tarantulas in Kashgar, but the audience still got the gist of what was happening. They went berserk. As the spider crawled upwards the background murmur in the cinema got louder and louder. At the moment Bond tossed the beast off his chest and onto the floor, crushing it with his shoe, the cinema exploded. The Uigurs rose from their seats and bawled 'Allah-i-Akbar' (God is all powerful). A very old man next to me took off his shoe and started thumping the floor with it. Hats were thrown in the air. Urchins made wolf whistles. It was like the winning goal in the Cup Final. After that, even the twenty megaton nuclear explosion in the SPECTRE headquarters came as bit of an anticlimax.

William Dalrymple, In Xanadu, 1989

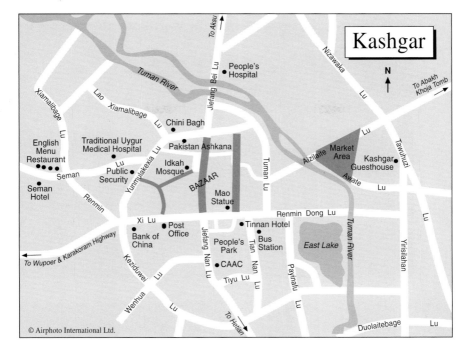

shave faces and scalps with an assortment of large knives and cleavers. The position of the cap or hat is also very important in achieving the desired careless effect. Dress is conservative and meant to cover the entire body: long sleeves and pants for the men, dresses and stockings for the women. Wearing the long brown veils over their heads to avoid exposure, the older women look like walking ghosts.

Silversmiths, bootmakers, porcelain menders and bakers labour in front of teashops and numerous stores that sell jewellery, silk, colourful wood-carved baby cradles and handsome wooden chests overlaid with strips of tin. In the residential quarter are high walls that protect small courtyards encircled by two-storey houses with carved wooden balconies, window shutters and doorways executed in classical Uygur style.

On Sundays, thousands of farmers driving carts flock from the countryside to the great Kashgar bazaar around Aizilaitie Lu, east of the Tuman River. There are numerous gates and fences demarcating the many sections within the market: silk and cotton in *aidelaixi* patterns, knives, hats, pots and pans, fresh vegetables, mountains of stacked Hami and Xiang (fragrant) melons, baskets of peaches and apricots. The overflow of people spills into the streets where horse and donkey carts jostle with each other, carrying people to and from the market. Uncured sheep skins, Karakul lambskins, boiled and dyed eggs, red twig baskets, glazed jars and water ewers, felt carpets, coloured cut-glass jewellery and fresh meat, all can be found at the other stalls. Shows of acrobats and magicians attract large crowds of shoppers. The livestock and

(above and below) The holiest place in Xinjiang, Abakh Khoja's Tomb was built in 1640. The pictures show the Tombs Hall which contains a number of tombs covered in coloured cloth, including, traditionally, that of Xiang Fei, Abakh Khoja's grand-daughter, who was said to be the Fragrant Concubine of the Qing emperor Qianlong

horse section of the market, which once added to the spectacle, has now been moved 6 km southeast of the market.

Throughout the chaotic Sunday market are stalls selling noodles, *poluo*, *samsa*, boiled hunks of mutton and piles of fresh nan, yoghurt and *maroji*. To the cacophony of cries from enthusiastic traders is added *posh! posh!*, which means 'get out of the way!' Those who ignore it risk being run down by a cart loaded with yellow carrots or a devil-may-care horseman.

Idkah Mosque

his mosque, the largest in China, can see as many as 10,000 worshippers at prayers on Friday afternoon. Muslims come from towns as far away as Yengisar, many dressed in traditional *chapans* (three-quarter-length coats of striped cotton), embroidered *dopas* and knee-length leather boots. Veiled women and young children stand outside the mosque, holding teapots of water or pieces of nan in cloth. As the men stream out from prayers they bestow on these their holy breath or spit, blessing them; they will then be taken to feed a sick relative.

Built in 1442, the mosque dominates the central square, its tall rectangular doorway flanked by slim minarets at the centre of a yellow-and-white facade. The large prayer hall is supported by 140 carved wooden pillars. It is one of the liveliest places to be during the Korban festivities.

Abakh Khoja's Tomb

This *mazar* is the holiest place in Xinjiang and an architectural treasure. Built in 1640, it is reminiscent of the Central Asian artistic style of Samarkand or Isfahan. A handsome blue-and-white tiled gate leads into the compound, which includes a small religious school and the Abakh Khoja family tomb. The latter is domed and faced with multi-coloured tiles.

In the 17th century, Abakh Khoja was the powerful ruler of Kashgar, Korla, Kucha, Aksu, Hetian and Shache. A leader of the White Hat Sect of Islam, he was revered as a prophet and second only to Mohammed. The site was originally donated to Abakh's father, Yusup, a respected Muslim missionary who had travelled in Arabia and returned a greatly respected teacher of the Koran. Yusup set up his religious school here, and the mausoleum was built for him. But his son's fame was greater, and after Abakh's death in 1693 the tomb was renamed after him. All five generations of the family are buried within. There were 72 tombs until an earthquake in 1956 left only 58. The tombs are decked in coloured saddle cloths.

The different buildings include the Tombs Hall, the Doctrine Teaching Hall, and the Great Hall of Prayer. The Tombs Hall has a dome covered with glazed green tiles; the tombs below are decorated with beautiful flower patterns.

Among the many devotees attracted to the *mazar* are women who come to pray for a child; they tie strings of coloured cloth—black, white and blue for a boy; red and floral for a girl—to one of the window frames. During the Korban festival, many Muslims from all over Xinjiang make the pilgrimage to the tomb. Before the main entrance is a pool filled with lily pads, and behind the mausoleum is a large graveyard, where, it is said, Yakub Beg was buried in an unmarked grave. The graves are coffin-shaped, above ground and made of earth. Many have a small hole in them that allows the soul of the dead to travel. The tomb, about three kilometres east of the city, is easily accessible by horse cart or bicycle.

Chini Bagh

 his old British Consulate was the home for 26 years of the most famous of British India's representatives in Kashgar, Sir George Macartney and his wife. The Macartney's legendary hospitality was extended to weary foreign travellers of the Silk Road, including Sir Aurel Stein, Albert von Le Coq, Sven Hedin, Peter Fleming and Ella Maillart. Until 1948, its gates were guarded by turbaned soldiers of the Gilgit Scouts. Life at Chini Bagh is delightfully recalled in *An English Lady in Chinese Turkestan* by Lady Macartney. The gardens were destroyed to make room for a large tourist hotel, and behind it is the house where the Macartneys lived, now reserved for official visitors.

The once luxurious **Russian Consulate** (now the Seman Hotel) was the home of the powerful Nikolai Petrovsky, Macartney's chief adversary in the Great Game (see Special Topic on page 284). During the years they were stoically positioned at this desolate outpost the two consuls carried on an almost comic rivalry for political secrets as well as for manuscripts and antiquities dug up by locals in the ancient buried cities of the desert. It is said that the extremely volatile Petrovsky did not speak a word to Macartney between November 1899 and June 1902.

Three Immortals Buddhist Caves (Sanxian Dong)

The turn-off for these caves is close to the ten-kilometre (six-mile) mark along Wuqia Lu, northwest of Kashgar. After following the track for three kilometres (two miles) along the south side of the Qiakmakh River, the three caves are visible, hewn from the cliff face some ten metres (30 feet) above the river bed. Dating from the second or third century, they are the earliest Buddhist caves extant in China. Each has two chambers, and traces of wall paintings survive in the left-hand cave. The caves are virtually inaccessible, especially at high-water periods. However, if you are intent upon seeing them, arrangements must be made with CITS and the fire department, as they are the only ones with ladders tall enough to reach the caves.

ANCIENT CITY OF HANOI

Thirty kilometres (18 miles) east of Kashgar lie the ruins of two dagobas and the city walls of this Tang-dynasty town, which probably dates from the mid-seventh century, when the Shule military governorship was established in the region. The site was abandoned after the 11th century. The remains of *karez* wells show how the town was supplied with water. Darkened soil indicates that the two dagobas constituting the Mor Temple, both a dozen or so metres high, were destroyed by fire. Porcelain sherds and Tang-dynasty coins have been found here.

OPAL

The tomb of the 11th-century Uygur philologist, Mohammed Kashgeri, is attractively situated in the rich agricultural oasis of Opal, a pleasant 45-kilometre (28-mile) excursion to the west of Kashgar. Kashgeri, a renowned scholar of Turkish culture in western Xinjiang and other parts of Central Asia, compiled a widely-acclaimed Turkic dictionary in Arabic. The present mausoleum of Opal's native son was rebuilt in 1983, and several rooms are devoted to an exhibition of his works and local archaeological finds, including a large pottery sherd showing a bearded foreign king crowned with vine leaves. In the bluff behind the tomb are several ancient Buddhist caves in complete ruin. To get to Hanoi or Opal, hire a car at Caravan Café or one of the hotels.

KASHGAR PRACTICAL INFORMATION

There are several different ways of getting around Kashgar: by foot, bicycle or taxi. Normal business hours are 10:30am–2:30pm, 5pm–9pm, Beijing time.

TRANSPORTATION

There are two flights a day to/from Urumqi as well as flights to Bishkek and Almaty (CAAC booking office at 49 Jiefang Lu, tel 282-2113). Three trains per day to/from Urumqi, taking 23 hours, and one train per day to/from Turpan which takes 22 hours. Daily buses to/from Tashkurgan, Yengisar, Yecheng, Hetian, Aksu, Kucha, Yining, Korla, Turpan and Urumqi (main bus station is on Tian Nan Lu, luxury bus available to Urumqi); chartered buses to/from Sost, Pakistan depart from the International bus station in the morning (with an overnight in Tashkurgan).

ACCOMMODATION

Kashgar Guesthouse (Xin Binguan)
Tawuhuzi Lu. Tel (0998) 261-2363; fax 282-4679
喀什宾馆
Large hotel complex three kilometres from city centre; comfortable accommodation geared for groups; Muslim restaurant; ticket services and bicycle rental.

Seman Hotel (Lao Binguan)
Seman Lu. Tel (0998) 255-2129, 255-2147; fax 255-2861
色满宾馆　色满路
Former Russian consulate; good location, perhaps a little run-down; traditional Uygur restaurant; outdoor garden café; ticket services and cars for hire; more expensive rooms and suites are available.

Chini Bagh (Qini Bake)
144 Seman Lu. Tel (0998) 282-5929; fax 282-3087
其尼巴合宾馆　色满路 144 号
Former British consulate; recently renovated and comfortable; popular with Pakistani traders; chartered buses to Sost, Pakistan; Chinese, Western, and Muslim restaurants; CITS on the grounds. Bike hire available.

Tiannan Hotel (Tiannan Fandian)
Renmin Dong Lu. Tel (0998) 282-4023
天南饭店　人民东路
Basic Chinese accommodation (communal toilets and public shower); close to the main bus station.

FOOD AND DRINK

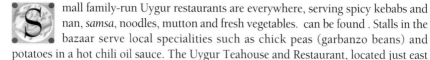

mall family-run Uygur restaurants are everywhere, serving spicy kebabs and nan, *samsa*, noodles, mutton and fresh vegetables. can be found . Stalls in the bazaar serve local specialities such as chick peas (garbanzo beans) and potatoes in a hot chili oil sauce. The Uygur Teahouse and Restaurant, located just east of the mosque at a busy intersection, serves pots of *chai*, *laghman* and *chushira* eaten with a large wooden spoon. Spend a cool afternoon on the second storey balcony watching the chaotic market scene below. There are several Chinese restaurants with English menus opposite the Seman Hotel. *Durap* and *maroji* are popular on hot summer days.

For a change in flavour, try the Pakistani Ashkana (opposite the Chini Bagh and slightly to the north), equipped with a series of wicker-chair booths, swirling ceiling fans, and friendly Ugyurs that serve excellent Pakistani cuisine. In the morning (afternoon, Beijing time), many of the Pakistani traders congregate for a leisurely breakfast of sweet milk tea, scrambled eggs and *prata*, fried dough dipped in sugar; a typical midday meal consists of chapatis with chicken or mutton curry, fresh yoghurt served with a small plate of tomatoes, cucumbers and onions. An excellent place to relax and avoid the mid-afternoon sun, you are in the right place if, upon the wall, there is a sign exhorting you to 'Live like Ali, Die like Hussein'.

The horse and livestock section of the Kashgar Sunday market, where horsemen test mounts and show off their riding skills, is now located 6 km to the southeast of the main market on the edge of town

THE GREAT GAME

I n the early 19th century, Russian troops began a great expansion south through the Caucasus Mountains (now in Georgia) towards Persia. Initially, when Napoleon Bonaparte temporarily aligned himself with Tsar Alexander I and planned to march across Persia and Afghanistan into British India, London was not alarmed. But Britain was immediately alert to the vulnerability of the no-man's land north of the subcontinent and its strategic importance to both Britain and Russia. Although nothing came of Napoleon's elaborate plan, Russia continued its drive through the khanates of the former Silk Road in Central Asia for the next 50 years.

Until the early 20th century, the two rival imperialist powers were locked in an often subtle, sometimes overt struggle for control of the region, stretching from the Caucasus in the west through Central Asia to Chinese Turkestan and Tibet in the east. Russia was determined to gain access to the fabled riches of India—the source of Britain's power and wealth—through the uncharted mountain passes of the Pamir and Karakoram Mountains, while Britain fought to keep the Russians out by maintaining a loyal string of buffer states along the Indian borders. Power in this remote area rested more upon gathering intelligence and surveying the uncharted mountain passes than on high-level diplomacy. Despite the dangers involved, mostly from hostile tribes and khanates in the region, adventurous and patriotic British officers eagerly volunteered to map the region, report on Russian movements and try to entice the suspicious khans into aligning themselves with Britain. Explorations were carried out under the guise of 'shooting expeditions' or 'geographical surveys' by the British, and 'scientific expeditions' by the Russians. They ventured into dangerous and unknown territory, often in clever disguises; many never returned and lie in unmarked graves throughout the dry mountain passes of Central Asia.

Pundits, Indian explorers highly trained in secret surveying techniques, were employed by Captain Thomas Montgomerie of the Indian Survey, a mammoth agency in charge of providing the government with maps of the subcontinent and surrounding regions. It was politically sensitive for British officers to travel into the dangerous regions of Afghanistan, Turkestan and Tibet, beyond India's borders. Their deaths could not be avenged if they were accused of spying and murdered by suspicious khanates, wary of foreign threats to their power. *Pundits*, as native Indians, were less likely to be detected and could be more readily disowned if they were caught or killed. Disguised as Buddhist pilgrims, they mapped unknown regions, keeping track of their paces per day, counting them on prayer beads to measure distances, and noting these measurements on scroll paper hidden inside hand-held prayer wheels. A compass was concealed in the lid of the prayer wheel, and thermometers, for estimating altitudes, were hidden in the lid of the stave. Although the *pundits* were rarely rewarded for their bravery and cunning, this dangerous work was immortalized in Rudyard Kipling's *Kim*.

The theatrics and intrigue of this Great Game, as it was called (*bolshaya igra* in Russian), was as exciting for armchair strategists as it was for the players. Volumes of books, articles, pamphlets and editorials written about the perceived threat of the enemy's position in Central Asia dictated official foreign policy, and intrigued the public with stories about politics and adventures in the exotic kingdoms of Ladakh, Bokhara, Khokand and others.

An early player in the Great Game was William Moorcroft, a veterinarian with the British East India Company, who passionately advocated a more aggressive policy against Russian advances. He was posthumously lauded for his contributions to geography and vindicated for his warnings of the Russian threat. However, few British officals at the time wanted to hear his hawkish position. In 1819, Moorcroft went on a mission to Bokhara through the Karakorams to purchase the fabled Turcoman steeds. Alarmed by the presence of a native trader who had been recruited as a Russian scout, Moorcroft established an unauthorized commerical treaty with the ruler of Ladakh in northern India, enraging the neighbouring ruler of the Punjab. Moorcroft was disowned by the East India Company but continued on to Bokhara, where he found Russian goods in the markets and no horses. He reportedly died of fever some weeks later, though some think he was poisoned; other reports concerned an Englishman who lived in Lhasa disguised as a Kashmiri, and who possessed maps and plans with Moorcroft's name on them.

continues

Another early protagonist was a young Scotsman, Lt (later Sir) Alexander Burnes, fluent in Persian, Arabic and Hindustani. In 1832, disguised as a trader, Burnes also entered the dangerous Khanate of Bokhara, the leading Islamic cultural centre in Central Asia, on a mission to discover the ruler's political leanings. He brought back stories of the curious Grand Vizier and of the city's barbaric customs (throwing criminals to their deaths from the tops of minarets) and wrote a best-selling epic in three volumes on the mystery and excitement of Central Asia.

A Russian secret mission reached Kashgar in 1858, and in the 1860s Russia occupied Tashkent (one of the richest cities in Central Asia), Samarkand and Bokhara. At the same time, Yakub Beg established himself as ruler in Kashgar and played Russia and Britain against each other, establishing treaties with both powers in an effort to gain international recognition for his kingdom (which neither would do publicly for fear of angering the Chinese government). Yakub Beg's control spread, and soon threatened the Yili region with its strategic access to the southern Russian frontier and rich minerals. In 1871, to the consternation of the Chinese government, the Russians occupied Yili. Six years later, a Chinese army under the command of General Zuo Zongtang finally defeated Yakub Beg and restored Chinese command in the region.

In the 1870s, the Russians took Khiva and Khokand. In 1884, Russia's annexation of Merv near the Persian border gave them access to Persia and Afghanistan. Strategically close to British India, they were blocked only by the formidable High Pamirs and Karakorams; Britain and Russia came close to war. By the end of the 1880s the Russians were sending intelligence-gathering sorties into the Pamir region. British Indian forces subdued the unreliable tribes along the Indian frontier in an attempt to block Russian encroachment.

In 1888, Captain Gromchevsky, a Russian explorer, entered the remote Kingdom of Hunza (now in Pakistan) and was favourably received by the volatile khan in an area considered to be within the British sphere of

continues

Colourful Uygur architecture in Artush, near Kashgar

influence. Worse, Hunza raiders, later discovered to be envoys of the khan himself, were using a secret pass to attack trade caravans in the mountains between Leh and Shache. Determined to find this important pass before the Russians, Lt (later Col Sir) Francis Younghusband set out for Hunza. He ran into Gromchevsky high up in the Karakorams and shared a meal of vodka and *blinis* with him while discussing the rivalry between their two countries. The next day, Younghusband proceeded on to Hunza to secure British interests there. According to Younghusband, the notorious Khan of Hunza, Safdar Ali (who had seized power by killing his mother and father and throwing his two brothers over a cliff) was 'under the impression that the Empress of India, the Czar of Russia and the Emperor of China were chiefs of neighbouring tribes'.

With the establishment in 1890 of a British Indian Agency in Kashgar, the city became a crucial listening post for the British. George (later Sir George) Macartney spent 26 years here as the British consul-general, creating a vast intelligence-gathering network that kept a particularly wary eye on the Russians while forging closer ties with the Chinese governor. Relations with the all-powerful Russian consul, Nikolai Petrovsky, were tenuous. Petrovsky also had a network of spies whose tentacles spread everywhere. Younghusband came to Kashgar with the young Macartney to persuade the Chinese to occupy the Pamir region directly west of their territory, thereby filling in the gap between China and Afghanistan. The Russians learned of this plan (via Petrovsky) and moved in first.

The easy defeat of Tsar Nicholas's navy by the Japanese in 1905 so demoralized the Russians and crushed their dreams of a Far Eastern Empire that they signed the historic Russo-British Convention in 1907, which ended the first round of the Great Game. The terms of this treaty give a good indication of the imperialist manner in which both countries managed their international affairs. Both Britain and Russia agreed to stay out of Tibet except officially through China; Afghanistan was considered to be within Britain's sphere of influence, but she agreed not to interfere in Afghanistan's domestic politics; and lastly, both agreed to leave the territory that was to become Pakistan independent but divide it in two, the north and centre to Russia, the south and Arabian Gulf access to Britain.

T he Russian Revolution of 1917 began the second phase of the Great Game. The Russian eastern front collapsed and the Bolsheviks tore up the landmark treaty. Lenin planned to subdue the East with Marxism and stated bluntly: 'England is our greatest enemy. It is in India that we must strike them hardest... The East will help us to conquer the West.'

The White Russian armies retreated westwards, setting up resistance fortifications in Central Asia, where Muslims were trying to throw out the Russians altogether. The fabulously wealthy Emir of Bokhara approached Colonel Percy Etherton in Kashgar with a plan to secretly deposit his fortune of some £35 million in gold and silver for safekeeping in the Consulate-General.

Etherton could not accommodate so great a treasure but did assist in the escape of the emir, whose treasure fell into the hands of the Bolsheviks. Etherton widened his network of spies and his propaganda efforts were formidable; the Russians in Tashkent put a price on his head.

Another extraordinary player in the Great Game was Colonel F M Bailey, a linguist, explorer and naturalist, who spent almost a year and a half dodging the Bolshevik secret police in Tashkent in 1919–1920. His task was to thwart communist control in Central Asia. A master of disguises—posing as an Austrian cook, a Romanian officer, a Latvian official and a German prisoner-of-war—he was actually recruited by Bolshevik counter-intelligence to find a British master spy named Bailey!

B y the mid-1930s Russia and Britain were preoccupied with the growing threat of fascism in Europe, and at the end of the Second World War Britain faced the disintegration of her empire, including the loss and partition of India in 1947. In China, the Communist Party came to power two years later, completing the turnover of players and inaugurating a new phase in the Great Game, surprisingly similar in attitude and strategy to the one of a hundred years earlier.

These two young girls illustrate the colourful clothing and variety of headgear worn by women of ethnic minorities, both young and old, in China's northwest region

TWO EARLY FOREIGN TRAVELLERS

Marco Polo (1254–1324): The most famous foreigners to make the great overland journey were the Polo family. Around 1263 the Venetian traders, Nicolo and Maffeo Polo (Marco's father and uncle), set off to sell their luxury goods in the Volga River region. Unable to return home due to a war, they joined a Mongol tribute mission to Khanbalik, Kublai Khan's capital at Beijing. The Great Khan took a liking to the Polos and through them asked the Pope to send 'a hundred men learned in the Christian religion, well versed in the seven arts, and able to demonstrate the superiority of their own beliefs.'

In 1271, Marco, then 17, joined the Polo brothers on their return journey, which carried blessings and credentials from the Pope. They took the overland route via Persia and Central Asia to the Oxus River, across the Pamirs into present-day Xinjiang, and along the southern Silk Road to Dunhuang, finally arriving at the Great Khan's court of Shangtu in 1275. The Polos were to remain in China for about 17 years, and Marco, who became something of a court favourite, is believed to have held an official post. They left in 1292 by sea, escorting a Mongol princess to Persia and arriving back in Venice in 1295.

Benedict de Goes (1562–1607): Even as late as the early 17th century, the debate continued whether or not Marco Polo's Cathay and the Empire of China were one and the same. In 1602, Benedict de Goes, a lay Jesuit from the Azores, was chosen by his order to follow in Marco Polo's footsteps. He set off from India disguised as an Armenian trader. He was haunted by the constant fear of being exposed as a non-Muslim but managed to join a caravan of 500 merchants bound for Kabul. There, he joined another caravan, which in spite of great caution was attacked, and its remnants struggled over the Pamir passes to reach Shache (Yarkand) in 1603. A year later, he joined an eastbound merchant caravan and, from travellers along the way, learnt that Jesuits had found favour at the Ming Court. This convinced him that Cathay was indeed China. While his caravan waited in Jiuqian for permission to continue, de Goes was made impoverished by Muslim merchants. Despondent at not hearing from the Jesuits in Beijing, he soon fell ill. The Jesuits' emissary arrived in 1607, just in time to watch brave de Goes die.

THE SOUTHERN SILK ROAD

he trail along the southern oases of the Taklamakan—the oldest Silk Road route—winds its way between foothills of the Kunlun Mountains and the southern rim of the Taklamakan, from **Miran** to **Endere, Niya, Keriya, Hetian** and **Shache**, where it turns to meet the northern route in Kashgar. From Kashgar the route continues to the High Pamirs, then into Central Asia and the towns of Khokand, Samarkand, Bokhara, Merv, through Persia and Iraq to the Mediterranean Sea, ending up at the markets of Rome and Alexandria. Another Silk Road route begins at Shache, and continues south to the Karakorams, down to Leh and Srinagar, then on to Bombay (Mumbai).

The cities along the present Southern Silk Road are officially open to foreigners, including **Shache (Yarkand), Yecheng (Karghalik), Hetian (Khotan) Qiemo (Cherchen)** and **Ruoqiang (Charkhik)**. The 510 km road journey from Kashgar to Hetian once took several weeks but can now be accomplished comfortably in ten hours by Landcruiser. The tarred road continues throughout to Ruoqiang. There are several flights a week from Urumqi to Hetian via Aksu and to Qiemo via Korla. Both flights take about three and a half hours. In winter, the flight frequency is reduced.

However, access to major archaeological sites such as Dandan Oilik, Karadong, Yuan Sha, Niya, Endere and Loulan—which are all off the beaten track—is forbidden. To visit these places, a special permit issued by the Cultural Relics Bureau in Urumqi is required. The permit must be applied for at least one month prior to leaving Urumqi; they are seldom granted and include a fee of hundreds or even thousands of US dollars, depending on the site. An official will accompany the visitor to the site. Permits to visit sites of secondary archaeological importance like Mazar Tagh or Rawak near Hetian may be obtained within one or two days for a modest fee at the local Cultural Relics Bureau, or with the help of the Hetian District Museum. Places which are near cities like Yotkan or Melikawat next to Hetian are open. Regardless of where you go, however, picking up ancient objects and carrying them out of China is strictly prohibited.

There is neither public transport to nor accommodation at any of the archaeological sites, and should you be intent on visiting them, it is mandatory to plan expeditions well ahead in cooperation with a Chinese travel agent. Equipment like tents, cooking gear, etc can be rented in Urumqi. To get to Mazar Tagh, Rawak and Miran, 4WD vehicles are sufficient, but the other sites require either UNIMOG trucks, camels, or special Chinese-made trucks called "Shato", used by the oil drilling companies. These trucks can be rented in Korla at a cost of US$280 per day including a driver.

YENGISAR

 ixty-eight kilometres southeast of Kashgar is the small town of **Yengisar**, whose 400-year history of knife-making has made it famous throughout Xinjiang. A Yengisar knife is essential for every Uygur man, who wears it slung around his waist. A knife is especially important during the melon season, when it is produced with a ceremonial flair and thoroughly cleaned before use by cutting off the base of a melon. Knives are carefully chosen; hand-made ones encrusted with stones and inlaid with silver are highly valued, but just as effective are the sturdier ones with bone or horn handles and carvings on the blade.

The knife-crafting skill has been handed down from father to son. The best knives were made before 1968, when silver was still available and fine craftsmanship was employed in honing the wide blade, decorating and inlaying the handles with mother of pearl. These are now rare and cherished by their makers, who will part with one—reluctantly—for Rmb500 or more.

Most knives now found in the markets of northwest China are factory produced, but the Yengisar County Small Knife Factory (Yingjisha Xian Xiao Dao Chang) employs about 50 craftsmen who hand-operate the simple lathes and decorate the handles with horn or plastic. The factory is a small state-run compound located in the main bazaar. The workers take about two days to complete one knife, many of which are shipped all over Xinjiang. You can purchase knives directly from the factory.

The road leads on southeast towards Shache through flat country, with the snow-covered peaks of the Pamirs visible off to the west. Apart from the bazaar and knife factory there is little to see in Yengisar. There are several guesthouses in the town that offer basic Chinese accommodation.

SHACHE (YARKAND)

Until recent decades, **Shache** was larger than Kashgar due to its extensive commercial trade with India via Leh, in Ladakh. Silk Road caravans carried silks, tea, precious stones, gold, furs and skins and, in the Qing dynasty, opium from India. Kashmiri merchants taught the Yarkandis to clean and treat wool fleeces, and soon the quality of Yarkand's shawl wool surpassed that of Kashmir. Hindus, Pathans, Tibetans, Baltis, Afghans, Kokandis and even Armenians were among the many foreign traders who swelled the city's population.

On a perilous journey in 1895, Sven Hedin set out on an expedition to chart the southwest Taklamakan between the Shache and Hetian rivers. Twenty days out of Merkit, the point of departure 60 km to the north of Shahe, his expedition ran out of water and struggled through the Taklamakan for six days. Hedin finally crawled

(preceding pages) A pair of wild camels wander in a river valley along the Southern Silk Road between Xinjiang and Tibet

No Way Out

During the long summer Turfan is undoubtedly one of the hottest places on the face of the earth, and the thermometer registers around 130° Fahrenheit in the shade, but it is not hot all the year round and in winter the temperature falls to zero Fahrenheit. The heat is accounted for by its geographical location, which is in a depression watered by no river of any size, and lying below sea-level. Between May and August the inhabitants retire underground, for the mud or brick houses, even though they have deep verandahs and spacious airy rooms, are intolerable by day. In each courtyard there is an opening which leads by a flight of steps to a deep dug-out or underground apartment. Here are comfortable rooms and a kang spread with cool-surfaced reed matting and grass-woven pillows which help the people to endure the breathless stagnation of the midday hours; they eat and sleep underground and only emerge at sunset. The shops, which have been closed during the hot hours, are opened by lamplight, and all necessary business is done then, but people avoid the living and sleeping rooms of their houses because they are infested with vermin. There are large and virulent scorpions which creep under sleeping-mats, drop on to the unconscious sleeper from the beams or hide themselves in his shoes. One jumping spider with long legs and a hairy body as large as a pigeon's egg leaps on its prey and makes a crunching noise with its jaws. Turfan cockroaches are over two inches in length, with long feelers and red eyes which make them a repulsive sight. All these creatures know how to conceal themselves in sleeping-bags and rolls of clothing, so that man is handicapped in dealing with them. Apart from these virulent monsters, the inns provide every variety of smaller vermin such as lice, bugs and fleas, and each is of an order well able to withstand all the patent nostrums guaranteed to destroy them. On account of these pests the people of Turfan sleep on wooden beds in the courtyards, but the constant watering of the ground results in swarms of mosquitoes, which torment the sleeper almost beyond endurance.

Mildred Cable, The Gobi Desert, c.1930s

A carpet maker in Hetian

to the Hetian River and brought back water to save the life of his one remaining assistant. Hedin's most famous discovery was on a later expedition to chart the Shache River and its continuation, the Tarim River, when he discovered the secret of the 'wandering' Lop Nor Lake.

Visiting Shache in 1923, the British consul-general in Kashgar, Sir Clarmont Skrine was amazed 'by the size and spaciousness of the long roofed bazaars, far better-built than those of Kashgar. . . courtyards of houses, weeping willows drooping over them, eating shops and groceries, smithies and old-clothes shops and carpenters' shops, and everywhere masses of picturesquely-garbed people.'

In *News from Tartary* (1936), Peter Fleming wrote of a tenser city in the wake of a Muslim rebellion:

> **P**arts of the bazaar were still in ruins; the bastions of the New City were pockmarked with bullets, and the walls of the houses round it with loop-holes; Chinese inscriptions were defaced. Here a Chinese garrison held out with some gallantry against the fanatical insurgents from Hetian, and after a siege of several weeks was granted a safe-conduct; in the desert they were massacred almost to a man. The incident is typical of a Province whose whole history stinks with treachery.

continued on page 306

(left) The Uygur men of western Xinjiang place great importance in the wearing of a knife. Consequently, knife craftsmen are highly respected and in places like Yengisar, on the Silk Road's southern route, the skill has been developed to a fine art

THE SILK SECRET

C hinese legend gives the title Goddess of Silk to Lei Zu (Lady Xiling), wife of the mythical Yellow Emperor, who was said to have ruled China in about 3000 BC. She is attributed with the introduction of silkworm rearing and the invention of the loom. Rituals and sacrifices to Lei Zu were made annually by the imperial court. Court regulations of the Zhou dynasty decreed that 'the empress and royal concubines fast before making their offerings and gather mulberry leaves in person in order to encourage the silk industry'. During the Han dynasty, the heyday of the Silk Road, the annual celebration of Lei Zu was held during the third lunar month in splendid style. The empress and the ladies of the court rode in grand procession to the Temple of Silkworms in horse-drawn carriages, accompanied by 'tens of thousands of horsemen' carrying dragon banners and silk pennants to the Altar of the Silkworms. In Beijing's Beihai Park, once part of the Forbidden City, stands a temple to the Goddess of Silk built in 1742. The age-old annual silk ritual continued until the fall of the Qing dynasty in 1911.

Half a silkworm cocoon unearthed in 1927 from the loess soil astride the Yellow River in Shanxi Province, in northern China, has been dated between 2600 and 2300 BC. More recent archeological finds—a small ivory cup carved with a silkworm design and thought to be between 6,000 and 7,000 years old, and spinning tools, silk threads and fabric fragments from sites along the lower Yangzi River—reveal the origins of sericulture to be even earlier. Some Shang-dynasty (1600–1027 BC) oracle-bone inscriptions bear the earliest known pictographic characters for 'silk', 'silkworm' and 'mulberry'.

The fifth-century BC Book of Annals catalogued tributes to Emperor Yu of 'lengths of silk of blue or red' from six provinces of China. At that time, not only was the production of silk widespread, but the colours and designs were rich and varied. By the Han dynasty sericulture was practised from Gansu in the west, where painted tomb bricks show scenes of silkworm breeding and silk weaving, to Sichuan in the south, where the ancient capital of Chengdu was dubbed 'Brocade City', and to Shandong on the east coast, which was famous for its wild silk.

From about the fourth century BC, the Greeks and Romans began talking of Seres, the Kingdom of Silk. Some historians believe the first Romans to set eyes upon the fabulous fabric were the legions of Marcus Licinius Crassus, Governor of Syria. At the fateful battle of Carrhae near the Euphrates River in 53 BC, the soldiers were so startled by the bright silken banners of the Parthian troops that they fled in panic. Within decades Chinese silks were widely worn by the rich and noble families of Rome. Its production remained a mystery, however; Pliny, the Roman historian, believed that silk was obtained by 'removing the down from the leaves with the help of water'.

The flimsy transparency of the silken 'glass togas' so loved by the Roman élite was soon to bring moral condemnation. Seneca, the Roman philosopher, wrote in the first century: 'I see silken clothes, if one can call them clothes at all, that in no degree afford protection either to the body or the modesty of the wearer, and clad in which no woman could honestly swear she is not naked.' Silk drained the Roman Empire of its gold, and by the fourth century one-third of the Byzantine Empire's treasury went to imports of luxury items from the East. High court and church dignatories dressed lavishly in imperial purple silk, and important personages were buried in silk winding sheets.

The Chinese zealously guarded their secret, but around AD 440 (according to legend) a Chinese princess hid silkworm eggs in her head-dress and carried them to Hetian upon her marriage to the king, bringing the art to present-day Xinjiang. Around AD 550, two Nestorian monks introduced the silkworm to Byzantium, where the church and state created imperial workshops, monopolizing production and keeping the secret to themselves. By the sixth century the Persians, too, had mastered the art of silk weaving, developing their own rich patterns and techniques. It was only in the 13th century—the time of the Second Crusades—that Italy began silk production with the introduction of 2,000 skilled silk weavers from Constantinople. By that time silk production was widespread in Europe.

In the Tang dynasty the main silk centres were south of the Yangzi River around Taihu Lake, where factory looms produced exquisite brocades highlighted with gold

continues

thread. To stock the wardrobe of Yang Guifei, Precious Consort of Emperor Xuanzong, 700 weavers were employed full time. While in Beijing, Marco Polo noted that 'every day more than 1,000 cart-loads of silk enter the city'. Bolts of silk and silken robes were essential gifts to political envoys, princes and tribute missions to the Tang, Ming and Qing courts. A mission of 2,000 men to the Ming-dynasty capital of Beijing returned laden with 8,000 bolts of coarse silk, 2,000 lined satin robes and 2,000 pairs of boots and leggings, as well as many other presents.

The breeding of silkworms is a side-line of the Chinese peasant—one that has remained unchanged through the ages. During the summer families take care of large round rattan trays of voracious bombyx mori caterpillars, which feed day and night on fresh, hand-picked mulberry leaves. Around Tai Lake and the Grand Canal—China's main silk-producing area—the mulberry tree grows to about a man's height, making it easy to pick the leaves.

The newly hatched silkworm, like a tiny piece of black thread, multiplies its weight up to 10,000 times within a month, changing colour and shedding its whitish-grey skin several times. After 30-odd days the peasants place the silkworms on bunches of straw or twigs, to which the worms attach the cocoons they spin from a single thread of silk about a kilometre (half a mile) long. The cocoons are then heated to kill the pupa and sent to the silk-reeling mills. There, they are sorted by hand and boiled at 48°C (120°F) for softening and releasing the thread. The workers plunge their hands continually into the hot water, plucking the threads from about eight cocoons and feeding them into the reeling machine to form a single strand. The rewinding process, resulting in skeins of pure white silk, is usually automatic. The silk from rejected cocoons is made into floss silk, and the pupae are a source of protein for animal fodder.

(right) Silkworms spin cocoons, which women sort and a young woman reels. The silk is skeined and, after being dyed, fed onto a warp drum

THE MOMENT OF TRUTH

With the approach of the harvesting time for silkworms, the tension grew. The atmosphere became more sharply charged throughout this tiny village and its twenty-odd inhabitants. Determination, boldness, hope, tempered by fear and suspense. Hunger seemed to be forgotten. Days went by quickly. In Old T'ung-pao's family they lived on whatever scraps they could find, on pumpkins and potatoes. Nor was his family alone in this, for who in the whole village could afford to store two or three piculs of rice? There had been a fine harvest last year but it was hardly off the ground before the landowners, the creditors, and the tax collectors came and their harvest dwindled to nothing. Their only hope now was in the spring silkworm harvest. Every short-term loan they'd contracted in the interim had to be paid back at that time. Everyone was alive with hope and fear, facing the coming battle for the cocoons.

With the approach of Ku Yü, the day of the Great Rain, little specks of stirring green appeared in the black of the eggs on their pieces of cloth. Women talked to each other with joy and anxiety as they compared notes.

"The eggs will soon be hatched at Lu Pao's house."

"Ho-hua said hers will be out tomorrow. How fast!"

"Taoist Huang went to the fortune teller. He heard that leaf would go up to four dollars a picul."

Mrs. Ah Szu studied their egg patches closely. Nothing yet. The hundreds of black dots remained unbroken in color. Not a trace or speck of green among them. Ah Szu impatiently took them out into the light. But neither could he find any sign of moving green. His wife fretted with worry.

"You'd better start trying to hatch them." He tried to speak reassuringly. "These eggs come from Yu-hang, you know. Maybe it takes them longer." His confident tone made no impression upon her. She made no reply. Old T'ung-pao's dry wrinkled face was long and sad. He said nothing although his heart was heavy with foreboding.

Next morning Mrs. Ah Szu looked anxiously at her piece of cloth and found dots of bright green shining against the black! She ran with them to her husband. She shouted to Old T'ung-pao, to Ah-to, to her son, Hsiao Pao. She tucked the three pieces *of cloth to her breast and sat there motionless, hugging them like a mother her suckling babe. At night she kept the pieces of cloth with her, warm under her cover. She made Ah Szu go over and sleep with Ah-to. On each patch the tiny things moved and made her flesh creep when they touched her. But Mrs. Ah Szu was mad with joy and trepidation. She felt as she did when her child was within her, half-anxious, half-relieved when the little being inside her first moved and she felt him. The whole family was uneasy and excited, waiting for the critical days to come. Ah-to was alone unruffled. "Sure, the harvest will be fine," he said. "But getting rich is out of the question. The fates are still a long way off!" Old T'ung-pao raged at him to keep still, but he paid no attention.*

Everything was already in order in the silkworm shed. The day after the eggs began hatching Old T'ung-pao took a large bulb of garlic plastered in mud and set it down on the ground against one wall of the shed. He did this every year, but this time he was especially careful. His hands trembled. The bulb he had set down last year had enabled him to gauge the harvest quite closely. He hardly dared hope for another true forecast this year.

By now every family in the village was wholly absorbed. The paddies and the banks of the streamlet, so often alive with the chatter and laughter of the women, were deserted. By tacit and mutual consent everyone observed the rule of mutual avoidance. There was no visiting, even among close friends, for it was no joke if a guest should frighten off the silkworm god. Most people exchanged only a few whispered words on the threshing ground and then separated. This was a sacred period. In the house of Old T'ung-pao bits of life were already crawling on the three patches of cloth. Tension filled the house. It was but one day before the Ku Yü. Mrs. Ah Szu carefully placed the cloths in the shed instead of under the quilt, for they no longer needed warmth. But when Old T'ung-pao stole a look at his bulb of garlic against the wall, his heart jumped with fear, for only two short sprouts had appeared. He didn't have the courage to look again.

Mao Tun, Spring Silkworms, 1932

Shache is 126 kilometres south of Yengisar, and its character is more subdued than in previous days. The town is surrounded by an oasis of trees, fields and rice paddies. On Sundays, a large market sprawls over the streets and alleys of the east (old) end of the city. Try a delicious cold bottle (no label) of the locally made plum soda (meigui xiangjiu). The only accommodation available to foreigners is at the Shache Hotel (4 Xincheng Road, Tel: 998 851 2365, Fax: 998 851-2356, dorm Rmb7, double Rmb26), south of the bus station.

Yecheng (Karghalik)

he road continues through the well-watered agricultural zones of **Posgam** (**Zepu**) and Yecheng, the assembly point for mountaineering expeditions climbing up the Chinese side of **K-2**, in the Karakoram Range, which was opened to foreigners in 1980. The base camp is a journey of two days by car and a further nine days by camel from Yecheng (the ascent usually takes two to three months). The road curves around the north side of Yecheng after passing the bus station and crossing the river. The mosque and bazaar are in the southwest. The Yecheng County Mountain Climbers Hotel offers accommodation to foreign nationals (Tuan Jie Road, Tel: 998 728 2652). Just east of town is the turnoff south to the Ali region of Western Tibet.

The verdant strip gives way to stony desert, and the road, subject to severe damage from flash flooding, leads to **Goma** (**Pishan**). Skrine wrote:

> oma is on the very verge of the Takla Makan . . . It is a great place for the treasure seekers known as 'Taklamakanchis', who are to be found all along the fringe of the great desert; ragged, ever-hopeful men of the tramp type who spend their lives ransacking the remains of ancient Buddhist tombs and temples far out among the sands of the Takla Makan. Occasionally these men find a few coins or seals, one of them becoming rich in the process. From the archeological point of view, the activities of the ubiquitous Taklamakanchis cut both ways; Stein acknowledges many debts to them including assistance, direct or indirect, in the discovery of his chief sites; but he had far oftener to deplore the damage done by them to tombs and temples, stupas and dwelling-houses.

Hetian (Khotan)

Hetian is famous for its jade, carpets, silk and embroidery. For almost 2,000 years it was the principal supplier of precious nephrite, much cherished by the Chinese. White jade came from the bed of the White Jade River, dark-green jade came from the Black Jade River, and was transported by caravans to the heartland of China

Gathering mulberry leaves in Hetian

where it was then exquisitely carved. Hetian's gem markets also dealt in cornelian and lapis lazuli. Today, Hetian is a collection centre for the raw white jade still found by individuals along the river; however, finds of good jade amount to only a few kilos annually. Some mining is carried out in the Kunlun Mountains during the summer months, but the yield is also very low.

Sericulture was introduced to Hetian by a Chinese princess betrothed to the King of Hetian more than 1,500 years ago. She concealed the eggs of the silkworm and the seeds of the mulberry tree in her headdress to avoid discovery by border officials instructed to zealously guard this national secret. The industry thrived in Hetian, and examples of the city's magnificent silks can be seen in Xinjiang's museums. Hetian is the centre of the traditional hand-woven aidelaixi silk that is produced by small family units and is a favourite of Uygur women.

The rich natural colours and designs of Hetian carpets have been treasured all over Central Asia for centuries. They are especially valuable because of the city's especially long, thick wool. Villagers make carpets as a sideline, selling them at the bazaar or to private buyers from other parts of Xinjiang. Pieces of chain-stitch embroidery made with a hooked needle are much prized.

he Kingdom of Hetian, which formerly went by the names of Yutian and Kustana, was one of the 36 kingdoms of the Western Regions. General Ban Chao drove out the Xiongnu from the oases of Xinjiang in the first century AD, during the time the King of Hetian was under the influence of a Xiongnu court shaman. The king and the shaman plotted the humiliation and death of Ban Chao; they demanded that he surrender his prize war horse to be sacrificed to their gods, to which Ban Chao consented if the shaman himself would lead the horse away. When the shaman appeared, Ban Chao had him decapitated and sent the head to the King of Hetian, who immediately surrendered to the Chinese.

During the second century AD, Hetian was ruled by the Indo-Scythian kingdom of the Kushans, whose King Kanishka was a devout Buddhist. Hetian flourished as an important centre of Mahayana Buddhism in the fifth century, and its inhabitants remained Buddhist until the early 11th century.

The Buddhist pilgrim, Fa Xian, left a vivid account of the Kingdom of Hetian when he passed through in 399: 'This country is prosperous and happy; its people are well-to-do; they have all received the faith and find their amusement in religious music. The priests number several tens of thousands.' Fa Xian stayed in Hetian for three months and visited the king's new monastery, which had taken 80 years and three reigns to build. 'It is about 250 feet in height, ornamentally carved and overlaid with gold and silver, suitably furnished with the seven preciosities [gold, silver, lapis lazuli, crystal, ruby, emerald and coral]. Behind the pagoda there is a Hall of Buddha which is most splendidly decorated.'

a Xian recorded that there were 14 large monasteries, not including the smaller ones. During his visit he attended an important Buddhist festival in which the royal court took part. 'Beginning on the first day of the fourth moon, the main streets inside the city are swept and watered, and the side streets decorated. Over the city gate they stretch a large awning with all kinds of ornamentation, under which the king and queen and court ladies take their places.' A procession followed, led by the Buddhist priests. Outside the city was a float 'over thirty feet in height, looking like a moveable Hall of Buddha and adorned with the seven preciosities, with streaming pennants and embroidered canopies'. A figure of the Buddha was placed on this 'image car', followed by two bodhisattvas 'all beautifully carved in gold and silver and suspended in the air,' Fa Xian noted. The parade halted before the city gate and the king exchanged his royal robes for simple clothes. 'Walking barefoot and holding flowers and incense in his hands, with attendants on either side, he proceeds out of the gate. On meeting the images, he bows his head down to the ground, scatters the flowers and burns the incense.' The festival lasted for 14 days, with each monastery assembling a Buddha float on a different day, after which the king returned to his throne, and Fa Xian continued northwest to Kashgar.

During the early Tang dynasty (618-907) Hetian paid tribute to the Chinese court, on one occasion sending 717 pairs of polo ponies to Chang'an. Having been summoned to the imperial presence in 648, the King of Hetian returned home laden with titles and gifts, including 5,000 rolls of silk.

In the seventh century, Xuan Zang passed through Hetian on his return from India and reported a strange legend. West of the town were a range of small hills that locals said had been formed by a tribe of sacred rats. These precious vermin and their rat king were protected and fed by locals because they had once saved the Buddhists of Hetian from an army of Huns by gnawing their leather harnesses and armour, thereby rendering them helpless in battle.

etian was part of the Kharakhanid Kingdom between 1006 and 1165 when it fell to the Kara Kitai rulers, and as the only oasis in Kashgaria to defend itself against Genghis Khan, it was consequently devastated to set an example to other recalcitrant states. Wars raged between Buddhist and Muslim rulers during the late tenth and early 11th centuries, and the kingdom was enmeshed in all the power struggles of the next eight centuries, including those of the Chagatai Khanate and the khojas of Kashgaria. Marco Polo travelled through the kingdom in 1273, noting that it was 'eight days' journey in extent'.

In the 19th century, the kingdom became part of Yakub Beg's Kashgaria after a desperate stand against the army by the proud women of Hetian; offerings of packhorses laden with silver bullion, 70 camel-loads of gifts and 14 racing camels were subsequently made to placate Yakub Beg.

H etian was one of the first cities to be excavated by foreigners in the late 19th century. One of the first Western explorers to visit Hetian was William Johnson. A civil servant with the British Survey of India, he was following up on the report of a native who had been conducting surveys in Hetian in 1864 and had run across some old ruins. According to the native, 'Hetian . . . was long ago swallowed up by the sand' and now the local inhabitants were digging out artefacts from those houses left uncovered. The man reported that 'it would appear as if the city had been buried suddenly before the inhabitants had time to remove their property'. Johnson braved the territory of the wild Kirghiz nomads to visit the Khan Badsha of Hetian (who held him hostage in the hope that the British government would send him troops with which to fight the encroaching Russians). Johnson came to learn of tea bricks 'of great age', and of gold coins weighing four pounds that had been dug up, and of buried cities whose locations were 'known only to a few persons who keep it secret in order to enrich themselves'.

As fantastic as Johnson's information was, scholars did not venture into the Chinese Turkestan for another 20 or more years. This was partly because archaeologists were occupied with rich finds being made in Greece, Palestine, Mesopotamia and Egypt, partly because the area was considered dangerous and risky to travel in, and lastly because of the assumption that any buried cities beneath the Taklamakan were likely to be Islamic rather than Buddhist.

After the discovery of the Bower Manuscript and other finds by Xinjiang treasure seekers, foreign travellers and scholars became more intrigued with the Taklamakan region. In 1892 two Frenchmen, Jules Dutreuil de Rhins and F. Grenard, came to Hetian where they bought an ancient Buddhist manuscript written on birch bark in the Indian Kharoshthi script and dating from the 2nd century AD. Then, in 1895, Sven Hedin arrived in Hetian determined to be the first European to explore the lost Silk Road cities. Hedin was taken to an ancient village called Borasan (Yotkan), where he discovered—and bought from local treasure-hunters—manuscripts, coins, terracotta images of the Buddha, figurines of people and camels, a copper cross, and other antiquities. He then went on to explore a city northeast of Hetian, simply called 'Taklamakan' by locals, a collection of ruins in the dunes. Hedin discovered on one of the walls protruding through the sand images of the Buddha and Buddhist deities. He wondered if he had discovered the ancient

(above) Silver hairpins decorated with bird and peony designs. (right) Painted pottery figure of a woman holding a mirror (Tang dynasty, AD 618–907)

city that Fa Xian had described in such detail. He said of his discovery, 'The scientific research I willingly left to the specialists. For me it was sufficient to have made the important discovery and to have won in the heart of the desert a new field for archeology.' Hedin's digging produced the remains of apricot trees in the barren desert, houses, and a temple that contained wall paintings with Indian, Greek, Persian and Gandharan influences.

ir Aurel Stein explored the sites of Yotkan, Niya, Dandan Oilik, Endere and Rawak. In 1901, he unmasked the forger, Islam Akhun, whose 'ancient scripts' had caused many a Western orientalist in India and Russia to waste years in attempting to decipher his manufactured 'old books'. An old treasure hunter showed Stein pieces of fresco with Indian Brahmi characters and Buddhist designs. Stein determined that these were from Sven Hedin's 'Taklamakan', which locals called Dandan Oilik. Subsequent work at the site produced Sanskrit texts of the Buddhist canon from the fifth and sixth centuries, and documents in Chinese from the 8th century AD. He also found several paintings on wood in a few temple complexes. One of them, a human figure, is depicted with the head of a rat, flanked on either side by attendants. Stein realized this was the sacred King of Rats who had saved Hetian, a story that Xuan Zang had heard about 1,300 years earlier.

In 1935, when Peter Fleming and Ella Maillart arrived in Khotan (nowadays called Hetian) on their daring overland journey to India, the city was hand-printing its own currency on paper made from mulberry trees. They had the delightful experience of witnessing the arrival by mule of the British Indian postman with documents for the local Indian merchants and three-month-old copies of The Times brought all the way from Kashmir.

The Hetian region consists of seven counties with a population of 1.2 million, of whom 96 per cent are Uygur. Twenty-four rivers flow during the summer months when the snows from the Kunlun Mountains melt to fill them, and ample water is available to grow maize, wheat, rice, cotton and oil-bearing plants. Mulberry and fruit trees are also abundant.

SIGHTS

This city of 80,000 has no historic structures except some sections of the crenellated city wall that once surrounded the 'New City' or Chinese cantonment. (The Uygur 'Old City' had no fortification.) Most of the shops are yellow-fronted and single-storey, and stock only basics. The **Cultural Palace** is a handsome red-brick building arched in Uygur style. The pace of the city is pleasantly relaxed, and strolls around the unpaved lanes of the old residential area afford glimpses of daily life lived in tree- and vine-shaded courtyards. The Sunday bazaar is held in the eastern part of the city.

ISLAM AKHUN

n Aurel Stein's first expedition, he wanted to verify the validity of certain ancient books the Anglo-German oriental scholar, Rudolf Hoernle of Oxford University, had obtained through Islam Akhun, a local Kashgar trader. Soon after the discovery of the Bower Manuscripts, local treasure seekers became acutely aware of British and Russian interest in old books and artefacts, and realized a small fortune could be made in delivering them. Islam Akhun and his partner provided both George Macartney and Nikolai Petrovsky, the consul-generals in Kashgar, with several manuscripts that had baffled scholars because the texts were written in an unknown language. Suspecting a hoax, Stein found his proof in the desert between Hetian and Guma, where Akhun's supposed source contained nothing more than empty ruins in sands.

Upon confronting the spurious historian with his artifically discoloured paper and a fictitious report of the site, the terrified Islam Akhun admitted to having falsified the book prints. He and his partner were desperate to find more manuscripts to sell to the foreign collectors and decided to write their own. The first was handwritten, a collection of odd characters that learned scholars believed to be related to ancient Greek. Realizing the foreigners couldn't distinguish the fake characters from authentic ancient scripts, Akhun stopped imitating actual ancient letters and symbols and invented his own (which explained the odd discrepancy in the texts). As this method proved time-consuming, Akhun eventually came up with the idea of block-printing. Using local paper stained yellow, the two entrepreneurs then block-printed books, hung them over a fire to give the paper an authentic, ancient look, then washed them with desert sand, suggesting that the texts came from a buried site.

Although Akhun was not prosecuted by the Chinese, his enterprise caused considerable embarrassment to the academic world, as all 90 volumes of his forgeries had been bound and now rest, forgotten, in the British Library's oriental department. To be fair to the deceived academics, the texts were amazingly authentic and sophisticated; the neat script seemed scholarly or at least artistic. Some of the blame must lie with the two consul-generals of the time, who indiscriminately bought up all offered books in their eagerness to procure artefacts for their respective nations.

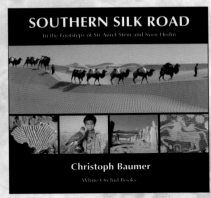

Christoph Baumer is a Fellow of the Royal Asiatic Society of Great Britain and Ireland. Since 1971 he has travelled extensively in Central Asia, China and Tibet and publishes books and articles on themes relating to the history, archaeology and religions of these areas. He has led three international archaeological expeditions into the Taklamakan Desert during which he made several important discoveries. His book Southern Silk Road: In the footsteps of Sir Aurel Stein and Sven Hedin (Orchid Press, 2000) provides a beautifully illustrated insight into the history of the civilizations which flourished and died along the edge of the Tarim Basin.

All my life I have wanted to trick blood from a rock. I have dreamed about raising the devil and cutting him in half. I have thought too about never being afraid of anything at all. This is where you come to do those things.

I know what they tell you about the desert but you mustn't believe them. This is no deathbed. Dig down, the earth is moist. Boulders have turned to dust here, the dust feels like graphite. You can hear a man breathe at a distance of twenty yards. You can see out there to the edge where the desert stops and the mountains begin. You think it is perhaps ten miles. It is more than a hundred. Just before the sun sets all the colors will change. Green will turn to blue, red to gold.

Barry Holstun Lopez, Desert Notes, 1976

Traditional sericulture in Hetian. While the man bundles up the 25-30 silk threads into skeins, the woman winds the actual silk thread onto a reel

The Hetian Jade Factory, located next to the District Museum on Tanayi Nan Lu, consists of one room where six to eight artists casually carve jade pieces of varying shapes and sizes with lathes. The second-floor gift shop has an excellent selection of carvings.

HETIAN DISTRICT MUSEUM (HETIAN BOWUGUAN)

This small two-room museum houses a good exhibit of Hetian area artefacts, including pottery animals and figures, clay figures, money, clothing, carved wooden beams from Niya, silk and carpet fragments, fresco samples, jade lamps, Tibetan bronzes, jewellery, chased silver and gold utensils, and documents. The well-preserved corpses of two Buddhist monks, one aged 30-35, the other aged 10-12, are resting in decorated coffins of wood (assembled without nails), their feet tied together so as to achieve final peace without any further wandering. They date from the fifth or sixth century and were unearthed in recent digging within the city limits. The main treasure of the museum is a 45 cm high bronze statue of a seated Buddha which was either imported from Kashmir or made by an Indian artist in Hetian in the 7th/8th century. It is not on display but stored in a safe. The museum is located on Tanayi Nan Lu next to the Jade Factory.

SILK AND MULBERRY RESEARCH CENTRE

The centre, located five kilometres north of town, operates between April and October, conducting experiments to improve the quality of local silk. The factory employs over 1,000 workers and produces 150 million metres of silk a year. The compound has dorms, cafeterias and schools, and recruits workers from all over Xinjiang. Products include raw or dyed spun silk for the international market, velour and velvet-patterned comforters shipped to the CIS, and synthetic fabrics for domestic use. Silk pupas are brought in from the countryside and boiled; the silk thread is extracted with the use of machines and then wound. The thread is taken to other buildings to be spun, dyed and woven, all by heavy machinery. Tours of the centre can be arranged through the FAO at the Number One Guesthouse, or it is possible to go yourself; take bus 1 to the end of the line.

The weaving of the aidelaixi silks favoured by Uygur women remains very much a cottage industry. In some villages nearby, the cocoons are boiled, the silk reeled, and the fabric woven and tie-dyed using traditional techniques. The finished fabric is sold in 3.25-metre (3.5-yard) lengths. Visits to these family workshops can also be arranged through the FAO.

ANCIENT CITY OF YOTKAN

 he remains of this ancient city, believed to be the capital of the Kingdom of Hetian between the third and tenth centuries, are ten kilometres (six miles) west of present-day Hetian, under four metres of accumulated mud, now planted with rice. Lovely sherds of decorated red pottery and pieces of jade can still be picked out of the sides of the water channels cutting through the site.

Historical records say the city once covered ten square kilometres. Both Sven Hedin and Aurel Stein visited **Yotkan**, and Hedin devoted a chapter to it (calling it Borasan) in his mammoth book Through Asia. In the late 19th century, finds of great value drew teams of local treasure hunters more interested in the gold and silver objects than in the richly varied sherds of pottery, which depicted animals and figures in a style heavily influenced by Indo-Hellenistic and Persian styles (some of these are in the Hetian Museum). Stein noted that much of the gold found was actually gold leaf, and concluded that the statues and some of the buildings must have been lavishly coated with it. Among the coins he found were 'bilingual pieces of the indigenous rulers, showing Chinese characters as well as early Indian legends in Kharoshthi, struck about the commencement of our era, to the square-holed issues of the Tang dynasty'.

ANCIENT CITY OF MELIKAWAT

Thirty-five kilometres (22 miles) south of Hetian by the banks of the White Jade River lie the broken walls of this ancient city. In 1977, the remains of what are believed to have been an imperial hall and a collection of pottery were excavated. Archaeologists, referring to historical records, think that the site was the capital of the Yutian Kingdom during the Han dynasty, and was inhabited until the Tang. The desert surface is covered in sherds—a playground for small lizards. The sites of Yotkan and **Melikawat** are accessible by car (available at the FAO), yet very little remains.

ANCIENT STUPA OF RAWAK

 hile archaeological sites such as **Balawaste** or **Farhad Beg**—located a few dozens of kilometres to the east of Hetian and excavated by Sir Aurel Stein—offer little to see today, the large Stupa of **Rawak** is a rewarding target for a single day excursion from Hetian. It stands 32 km to the northeast and is accessible by 4WD vehicle but for the last 5 km, which must be tackled on foot. A permit and a local guide are needed. The 9 m high stupa, dating from the 3rd to 5th centuries, is one of the best-preserved Buddhist sanctuaries on the Southern Silk Road. In 1901 Aurel Stein excavated along the outer walls enclosing the stupa and discovered about 100 man-sized stucco statues featuring the Buddha and bodhisattvas. Unfortunately, when Stein returned in 1906, local treasure hunters had smashed the statues, hoping to find gold inside them. Even as recently as 1998, newly found torsos of figures were vandalized by indigenous treasure seekers. Nevertheless, this is an impressive site. Also worthwhile is the ruined, brick-built fort of **Aksipil** dating from the 5th to 6th centuries, about 18 km to the east of Hetian. Although less impressive than Rawak, Aksipil gives a fair impression of how other, less accessible sites located deep in the desert look.

Also to the east of Hetian, at a place called **Shanpul**, between 1983 and 1993 archaeologists discovered three graveyards containing 69 tombs dating from the 3rd century BC to the 4th century AD. Here unique, colourful woollen textiles were found featuring hunting scenes and animals such as winged stags, camels and birds of prey. The motifs seem to be influenced by the culture of the Saka people living in the Pamir Mountains and inspired by ancient Iranian mythology. There is not much to see above ground, and the excavated objects are now in the museums of Hetian and Urumqi.

HETIAN PRACTICAL INFORMATION

Hetian is an extremely dusty town with very little charm and almost everything is accessible by foot or bus.

TRANSPORTATION

By air or road: daily flights to/from Aksu (the airport is ten kilometres from town, FAO for bookings); daily buses to/from Yecheng, Shache, Yengisar and Kashgar (continuing on to Aksu, Kucha, Yining, Korla, Urumqi and Turpan) and Yutian, Minfeng, Qiemo and Ruoqiang in the other direction.

ACCOMMODATION

vailable at either the **Number One Guesthouse**, tel (0903) 202-2824, on Nuerwake Lu, a spacious garden compound with grape arbours and apricot trees in the courtyard, including a Chinese restaurant (dorm Rmb21 for three beds, double Rmb45), or the **Number Two Guesthouse**, tel (0903) 202-2063, on Tanayi Bei Lu, basic Chinese accommodation with communal toilets and no showers (dorm Rmb13 for four beds, double Rmb40). The **Hetian Bing Guan** (Hotan Hotel) is located at Urumqi Road (Wulumuqi Lu, Tel: 903 251 3564, 251 3570).

FOOD AND DRINK

Somewhat sparse: the bazaar area near the bus station features the usual Uygur specialities; there are also a number of small Chinese restaurants scattered throughout the town.

FOREIGN AFFAIRS OFFICE (FAO)

Located on the grounds of the Number One Guesthouse (tel (0903) 202-6090; open 10am-2pm and 4:30pm-8:30pm, Beijing time). Personnel here can arrange transport to the Jade River and its fruit fields for those wanting to pick their own fruit.

(above) The Buddhist stupa of Rawak near Hetian, built between the third and fifth centuries AD. The nine-metre-high, triple-floored stupa is crowned by a cylindrical building, to which steps lead from each of the four cardinal points. The cupola at the top has crumbled

(left) An exquisite woollen wall hanging from Shanpul east of Khotan, dated to the 3rd-2nd centuries BC. Such wall hangings were often cut up by Saka riders and used as leggings. The textiles found in the graveyards of Shanpul show not only Iranian but also Hellenistic influences, as can be seen in this head of a warrior

BEYOND HETIAN

In the desert east of Hetian, a tarred road leads towards Yutian (Keriya), Minfeng, Qiemo (Cherchen) and Ruoqiang (Charkhlik). There is not much to see on the road and the small towns offer little attraction but for their lively and colourful markets. On the road, fields and reed marshes are interspersed with large tracts of desert.

SIGHTS

North and east of Hetian are some 15 rivers, which once flowed more than 80 kilometres further into the Taklamakan than they do today; the Khotan and Keriya rivers even crossed the entire Taklamakan Desert and reached the Tarim River at its northern edge. Many of the prosperous towns watered by these rivers were abandoned to the sands between the third and ninth centuries due to climatic changes, rivers shifting their courses, and political disturbances which caused irrigation channels to be neglected and fall into decay. Over time the towns became buried treasure-troves.

MAZAR TAGH

bout 160 km as the crow flies to the north of Hetian stands the old fortress of **Mazar Tagh**, which controlled the north-south transverse trade road following the Khotan River and linking Hetian with Aksu. The well-preserved fortress sits on a rocky ledge and was built in the 7th century; it was occupied by Tibetan troops from 790 till about 850 and was thereafter abandoned. Aurel Stein found numerous documents here written on wood and paper in Chinese, Khotanese, Indian Brahmi, Sogdian, Tibetan, Arabic and Uygur.

Mazar Tagh can be reached in a one long day's drive with a 4WD vehicle, but make sure the car is in perfect condition! From Mazar Tagh you can continue to Aksu (another three days' driving), but make sure to drive with a minimum of two vehicles in case one breaks down. It's also possible to trek eastwards with camels to the small village of **Tunguzbasti** located near the dry riverbed of the Keriya River—a 100 km trip of six or seven days.

DANDAN OILIK

The Southern Silk Road continues from Hetian eastwards to **Qira**. About 115 km to the north, in the desert between the Khotan and Keriya rivers, is **Dandan Oilik**. This site was discovered in 1896 by Sven Hedin and excavated in 1900/01 by Aurel Stein, who identified 16 ruined structures, most of them Buddhist shrines or monasteries. The town, which may have been a religious centre, bloomed in the 5th to 8th centuries and was abandoned in 790 due to marauding Tibetan troops. Here Stein discovered Buddhist murals, painted wooden tablets donated by pilgrims as votives, and many ancient documents, among them a unique letter on paper written in Middle

continued on page 326

The fort of Mazar Tagh, 7th-9th centuries AD, with the Khotan River in the background. The fort controlled the transverse road linking ancient Khotan in the south with Aksu to the north

The fortified caravanserai of Karadong (first century BC until fourth century AD). In those times the Keriya River flowed near Karadong, but today it percolates into the desert 50-60 km to the south

THE TARIM HIGHWAY

ince early traders first guided their camel caravans along the Silk Road over two millennia ago, only a handful of intrepid archaeologists, lured by the prospect of discovering ancient cities and buried treasures, have dared to penetrate the fearsome Taklamakan Desert.

Beyond Dunhuang, on the eastern threshold of Xinjiang's deserts, the Silk Road divided. Some travellers and merchants took the route north of the Taklamakan, others skirted the great void to the south. Indeed there was no reason to go into the world's second largest sea of sand.

Centuries later, as socialist China's reforms took off, its economy thirsted for power resources, particularly oil. That was the reason to thoroughly explore the Taklamakan. After positive seismic surveys, wildcat wells were drilled, very expensively. Helicopters—normally used as a means of transport to service offshore wells—were used, together with surface access. Convoys followed a 1,200 kilometre route around the desert from the north, with special desert motor vehicles having to be used on the final leg of the detour.

By this tortuous and costly means, the Tazhong-4 Oilfield was discovered in the heart of the Taklamakan. But the China National Oil Corporation, a state consortium that exploits all of China's oil and gas resources, realized that an economical means of transport would be needed, if the recovery of oil from the field were to be profitable. A road was the only viable option.

With a budget of US$60 million, the China National Oil Corporation organized 17 research institutes and more than 100 experts—engineers, geomorphologists and botanists—to build a road across the Taklamakan. Nowhere in the world had a road ever been built across such a hostile terrain. Engineers faced two main problems: to build a solid roadbed, and to protect it from being buried by moving sand.

Experimentation began in late 1991. The most suitable roadbed formula was underlain with 'geotextile,' a heavy duty weave of tough plastic that was laid on compressed sand. This was topped with a gravel-asphalt surface, approximately 30 centimetres in depth.

As the road inched its way south from Luntai, researchers focused their efforts on finding the best way to protect it from wind blown sand. Shelter belts, consisting of two lines of defences, were built on both sides of the road. The first, about 100 metres from the road, was a 1.3 metre-high fence of interwoven reed stalks. The second line of defence lay just alongside the road itself: a checkerboard pattern of reed stalks 'planted' deep into the sand. This double defence proved effective because 90 percent of all windblown sand in the desert never rises more than one metre above the ground even in the most powerful of desert storms.

In total, the road building teams came up with 310 new desert-stabilizing and road-building techniques. Tens of thousands of labourers used thousands of square kilometres of geotextile and millions of tons of gravel. In summer they braved temperatures of 70 degrees Celsius, and in winter the mercury plummeted to minus 30.

Four sweating and shivering years of labour saw the a 522-kilometre road, seven metres in width, linking Highway 314, to the north of the desert, with Highway 315 in the south.

Designated Highway 312 and dubbed the Tarim Highway, this road building wonder was opened to traffic in September 1995 by Chinese vice-premier Zhu Rongji on the eve of the 40th anniversary of the establishment of the Xinjiang Uygur Autonomous Region. The road begins at the Lun Nan Oilfield to the west of Korla, and emerges south of the desert just east of Minfeng. In 2002 another road opened, branching off southeast from the Tazhong Oilfield and running 200 km to Qiemo. Yet another road from Tazhong to Ruoqiang is planned within the next few years.

There is no doubt that keeping the roads open will be a difficult, labour-intensive task. But one thing is certain—with so much oil beneath the sands, they will be maintained until the oilfields run dry.

(following pages) An ancient wooden door at the N VII group of ruined houses in Niya (3rd-4th centuries AD)

Persian using a fine cursive Hebrew script dated from 718. In 1998, the Swiss Christoph Baumer discovered three additional ruins, among them a small temple with murals featuring Sogdian and Buddhist deities. Chinese archaeologists removed these and other murals in 2002 and brought them to the Archaeological Institute of Xinjiang in Urumqi.

KARADONG AND YUAN SHA

Following the ancient Keriya River 170 km north from **Yutian** (**Keriya**), you reach the small village of Tunguzbasti. From here it's a leisurely one-day camel ride to the ancient fortified caravanserai of Karadong. Like Mazar Tagh, **Karadong** controlled a north-south traverse through the desert, but this site is much older, for it was already abandoned in the 4th century AD when the Keriya River changed its course eastwards and carried less water. Like Dandan Oilik, Karadong was initially explored by Hedin in 1896 and then excavated by Stein in 1901 and 1908. In 1993/94, a Sino-French team of archaeologists found Buddhist murals, which had already been noticed by Hedin but had been missed by Stein. These murals, dating from the first half of the 3rd century AD, display a noticeably Indian influence. They are in fact the world's oldest known Buddhist murals and are now kept at the Archaeological Institute of Xinjiang in Urumqi.

The same Sino-French team discovered the site of **Yuan Sha** (**Jumbula Kong** in the Uygur language) about 40 km north of Karadong. Dating from the Iron Age, this is the predecessor to Karadong and was already abandoned around 130 BC. The city was protected by a circular clay wall; outside were four graveyards situated at each of the four cardinal points. Naturally mummified corpses were discovered here, of which about half are of Indo-European stock. Even further north, two burial grounds from the Bronze Age (2,000-900 BC) were uncovered.

MINFENG (NIYA)

 he next oasis town after Yutian is **Minfeng**, also called New Niya. While Minfeng offers nothing of special interest, the Muslim pilgrimage site at the tomb of the saint Imam Jafer Sadik is worth seeing, especially in the latter part of summer and autumn when it is visited by thousands of pilgrims. The tomb is popularly called the 'Mecca of Turkestan' and is located 70 km north of Minfeng. Although legend tells that Imam Jafer Sadik was a descendant of the Prophet Mohammed, the shrine is no older than the 16th or 17th century. The Minfeng Niya Bing Guan (Minfeng Niya Hotel, Tel: 903 675 0259) offers rudimentary accommodation.

About 45 km north of the shrine is the ancient site of **Niya**, which formed part of the Kingdom of Shanshan till the 5th century AD. Stein led expeditions three times—in 1901, 1906 and 1913—to the site which he called "my little Pompeii". There he found huge wooden tablets (up to 2 m long) inscribed on both sides in the Indian scripts Brahmi and Kharoshthi. (Since paper was scarce at that time, ordinary letters and public records were written on wood.) Stein's work on a nearby rubbish heap ('I had to inhale its odours, still pungent after so many centuries, and to swallow in liberal doses of antique microbes luckily now dead') yielded wooden tablets sealed with the figure of Pallas Athene and other Greek deities. The discovery of tablets written in the early Indian scripts of Kharoshthi and Brahmi lent weight to the argument that the Southern Silk Road had until the middle of the 3rd century AD been under the cultural influence of Northern India, although since the 1st century BC it fell most often within the political and military zone of influence of China.

rom the various ruins and skeletons of houses and gardens Stein was 'able to reconstruct the physical aspects of the life once witnessed by these sites. Everything in the orchards and arbours dead for 16 centuries but still clearly recognizable; in the fences; in the materials used for buildings, etc, distinctly points to conditions of cultivation and local climate having been essentially the same as those observed in oases of the Tarim Basin.' Niya was abandoned in the 4th century AD due to lack of water and political instability. In 1995 a Sino-Japanese team of archaeologists not only discovered Buddhist murals dating from the late 3rd-early 4th centuries, but also a princely graveyard. In the following years a much older site dating from the Bronze Age (2000-900 BC) was discovered some 40 km north of Niya-it also contained Neolithic tools from pre-2000 BC. Excavations of this new site, called Niya North, are planned to start in the autumn of 2004 or early 2005. For this reason, access to Niya is especially restricted, and the same applies to Dandan Oilik.

About 170 km east of Minfeng the road passes through the village of Hortang, the starting point for a two-day camel ride to the ancient site of **Endere**. When the Buddhist monk Sung Yun passed through Endere in 518 AD he noticed a large monastery with more than 300 monks where a six-metre-high golden Buddha statue was kept. The main buildings of this huge site are 1.5 km apart, comprising an eight-metre stupa from the 3rd century AD and a circular fort built by the Chinese in the 7th century. Inside the fort stand the ruins of the administrative palace, built out of mud bricks; on one of its walls a Tibetan inscription dating from 791 AD informs of the victory of a Tibetan army over a Chinese one. When Aurel Stein excavated Endere in 1901 and 1906 he found Buddhist murals and stucco figures as well as numerous brief Buddhist texts which were offered by pilgrims as votive gifts. Unfortunately nothing remains to be seen of the murals, most of them having been vandalized.

M. III. viii.

An aerial view of the ancient riverbed of the Cherchen River north of Qiemo. This picture illustrates clearly the sea-like waves of sand dunes that so easily and inevitably swallowed whole cities

QIEMO AND ZAGHUNLUK

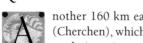nother 160 km east of Hortang, the main road hits the town of **Qiemo** (Cherchen), which is famous for sandstorms that can last for days and even weeks in spring and early summer. The ancient sites of Neleke—next to the Muslim cemetery Yulghuz Tugh Mazar—and Lalulik offer little to see, and the same goes for the small museum in the western suburb of Qiemo called Toghraklek Manor. More interesting is the small museum of **Zaghunluk**, located about five kilometres southwest of Qiemo. Here about 1,000 tombs were excavated between 1985 and 1999, many containing several bodies. Most of the people buried between the 12th and 7th centuries BC were cattle-breeding farmers of Indo-European stock whose ancestors originally came from Eastern Iran. For the burial of higher ranking people, horses, goats and even humans were sacrificed. The graveyard was used until the Eastern Han Dynasty (25–220 AD). The small museum is built directly above a pit containing 14 corpses and their ritual offerings, all left in place. The museum is usually closed; get the key from the small District Museum in the Tograklek Manor. Photography is strictly prohibited.

(left) A beautiful mural from shrine M III at Miran, (3rd century AD) depicting a princely disciple listening to the Buddha

In spite of the fact that the ancient city of Qiemo is described in several documents dating from the 1st century BC to the 9th century AD, the site has not yet been found; so far, four major expeditions have searched in vain for Old Qiemo. There are regular flights linking Qiemo with Korla and Urumqi, three times a week in summer and once in winter. Currently the only acceptable accommodation can be found at the Muertage Hotel on Yinbing Lu (Tel: 996 762-2687, 762-1499).

RUOQIANG (CHARKHLIK) AND MIRAN

 riving on to **Ruoqiang** (**Charkhlik**), you pass the village of Waxxari close to the ancient site of Washixia, Stein's Vash Shari from the time of the Tang (618-907 AD) and the Northern Song (960-1127 AD). The town of Ruoqiang is the most important in this vast region, encompassing the salt seabed of the dried-up lake **Lop Nor**. In the first century BC it formed part of the Kingdom of **Loulan**, which was later called Shanshan. At Ruoqiang the road divides, one branch heading north to Korla, the other taking a more southerly route than the original Silk Road, crossing into Qinghai Province through the fearsome Qaidam Desert and then turning northeast to Dunhuang. To the south lie the **Altun Mountains**, where a large nature reserve has been established. It was here in the 1880s that the great Russian explorer, Nikolai Przewalski, discovered the only existing species of the original horse, which was named Equus Przewalskii. Driven to extinction in the wild, the species is now being reintroduced from stocks bred in zoos. The Ruoqiang Bing Guan (Ruoqiang Hotel) is open to foreign travellers (Tel: 996 710-2542).

Northeast of Ruoqiang lies another archaeological site, **Miran**, which Stein visited in 1906, 1907 and 1914. Ancient Miran is 25 km north of the village of New Miran, itself 75 km away from Ruoqiang. The site is easy to reach by 4WD vehicle, and consists of the ruins of a huge circular fort—occupied between the eighth and ninth centuries by Tibetan troops—a stupa, a temple and a few other structures. It is now an official tourist site (tickets are Rmb350).

Here Stein unearthed not only manuscripts written in Tibetan, Chinese, Brahmi, Kharoshthi and even in a Turkic runic script, but also magnificent Buddhist murals dating from the 3rd century AD. Stylistic influences include Gandhara and the eastern Mediterranean area. In his book Desert Cathay, Stein noted: 'When the digging had reached a level of about four feet below the floor and a delicately painted dado of beautiful winged angels began to show on the wall, I felt completely taken by surprise. How could I have expected by the desolate shores of Lop Nor, in the very heart of innermost Asia to come upon such classical representations of Cherubim! And what had these graceful heads, recalling cherished scenes of Christian imagery, to do here on the walls of what was beyond all doubt a Buddhist monastery?' Some of those paintings are now on display in the National Museum of New Delhi; others were destroyed around 1912 by the Japanese spy Tachibana, who pretended to be an archaeologist and tried to remove them, but with no real skill succeeded only in ruining them.

LOP NOR

Lop Nor, to the north of Ruoqiang, was until the last century a shallow salt lake fed by the Tarim River and surrounded by salt marshes and a salt-encrusted plain. China conducted many of its nuclear tests in this area. Just west of Lop Nor once stood the important caravan trading city of Loulan. The Kingdom of Loulan was established before 176 BC and lasted until 330 AD, when it was abandoned due to lack of water. It had been a flourishing community, but when the Han dynasty fell in AD 220 it was overtaken by the Xiongnu, who cut the city off from all communication with Chang'an. It was reconquered by China around 260 AD.

Sven Hedin's greatest discovery came in the Lop Nor region in 1900. His expedition was financed by the King of Sweden and the millionaire Emmanuel Nobel, and originally planned to survey and map the **Shache River** and its continuation, the Tarim River. Hedin planned to follow the Tarim to Lop Nor, where the river emptied, and which had a mysterious habit of shifting over the course of years. Hedin's familiarity with the region enabled him to conclude that this 'wandering' was due to the many glacier-fed rivers that often changed course and hence the shape of the shallow lake.

fter three months of travelling along the Shache River, it froze over. Hedin's expedition marched on foot across the desert to Cherchen, then towards Marco Polo's 'Desert of Lop' in the eastern part of the Taklamakan. Digging in this area produced ancient paper with Chinese writing on it and documents written on wood with Buddhist designs. This turned out to be the ancient garrison town of Loulan, built to guard China's western frontier and the Silk Road traffic that passed through it. Stein came to Loulan in 1906 and 1914, guided by Hedin's first map of the area, and found many coins and documents written on both wood and paper. The international scope of Loulan's involvement was highlighted by the discovery of a fragment of a woollen textile featuring the Greek god Hermes which was used as a shroud, and was probably imported from the West.

In recent decades, Chinese archaeological teams have worked at this site and others nearby and unearthed lengths of tamped walls and timbers of an ancient roadway. Coins, jewellery, inscribed wood strips, wooden figures and pottery sherds have also been recovered. In the winter of 2002/3, tombs almost 2,000 years old were found, their walls decorated with murals. Unfortunately access to Loulan is forbidden, and a guard ensures that no illegal visits take place.

NATURE ALONG THE SILK ROAD
by William Bleisch

Before planes, trains and air-conditioned SUVs, travellers heading east from Kashgar on the Silk Road had to prepare themselves well for the long trek across the vast, forbidding Taklamakan Desert. It may at first have seemed that they were passing through a land devoid of life, but the natural world finds a way to blossom even in the harshest of landscapes, and this is still true today.

Travellers who take the northern route pass the Heavenly Mountains for the first half of their journey. While the desert dunes to the south seem almost lifeless, the mountain slopes to the north are covered

with forests and pastureland that is home to much wildlife. Ibex, a wild sheep with graceful horns that curve back over its neck, perch on tiny rock ledges and nimbly cross precipitous cliffs with the grace of acrobats. Wherever these wild prey are common, snow leopards may lie in ambush, protected from the mountain winds by their thick spotted coat.

Travellers taking the southern route find the great ranges of the Tibetan Plateau on their right, the Kunlun, Altun and Qilian

mountains. Few travellers cross this ranges; those who do find themselves in an inhospitable world that combines desert drought with the cold, sparse air of the high steppe, 4,000–5,000 metres above sea level. Protected by its remoteness, herds of hardy Tibetan wild ass, thick-haired wild yak and fleet Tibetan antelope migrate across a landscape of dune fields, salt lakes and grassy flatland.

Whether north route or south, the traveller has more than enough opportunity to view the desert. The Taklamakan, China's largest desert, fills a vast depression that alternates between unbearably hot summers and frigid winters. Rank upon rank of migrating dunes and even more monotonous gravel-covered flats known as *gebi* support only an occasional desert shrub or grass.

Yet even here, a few hardy creatures survive. Wild Bactrian camels, relatives of the two-humped local domestic camels, persist in the most remote deserts where hunters cannot track them (see pages 294–295). These hardy beasts can drink the water of desert salt lakes, ensuring survival where no other large mammal exists. Wherever there is fresh water, if only for a single season, life springs forth. From the dry

A herd of blue sheep on a ridge crest in the Arjin Mountains. These hardy animals keep close to cliffs that serve as their refuge. The elusive snow leopard is often present as well, but rarely seen

beds of intermittent rivers, fragrant desert shrubs such as wormwood and camel thorn grow luxuriantly. Goitered gazelle and kulan—sand-buff relatives of the Tibetan wild ass—derive much of the water they need from the desert vegetation they eat.

Where water is more reliable, woodlands of twisted diversified leaf poplar rise up from the sands. In these woodlands are found the endemic Tarim hare and Tarim deer, a small form of red deer with shorter hair than its mountain relatives. Where there is open water, such as on China's largest freshwater lake, Bosten Hu, red crested pochard, ruddy shelduck, common merganser and mute swans build their nests. Today, the great lake of Lop Nor and its marshes are gone, deprived of their source of water by distant irrigation projects. Still, along the river and around certain perennial springs fed by water from the mountains, marshlands dense with grasses still occur. These marshes are inhabited by abundant wild boar, which once served as prey for tigers. Unfortunately extinct in the region today, tigers were last recorded here in the 1950s, and were vividly described by Sven Hedin in his expedition memoirs of half a century earlier.

A pale rosefinch pecks a sunflower in a village garden on the edge of the Taklamakan. Like many desert animals, the rosefinch here is a paler version of its more colourful mountain relative. Its Chinese name translates as 'sand-coloured vermillion finch'

When travellers finally emerge from the western deserts and enter the plains of northern China, they find themselves in a fertile landscape of loess fields supporting farms of wheat and forests of poplar and pine. To the south, the high peak of Mt Taibei heralds a wall of green formed by the Qingling Mountains. The verdant

In full breeding colours a male Tibetan antelope, also known as chiru, struts in the cold winter air of the Tibetan Plateau south of the Southern Silk Road

KEY NATURE RESERVES ADJACENT TO THE SILK ROAD

Heaven Lake National Nature Reserve, Xinjiang (380 sq km): With its picturesque scenery below snow-capped Mt Bogda and its location near to the provincial capital Urumqi, this famous lake is a magnet for tourism. It protects forests of dragon spruce, a species characteristic of the Tian Shan.

Arjin Mountain National Nature Reserve, Xinjiang (45,800 sq km): Also known as the Altun Tagh, this remote high nature reserve protects the northernmost limit of typical Tibetan Plateau habitat. Stunning salt lakes, snow-capped peaks and large herds of wild ass, wild yak and Tibetan antelope. The reserve includes the peak of Muztagh Ulugh (6,973 m).

Lop Nor Wildlife Camel National Nature Reserve, Xinjiang: Most of this vast nature reserve is off-limits to tourists, but the fringes may be visited from Kuerla or Ruoqiang. The reserve protects one of the largest remaining populations of the world's only wild camel species.

Taibai Mountain National Nature Reserve, Shaanxi: Only 120 km southwest of X'ian, Taibai is famous not only for its high peak (3,767 m) but also for its ancient temples. Taibai Mountain is the pinnacle of a group of five contiguous nature reserves that protect a total of 1,731 sq km of the Qinling Mountains. Taibai's lush forests are more characteristic of the highlands to the south, and are home to golden monkeys, takin and giant panda.

forests of the Qingling are the farthest northern limit of much of the fauna and flora of the Oriental realm.

In these forests, with their dense growths of dwarf bamboo, roam many animals endemic to China. The rare crested ibis, with its odd down-curved bill and bare red face, still persists here and nowhere else in the wild, relying on the clear rivers and streams that drain the mountain slopes. Golden monkeys, the most colourful of the four species of snub-nosed langur, crash through the canopy in family groups of several dozen. On the ridges above, herds of great, cow-like takin push their way through the undergrowth, their massive horns showing their relationship to the muskoxen of the Arctic. And the flagship for all China's endangered wildlife, the giant panda, still roams these forests.

Dr William Bleisch has been working to conserve wildlife in China since 1987. Over the years, he has conducted research on several of China's most endangered species, including Western black gibbons in Yunnan, grey snub-nosed monkeys in Guizhou and Tibetan antelope in Xinjiang. He is currently China Programme Manager and Indochina Primate Programme Co-ordinator for Fauna and Flora International. When he is not travelling, he lives with his wife in Beijing.

arco Polo took 30 days to cross the 'Desert of Lop' to reach Dunhuang. This was the worst stretch of the southern caravan route. Apart from the lack of water, strange voices misled travellers, causing them to wander off:

And there were some who, in crossing the desert, have seen a host of men coming towards them and, suspecting that they were robbers, returning, they have gone hopelessly astray...Even by daylight men hear these spirit voices, and often you fancy you are listening to the strains of many instruments, especially drums, and the clash of arms. For this reason bands of travellers make a point of keeping very close together. Before they go to sleep they set up a sign pointing in the direction in which they have to travel, and round the necks of all their beasts they fasten little bells, so that by listening to the sound they may prevent them from straying off the path.

For those adventurous enough to complete the overland journey to Dunhuang from Ruoqiang, the route is now open. The approximate travel time is three days and permits for camping are available (there are no hotels, although travellers report that local Uygur families put them up).

RECENT DISCOVERIES

 everal important discoveries have been made in the last three decades in the northwestern region of Lop Nor. One is a 4,000-year-old female mummy called "The beauty of Loulan" found in 1980 in the graveyard of Qäwrighul. The woman was an Indo-European; she now rests in the Xinjiang Museum in Urumqi. Another spectacular discovery was made in 1995 at Yingpan, northwest of Loulan. This is an extremely well-preserved male mummy from the Eastern Han Dynasty (25-220 AD) who was covered by a red, woollen garment featuring pairs of naked putti fighting like Roman gladiators. This cloth was not imported, but locally made by artists familiar with Western patters. Finally, in 2002 a team of Chinese archaeologists started to systematically excavate the site of **Xiaohe** located about 150 km west of Loulan. Its graveyard was discovered in 1934 by Folke Bergman, a colleague of Sven Hedin who then excavated 12 tombs. The Chinese scientists have now identified about 200 graves, some of which are three to four storeys deep into the earth—the first graves of this kind ever found in China. The mummies are tentatively dated to the 1st millennium BC.

THE KARAKORAM HIGHWAY

he 1,284-kilometre Karakoram Highway linking Islamabad and Kashgar is a stunning roadway winding through some of the most inhospitable terrain in the world, past the region of Chinese Turkestan and the great mountain ranges of the Himalayas, Karakorams and **Pamirs**, following one of the ancient Silk Road routes to the valleys of the Indus, Gilgit and Hunza rivers. The highway, begun in 1967, is an incredible feat of engineering by Chinese construction teams. The passage through the Northern Territories of Pakistan was blasted out of sheer rock faces that rise high above deep canyons carved by the rushing waters of the Indus River and its tributaries. In some places men suspended by ropes hand-drilled the holes for the dynamite. More than 400 lives were lost in building the road, and small stone cairns mark the graves. It can still be unpredictable—rock slides and flash floods are a constant threat and frequently hold up transportation. The Pakistan Frontier Works Organization has deployed 10,000 soldiers on the other side of the border for road maintenance and emergency clearance.

The Karakorams and the Himalayas are the newest mountain ranges in the world; they began forming 55 million years ago when the Indian subcontinent collided with the northern Asian land mass. The subcontinent is still shifting north at a rate of five centimetres per year and the young mountains are still growing, which results in earth tremors every three minutes (on average). Karakoram means 'crumbling rock' in Turkish, an apt name for a highway that cuts through giant, snow-capped granite 4,733 metres high at the **Khunjerab Pass**.

outh of Kashgar the *gebi* (stony) plain gives way to foothills, and the road winds for several hours through the narrow gorge of the Gez River. Then it ascends to an altitude of 3,500 metres by the shores of **Karakuli Lake**, 196 kilometres from Kashgar. Horses, yaks and camels graze on the rich pasturage. This pristine spot is excellent for camping and hiking, though adequate gear is needed (it is possible to stay in yurts) as well as a travel permit (obtainable from CITS in Kashgar). Further on, the road rises by hairpin bends to around 3,900 metres, giving views dominated by the massive **Muztagata Mountain**, the 'Father of the Ice Mountains'. Here the glaciers and snowfields are overwhelming. The high, windswept plateaus between the parallel ranges that constitute the **Pamirs**, the 'Roof of the World' (called the Onion Mountains in early Chinese records), are home to a nomadic branch of the Kirghiz people known as the **Kara-Kirghiz**. Pack-camels amble between their encampments of round *ak-ois* (yurts covered in thick felts of goat or camel hair).

The Karakoram Highway along the Indus River

Dropping down to 3,200 metres one passes the Takhman checkpoint and enters Tashkurgan, the county seat of Tajik Autonomous County, 260 kilometres from Kashgar. As this is a frontier area, buses reach the town by sunset, and tourists travelling in either direction usually spend the night here.

TASHKURGAN

I n the second century AD, Ptolemy spoke of Tashkurgan as the extreme western emporium of the Land of Seres (China), for it stands on the trade route over the Taghdumbash Pamirs and the Karakorams to the ancient Buddhist kingdoms of Taxila and Gandhara. The inhabitants, then known as Sarikolis but today called **Tajiks**, are regarded as pure *Homo alpinus* stock, the occupiers of High Asia since earliest times. Their language belongs to the Iranian group of Indo-European languages, and they are followers of the Ismaili sect of Islam.

The Tajiks in Xinjiang number more than 26,000 and, apart from a small number in the cities of the Southern Silk Road, live in their traditional homeland in the High Pamirs. Unlike their nomadic neighbours, the Kirghiz and Kazakhs, the Tajiks engage in both animal husbandry and agriculture; they are semi-sedentary, building houses of stone and wood. Barley, beans, wheat and vegetables are planted during springtime. They become yurt-dwellers during the summer grazing season, when they tend flocks of sheep, goats and horses in the higher valleys, and return to their homes in autumn. At altitudes of over 3,000 metres crop yields are low. Hawking and *buzhashi* (rugby with a sheep carcass) are popular amongst the Tajiks, as are dancing and music. One of their traditional musical instruments is a three-holed flute made from the bones of eagles' wings.

Tashkurgan is Tajik for 'Stone City', referring to a stone fort just north of the town that was first built in the sixth century. The present ruins date from the Yuan dynasty and the fort was restored during the Qing. At the base of the wall is a narrow dirt road, said to be the ancient Silk Road itself. Xuan Zang, laden with 570 Buddhist sutras, spent 20 days here on his return journey.

O n top of a high mountain by the Tashkurgan River, about 80 kilometres southwest of the town, are the ruins of the Princess's Castle. The tamped-earth walls are crumbling, but piles of stones within are evidence of inner rooms. It was already in ruins when Xuan Zang told its legend. Once, the King of Persia became betrothed to a Chinese princess, but during her long journey to join him wars broke out, confining her to the Pamirs. Her escort built a temporary fortification on top of a steep mountain and guarded it night and day, and here she lived until peace was restored six months later. But, to the horror of the accompanying ministers, the princess had become pregnant, and an exhaustive investigation was demanded. The trusted handmaiden of the princess came forward: 'I know only that every day at noon a handsome young man comes from the sun to meet the princess. Afterwards, he mounts the clouds and departs.' Afraid to relate this to the court, the ministers decided to stay where they were and built a palace on the mountain top for the princess. The boy she bore was beautiful and intelligent. The princess established rule in the region, and her son eventually became king.

Tashkurgan Practical Information

Today, Tashkurgan is a small border town of 5,000 residents with one poplar-lined main street.

Transportation

By road: daily buses to/from Kashgar, Pirali and Sost, Pakistan.

Accommodation

Available at either the **Bus Station Guesthouse** or the more comfortable **Pamir Guesthouse**, tel (0998) 342-1085.

KHUNJERAB PASS

xit formalities take place before leaving Tashkurgan. Thirty kilometres south of Tashkurgan the road forks near a stone bridge, one route leading to the Wakhan Corridor of Afghanistan, only 80 kilometres away, the other heading for the Khunjerab Pass. Unless you are on a bus headed for Sost, you will have to catch another bus or rent a jeep from the respective official tourist agencies of China or Pakistan (extremely expensive).

The Khunjerab Pass and the simple stone Sino-Pakistani frontier marker are another 50 kilometres further on, one hour's drive. Though Sir Aurel Stein dismissed the crossing of the 4,733-metre pass as 'an excursion for the ladies', its name means 'Valley of Blood' in the Wakhi language, referring to the murderous raids on caravans and travellers staged from the neighbouring Kingdom of Hunza.

At this altitude both man and beast suffer altitude sickness, with nosebleeds a common occurrence. The traditional method of relieving horses of pain was to jab their muzzles with sharp iron spikes so that the blood ran. A young Scandinavian travelling this route in the 1940s was appalled: 'Along the whole pass there are dark-brown splodges on the stones. Once they were fresh streaming blood. Each drop is a message from the trembling horses that have foundered there.'

Over the pass, the road descends via hairpin bends to 2,500 metres, and then continues 86 kilometres through the closed Pakistan border zone to the checkpoint at **Sost**, Pakistan where entry formalities take place. Good accommodation is available here at the PTDC Motel.

RECOMMENDED READING

ARCHAEOLOGY

Barber, Elizabeth, *The Mummies of Ürümchi* (Macmillan, London, 1999)

Bergman, Folke, *Archaeological Researches in Sinkiang*
(Sven Hedin's Reports,Publication 7, Stockholm, 1939)

Debaine-Francfort Corinne and Abduressul Idriss, *Keriya, mémoires d'un fleuve*
(Editions Findakly, Paris, 2000)

Feng Zhao and Zhiyong Yu, *Legacy of the Desert King*
(China National Silk Museum, Hanghzou, 2000)

Lin, Yongjian, *Niya: Paradise Regained* (Minzhu Publishing House, Beijing, 1995)

Mair, Victor, *The Bronze Age and Early Iron Age Peoples of Eastern Central Asia*
(Institute for the Study of Man Inc. Washington, 1998)

Mallory J.P. and Mair Victor, *The Tarim Mummies*
(Thames & Hudson, London, 2000)

Stein, Sir Aurel, *On Central Asian Tracks* (Macmillan, London, 1933)
—*Ruins of Desert Cathay* (Macmillan, London, 1912)
see extract on pages 105–108, and Special Topic on pages 100–102
Republished as facsimile reprints by Dover Publications, New York, 1987

Stein, Sir Aurel, *Sand-Buried Ruins of Khotan* (Clarendon, Oxford, 1904)
—*Ancient Khotan* (Clarendon, Oxford, 1907)
—*Serindia* (Clarendon, Oxford, 1921)
—*Innermost Asia* (Clarendon, Oxford, 1928)

Sugiyama, Jiro, *Central Asian Objects Brought back by the Otani Mission*
(Tokyo National Museum, 1971)

von Le Coq, A, *Buried Treasures of Chinese Turkestan*
(Oxford University Press, Oxford 1985), see Special Topic on pages 109–111

Walker Annabel, Aurel Stein. *Pioneer of the Silk Road*
(J. Murray, London, 1995)

Yue Feng, *Archaeological Treasures of the Silk Road in Xinjiang Uygur Autonomous
Region* (Shanghai Translation Publishing House, Shanghai, 1998)

Art History

Abulat Abdulreshit, *A Grand View of Xinjiang's Cultural Relics and Historic Sites, China* (Suntime Intl. Cooperation Group, Urumqi, 1999)

Härtel, Herbert, *Along the Ancient Silk Routes*
(The Metropolitan Museum of Art, New York, 1982)

Knauer, E.R. *The Camel's Load in Life and Death* (Akhanthus, Zurich, 1998)

Li Kangning, *The Mystical Tarim*
(Xinjiang People's Publishing House, Urumqi, 1998)

Li Yuchun, *Xinjiang Museum* (Xinjiang Publishing Press, Urumqi, approx 1996)

Mu Shunying, *The Ancient Art in Xinjiang, China*
(The Xinjiang Art and Photography Press, Urumqi, 1994)

Piotrovsky, Mikhail, *Lost Empire of the Silk Road* (Electa, Milan, 1993)

Snellgrove, D, ed, *The Image of the Buddha*
(Kodansha International, Japan, 1978) see extract on pages 22–24

Sumner, Christina, *Beyond the Silk Road: Arts of Central Asia*
(Museum of Applied Arts and Sciences, 2000)

Talbot Rice, Tamara, *Ancient Arts of Central Asia*
(Thames and Hudson, London, 1963)

Warner, Langdon, *Buddhist Wall Painting: a Study of a Ninth-Century Grotto at Wanfo-hsia near Tun-huang* (Cambridge, 1938)

Whitefield, Roderick, et al *Cave Temples of Mogao: Art and History on the Silk Road* (Getty Trust Publications, 2001)

Whitfield, Roderick, *The Art of Central Asia*. The Stein Collection in the British Museum (Kodansha International, London & Tokyo, 1982)
  —*Cave Temples of Mogao. Art and History on the Silk Road*
    (The Getty Conservation Institute, Los Angeles, 2000)

Xia Xuncheng, *The Mysterious Lop Lake* (Science Press, Beijing, 1985)
  — *Wondrous Taklimakan* (Science Press, Beijing, 1993)

HISTORY

Baumer, Christoph, *Southern Silk Road: In the Footsteps of Sir Aurel Stein and Sven Hedin* (White Orchid Books, Bangkok, second revised edition, 2004)

Boulnois, Luce, *Silk Road: Monks, Warriors & Merchants on the Silk Road* (Odyssey, Hong Kong, 2004)

Chen, J, *The Sinkiang Story* (Macmillan, New York, 1977)

Dubbs, Homer H, *A Roman City in Ancient China* (The China Society, London, 1957)

Foltz, Richard C, *Religions of the the Silk Road* (Griffin Trade Paperback, 2000)

Giles, H A, *The Travels of Fa-hsien* (Cambridge, 1923)

Hedin, Sven, *Central Asia and Tibet*, 2 vols (Hurst and Blackett, London, 1903)
   —*My Life as an Explorer* (Cassel, London, 1926)
   —*Through Asia*, 2 vols (Methuen, London, 1898), see Special Topic on page 112

Hedin, Sven, *Scientific Results of a Journey in Central Asia, 1899-1902*
   (Lithographic Institute of the General Staff of the Swedish Army, Stockholm, 1904-1907)

History of Civilizations of Central Asia, six volumes
   (UNESCO Publishing, Paris, 1992)

Hopkirk, P, *Foreign Devils on the Silk Road* (Oxford University Press, Oxford 1986)
   —*The Great Game. On Secret Service in High Asia*
      (John Murray, London, 1990), see Special Topic on page 284–289
   —*Trespassers on the Roof of the World, The Race for Lhasa*
      (Oxford University Press, Oxford, 1982)
   —*Setting the East Ablaze. Lenin's Dream of an Empire in Asia*
      (John Murray, London, 1984)

Montell, Gösta, *Sven Hedin's Archaeological Collections from Khotan*
   (Museum of Far Eastern Antiquities, Stockholm, 1935)

Nagel's Encyclopedia Guide to China (Nagel Publishers, Geneva, 1979)

Orr, Robert G, *Religion in China* (Friendship Press, New York, 1980)

Przewalski, Col N, *Mongolia* 2 vols (trans from Russian, 1876)
   — *From Kulja. Across the Tian Shan to Lob-nor* (trans 1879)

Puri, B.N., *Buddhism in Central Asia* (Banarsidass, Delhi, 1993)

Schaefer, Edward H, *The Golden Peaches of Samarkand. A Study of T'ang Exotics* (University of California, 1963)

Skrine, C P and Nightingale P, *Macartney at Kashgar* (London, 1973)

Tucker, Jonathan, *The Silk Road. Art and History*
(Philip Wilson Publishers, London, 2003)

Wang Binhua (editor), *The Ancient Corpses of Xinjiang: The Peoples of Ancient Xinjiang and their Culture* (CIP, Urumqi,1999)

Whitefield, Susan, *Life along the Silk Road* (University California Press, 2000)

Wood, Frances, *Did Marco Polo Go to China?* (Westview Press, 1998)

Wood, Frances, *The Silk Road* (The Folio Society, London, 2002)

Wu, Aitken, *Turkistan Tumult* (Oxford University Press, Oxford, 1984)

LITERATURE

Bishop, Kevin, *Xi'an, China's Ancient Capital* (Odyssey, Hong Kong, 2000)

Dalrymple, William, *In Xanadu* (Harper Collins, London, 1989)
see extract on pages 275–276

Inoue, Yasushi, trans Jean Odo Moy, *Tun-huang* (Kodansha International, 1978)

Isaacs, Harold (translated by), *Straw Sandals; Chinese Short Stories 1918–1933*
(Massachusetts Institute of Technology, 1974)
see extract on pages 304–305

Laozi, *Dao De Qing*

Pilkington, John, *An Adventure on the Old Silk Road* (Random Century, 1989)
see extract on page 254

Saha, Dr Kshanika, *Buddhism and Buddhist Literature in Central Asia* (Calcutta, 1970)

Seth, Vikram, *From Heaven Lake* (Chatto & Windus, London, 1983)
see extract on page 224–225

Wu Ch'eng En, *Monkey,* trans Arthur Waley (Penguin Books, London, 1961)
see extract on page 174–175

SILK ROAD TRAVELLERS

Bruce, C.D., *In the Footsteps of Marco Polo* (Blackwood, Edinburgh, 1907)

Cable & French, *The Gobi Desert* (Hodder & Stoughton, London)
see extract on page 297

Dabbs, J.A., *History of the Discovery and Exploration of Chinese Turkestan*
(Mouton, The Hague, 1963)

Fleming, Peter, *News from Tartary* (Jonathan Cape, London, 1936)

Hedin, Sven, *Across the Gobi Desert* (Routledge & Sons, London, 1931)

Hedin, Sven, *The Silk Road* (Butler & Tanner, London, 1938)

Huc, Evariste-Régis and Gabet, Joseph, (trans William Hazlitt)
    Travels in Tartary, Thibet and China 1844–1846 (Routledge)

Macartney, Lady, *An English Lady in Chinese Turkestan*
    (Oxford University Press, Oxford, 1985)

Macleod, C and Mayhew, B, *Uzbekistan: The Golden Road to Samarkand*
    (Odyssey, Hong Kong, 2004)

Maillart, Ella, trans Thomas McGreevy, *Forbidden Journey*
    (Century, London, 1987)

Mannerheim, C.G., *Across Asia* (Suomalais-Ugrilainen Seura, Helsinki, 1940)

Neville-Hadley, Peter, *China: The Silk Routes* (Globe Pequot Press, 1997)

Polo, Marco, *The Book of Ser Marco Polo*, edited by Sir Henry Yule
    (Scribner's Sons, New York, 1926)

Polo, Marco, trans R E Lathan, *The Travels of Marco Polo*
    (Penguin Books, London, 1958)

Skrine, C P, *Chinese Central Asia* (Methuen & Co, London, 1926)
    see extract on page 142–143

Shaw, Robert, *Visits to High Tartary, Yarkand and Kashgar*
    (Oxford University Press, Oxford, 1984)

Stewart, Rowan and Weldon Susie, *Kyrgyz Republic* (Odyssey, Hong Kong, 2004)

Sykes, Ella and Sir Percy, *Through Deserts and Oases of Central Asia*
    (London, 1920)

Teichman, Sir Eric, *Journey to Turkistan* (Hodder & Stoughton, London, 1937)

Vincent, Irene V, *The Sacred Oasis* (London, 1953)

Warner, Langdon, *The Long Old Road in China* (Arrowsmith, London, 1927)

Xuan Zang, *Buddhist Records of the Western World translated from the Chinese of
    Hsuen Tsiang (AD 629) by Samuel Beal*
    (Reprinted, Chinese Materials Centre Inc, San Francisco, 1976)

INDEX OF PLACES

INDEX OF MINORITY NATIONALITIES

**Specialists in tailor-made travel
and small group tours to Uzbekistan,
all the countries of Central Asia
and Iran, Azerbaijan, Armenia,
Georgia, Russia and China**

Steppes East

WILD FRONTIERS

*Wild Frontiers runs a number of fixed-date, group tours
through Kyrgyzstan, Uzbekistan, Tajikistan and the Chinese
province of Xinjiang (Kashgar); tailor-made itineraries
through the whole region and horse treks in Kyrgyzstan.*

WILD FRONTIERS ADVENTURES TRAVEL LTD.